'·· good book which deals with its subject in a clear, thorough,
·r anized, and distinctive manner.'
      – **Jonathan Boulton**, *University of Notre Dame, USA.*

edieval France presents a new analysis of political change
    ⸱he kingdom of the Valois monarchs during the turbulent
period of the Hundred Years' War. Graeme Small:

- ' ⸱es into account social, economic and religious dimensions
- ⸱: ores the interests of a wide variety of powers in political soci-
    ⸱ ⸱v⸱ not just the monarchy but prelates, noble networks and the
    ϵ ⸱ging municipalities
- des a fresh appraisal of the sources and historiography
- lers the wider context of European history during the
    i, and of earlier and later developments in the French
    om.

One of the few single-authored studies of late medieval France in
English in the last forty years, this is a timely and essential text for
readers wishing to engage with a fascinating era of French history.

Graeme Small is Senior Lecturer in History at the University of Glasgow. His previous publications include *Court and Civic Society in the
Burgundian*

European History in Perspective
General Editor: Jeremy Black

Benjamin Arnold   *Medieval Germany*
Ronald Asch   *The Thirty Years' War*
Nigel Aston   *The French Revolution, 1789-1804*
Nicholas Atkin   *The Fifth French Republic*
Christopher Bartlett   *Peace, War and the European Powers, 1814-1914*
Robert Bireley   *The Refashioning of Catholicism, 1450-1700*
Donna Bohanan   *Crown and Nobility in Early Modern France*
Arden Bucholz   *Moltke and the German Wars, 1864-1871*
Patricia Clavin   *The Great Depression, 1929-1939*
Paula Sutter Fichtner   *The Habsburg Monarchy, 1490-1848*
Mark R. Forster   *Catholic Germany from the Reformation to the Enlightenment*
Mark Galeotti   *Gorbachev and his Revolution*
David Gates   *Warfare in the Nineteenth Century*
Alexander Grab   *Napoleon and the Transformation of Europe*
Nicholas Henshall   *The Zenith of European Monarchy and its Elites*
Martin P. Johnson   *The Dreyfus Affair*
Tim Kirk   *Nazi Germany*
Ronald Kowalski   *European Communism*
Paul Douglas Lockhart   *Sweden in the Seventeenth Century*
Kevin McDermott   *Stalin*
Graeme Murdock   *Beyond Calvin*
Peter Musgrave   *The Early Modern European Economy*
J. L. Price   *The Dutch Republic in the Seventeenth Century*
A. W. Purdue   *The Second World War*
Christopher Read   *The Making and Breaking of the Soviet System*
Francisco J. Romero-Salvado   *Twentieth-Century Spain*
Matthew S. Seligmann and Roderick R. McLean
Germany from Reich to Republic, 1871-1918
David A. Shafer   *The Paris Commune*
Graeme Small   *Late Medieval France*
David Sturdy   *Louis XIV*
David J. Sturdy   *Richelieu and Mazarin*
Hunt Tooley   *The Western Front*
Peter Waldron   *The End of Imperial Russia, 1855-1917*
Peter Waldron   *Governing Tsarist Russia*
Peter G. Wallace   *The Long European Reformation*
James D. White   *Lenin*
Patrick Williams   *Philip II*
Peter H. Wilson   *From Reich to Revolution*

European History in Perspective
Series Standing Order
ISBN 0-333-71694-9 hardcover
ISBN 0-333-69336-1 paperback
(outside North America only)

You can receive future titles in this series as they are published by placing a
standing order. Please contact your bookseller or, in the case of difficulty, write to
us at the address below with your name and address, the title of the series and the
ISBN quoted above.

Customer Services Department, Palgrave Ltd
Houndmills, Basingstoke, Hampshire RG21 6XS, England

Late Medieval France

GRAEME SMALL

First published 2009 by
PALGRAVE MACMILLAN

Palgrave Macmillan in the UK is an imprint of Macmillan Publishers Limited, registered in England, company number 785998, of Houndmills, Basingstoke, Hampshire RG21 6XS.

Palgrave Macmillan in the US is a division of St Martin's Press LLC, 175 Fifth Avenue, New York, NY 10010.

Palgrave Macmillan is the global academic imprint of the above companies and has companies and representatives throughout the world.

Palgrave® and Macmillan® are registered trademarks in the United States, the United Kingdom, Europe and other countries.

ISBN-13: 978–0–333–64242–9 hardback
ISBN-13: 978–0–333–64243–6 paperback

This book is printed on paper suitable for recycling and made from fully managed and sustained forest sources. Logging, pulping and manufacturing processes are expected to conform to the environmental regulations of the country of origin.

A catalogue record for this book is available from the British Library.

A catalog record for this book is available from the Library of Congress.

10   9   8   7   6   5   4   3   2   1
18   17   16   15   14   13   12   11   10   09

Printed and bound in China

For Ken Fowler

Contents

List of Maps

Acknowledgments

The largest debt I must acknowledge is to Philippa, Jamie, Louis and George, for their support while I was writing this book.

Among the scholarly debts I owe, the first is to Peter Lewis, whose influence will be apparent throughout: not just that of his *Later Medieval France: The Polity* (1968), a work which made a profound impact on both sides of the Channel, but also the seminal articles he wrote before and after. My main ambition in this volume has been to bring to an Anglophone audience as much of the scholarship of the intervening 40 years as I can, especially where it was written in French. A second debt is to David Potter, whose invitation to join a panel of collaborators in the late medieval volume of *The Shorter Oxford History of France* helped me decide the kind of book I should write. What follows is intended to complement, rather than compete with, the result of that collaboration, published in 2003 under the title *France in the later Middle Ages*. At an early stage, Anne Curry and Malcolm Crook very kindly shared their ideas with me about writing a book like this, and at later points Christopher Allmand, Jean-Philippe Genet and Craig Taylor organised conferences which helped shape my ideas in one way or the other. Michael Jones has been a constant source of encouragement while I have been working on the project, and I am most grateful to him for reading through the typescript at an advanced stage and saving me from several errors. Needless to say, those that are left are all mine.

This book could not have been written without a period of leave granted by the Department of History at Glasgow University, supplemented by an award under the Research Leave Scheme from the AHRC. Some of the work that was eventually used (in Chapter 5) was done with the help of a European Visiting Research Fellowship from the Royal Society of Edinburgh. Underpinning every chapter is the hard work of Joanne Findlay, Matthew Leavey, Paul Rowan and the rest of the team at Glasgow University Library's Document Delivery Service, to whom I express particular gratitude.

My work has benefited a great deal over the years from conversations and classes at the universities of Keele and Glasgow. Robin Studd gave me the opportunity to teach a course on late medieval France for the first time, and at Glasgow I have been fortunate to work with several historians whose knowledge of French history has brought me fresh insights, particularly Stuart Airlie, Sam Cohn, Thomas Munck, Matthew Strickland and Andrew Roach. Several cohorts of students at Keele and Glasgow have helped me wrestle with subjects discussed in the following pages. I am especially grateful for their many insights to Neil Murphy and Doug Aiton, and to Bryan Dick, whose high standards I am not always sure I have met.

This book is dedicated to Ken Fowler, who introduced me to many of the sources used in this book, and brought me to a fuller understanding of the terms 'Burgundy' and 'Armagnac'.

Note on Money

Most of the figures given in this book are in *livres tournois* (*l.t.*) or pounds of Tours. This was the main money of account used for record-keeping purposes in late medieval France, divided into 20 *sous*, each *sou* further divided into 12 *deniers*. On one occasion only, the *livre de Bordeaux* (*l.b.*) or pound of Bordeaux, a money of account used in English-ruled Guyenne, is referred to. The value of these monies of account in real coin could vary considerably at different times. The *écu*, referred to in Chapter 3 in relation to the ransom of John II, was one such coin, nominally valued at 1 *l.t.*, although in reality the value of the *écu* also varied.

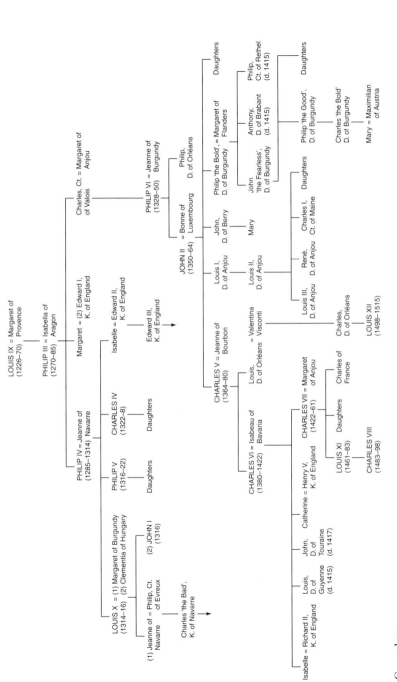

Genealogy

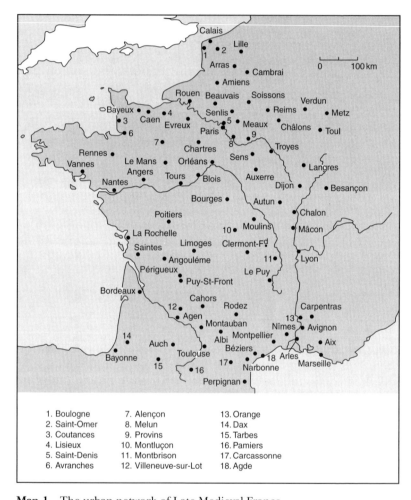

Map 1   The urban network of Late Medieval France

Source: Adapted from J. Dupâquier, *Histoire de la population française, I* (Paris, 1995), p. 394.

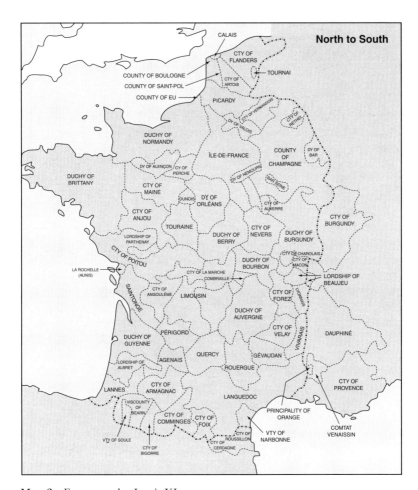

Map 2   France under Louis XI

Source: Adapted from J.-F. Lassalmonie, *La Boîte à L'enchanteur: Politique financière de Louis XI* (Paris, 2002), p. x.

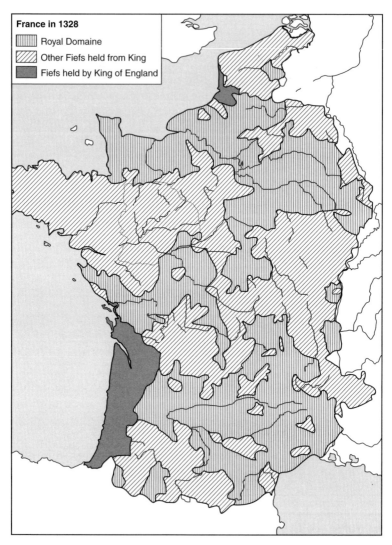

Map 3   France in 1328

Source: Adapted from Léon Mirot, *Manuel de Géographie Historique de la France* (Paris, 1947).

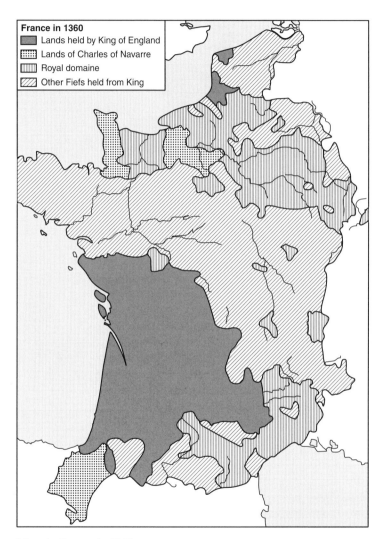

Map 4   France in 1360

Source: Adapted from Léon Mirot, *Manuel de Géographie Historique de la France* (Paris, 1947).

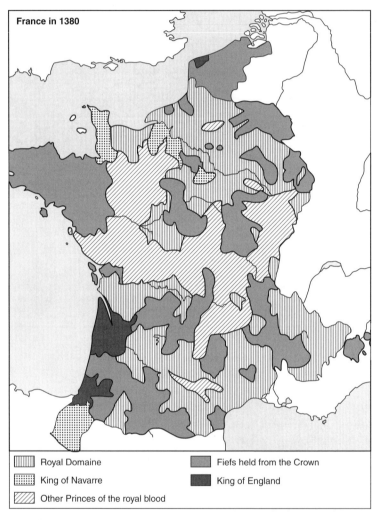

Map 5   France in 1380

Source: Adapted from Léon Mirot, *Manuel de Géographie Historique de la France* (Paris, 1947).

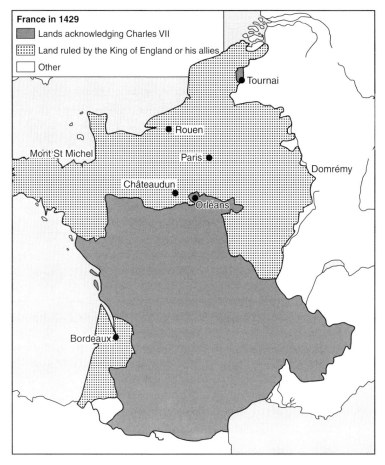

Map 6   France in 1429

Source: Adapted from Léon Mirot, *Manuel de Géographie Historique de la France* (Paris, 1947).

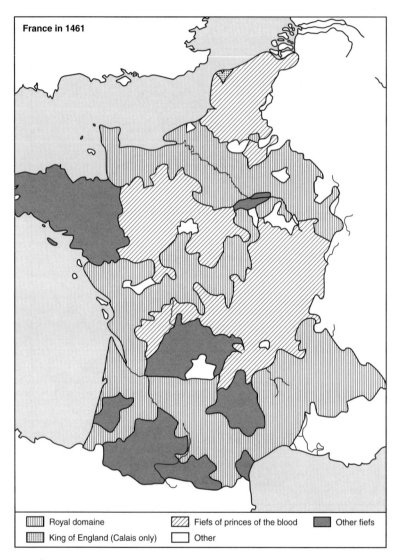

Map 7   France in 1461

Source: Adapted from Léon Mirot, *Manuel de Géographie Historique de la France* (Paris, 1947).

Introduction

Most histories of France begin with a reflexion on the themes of unity and diversity, and sadly this one is no different. Diversity is ever-present in the late medieval kingdom, in landscape and language, climate or custom – so much so that most scholars of the period would align themselves with Hervé Le Bras and Emmanuel Todd, whose study of a vast number of features in French life in later times concluded that 'by rights, France should not exist': it had to be 'invented'.[1] If so, the 'invention of France' was most likely to occur around the function and dignity of the king (or, as some were already putting it in the thirteenth century, the *status regis*, the king's state). After all, the monarchy was ultimately 'the sole symbol of unity in the kingdom, far above the many communities it ruled.'[2]

The first signs that the crown might become a source of unity in France are usually located in the twelfth and thirteenth centuries. The story of that period has been told in English by a number of scholars, notably Elizabeth Hallam, Jean Dunbabin and, most recently, Marcus Bull and his collaborators.[3] In the wake of the fragmentation of public authority that arose from the collapse of the Carolingian empire in the ninth century, Capetian kings gradually restored the monarchy's standing. They did so, first, by tightening their grip on the small but fertile region around Paris and Orléans which formed the core of the king's *domaine*, and subsequently by exploiting their rights as overlords within the wider kingdom to absorb the dominions of certain leading vassals, as opportunities presented themselves. These developments led to a remarkable expansion of the royal *domaine*, particularly in the period 1191–1271. The notion that the king was sovereign in his kingdom developed in the course of the thirteenth century, as men trained in Roman law began to identify the French king's powers with those of the Roman emperors of old. The lawyers' claims found practical expression in the belief that royal legislation applied across the realm. By 1300, as Beryl Smalley has it, 'we leave the French kings on the upgrade, extending their authority over a prosperous, civilized country.'[4]

But in the late Middle Ages, unity around the crown became problematic in a number of ways. The right to the throne itself was contested between two lines of descendants of the last Capetians: on the one hand, Philip count of Valois (1328–50) and his successors, known to posterity as the Valois kings of France; and on the other hand, Edward III king of England (1327–77) and his successors, whose claim to the French throne was first affirmed in 1340. The dynastic contest which ensued is known as the Hundred Years' War, and it too has been the subject of several studies in English.[5] Underpinning that war – or rather, series of wars – was an older feudal struggle over the duchy of Gascony in south-western France. English kings held this land as a fief of the French crown from 1259 onwards. The conflict over respective rights in Gascony was one of several which erupted between French princes and their royal overlord and sovereign in late medieval France. Historians such as Édouard Perroy, John Le Patourel and André Leguai consider these struggles to be the salient characteristic of our period.[6] France is sometimes portrayed as having fragmented into a number of 'princely states', the rulers of which frequently made common cause with the kings of England after 1340, above all the dukes of Brittany (especially in the fourteenth century) and Burgundy (in the fifteenth century). Viewed in this light, unity under the crown could only be pursued once the English were defeated in 1453, and the last of the 'princely states' had finally sunk from view. A triumphant monarchy emerged from these contests, raised further than ever above its subjects by the permanent taxes and standing army which helped the king see off his rivals. A 'fair sixteenth century' of relative unity, stability and expansion followed, down to the start of the Wars of Religion in 1560.[7]

There is no doubt that the story of the Hundred 'Years' War and the roles of the princes of the realm should figure prominently in any history of late medieval France. The experience of war loomed large in the lives of the king's subjects, affecting their well-being and prosperity in a great many ways. War made the monarchy a natural focus for the formation of loyalties and identity, through the shared experience of mass processions to pray or give thanks for victory, for example. The princes were, after the king, undoubtedly the most important figures in political society. But to focus only on rulers is to present a narrow view of the political life of the realm in our period, and this book will take a broader approach.

Beyond the royal familial community and great fief-holders lay a wider polity made up of many other powers. Churchmen were among the oldest of these. One school of thought, under the influence of Georges de Lagarde's monumental work (1934–46) on the origins of a 'lay spirit' in the work of the theologian Marsilius of Padua and the philosopher William of Ockham, held that the role of the church in public life declined in our period.[8] Since that time, historians of the church such as Jean-Louis Gazzaniga and Vincent Tabbagh have rightly emphasised that clergy of varying descriptions continued to hold public office, own extensive lands, exercise jurisdiction and shape political ideas.[9] Below the level of the highest nobility there were tens of thousands of noble families whose members practised lordship and arms, as recent syntheses by Philippe Contamine and Marie-Thérèse Caron remind us.[10] The kingdom contained dozens of urban communities large and small which also had a significant role to play in political change, indeed more so in our period than ever before. This last point emerges clearly in surveys by Bernard Chevalier and Gisela Naegle.[11] Histories of rural France reveal developments that were surely part of the political life of the kingdom too, such as peasant revolts or community action against the widespread scourge of the soldiery.

Peter Lewis has called on historians to take account of the 'pluralistic nature of power distribution' in late medieval France, to show ways in which the 'political grass roots' related to royal and princely centres.[12] Clearly, a book like the one introduced here can only answer that call to a limited extent. But it can certainly attempt to incorporate the 'plurality of powers' into an account of the political life of France, and consider the interactions between them: kings and princes of course, but also nobles, churchmen, municipal authorities and peasant communities at the levels of village and parish. The picture which emerges is necessarily more complex than the roller-coaster, single-track story of the monarchy's 'progress', with its apparent crests (say, in 1300 or 1453) and its vertiginous plummets (for instance, in 1356–8, or 1407–29).

To situate this picture in an intelligble context for an Anglophone audience, I have sought to take account of broader social and economic change in the late Middle Ages. Understanding how money was found to pay taxes, rents and dues, build city walls and defray the cost of clerical services has meant considering issues as diverse as demographic change, peasant status, urban trade or seigneurial revenues. The sources available for the study of these subjects increase greatly in type and number from the fourteenth century on. For rural lordships, in addition to the cartularies used for some earlier periods, historians begin to find *censiers* (listing the *cens*, or dues, owed by tenants), detailed *dénombrements* (estimates of a fief's value presented by a vassal to his lord) and the first surviving lay seigneurial accounts (giving figures for income from dues and tolls, the sale of wood and so forth). Wills and notarial papers further extend the historian's scope, providing insight – among other things – into prices and land values. Life in towns becomes clearer too, thanks to the marked upturn in the production of municipal documentation during our period. The first sustained financial accounts and registers of council minutes were already appearing in the late thirteenth century, and were widespread from 1350 on – by which stage a plethora of documents pertaining to the raising of taxes was also emerging. These different kinds of material find analysis in the large number of regional studies of rural and urban life which have characterised French historiography in the twentieth century. The regional approach has the advantage of identifying elements of unity as well as diversity across the realm. The further subdivision of such studies into rural and urban histories is largely justified by growing evidence of differences between the two milieux, in matters as fundamental as mortality rates or religious practice. Contrasts between town and country will be a sub-theme in what follows.

Social and economic issues underpin the main thread of political history which runs through this book. At one time, writing political history meant studying institutions and their procedures, or else recounting history as a series of events (*histoire événementielle*). In the 1920s and 1930s, the *Annales* school of French historians famously found political history so described to be inadequate, and it was only from the 1960s onwards that the subject began to find its feet again through the work of scholars such as Bernard Guenée, Raymond Cazelles and Peter Lewis. The focus shifted away from 'institutions' and 'events' to the study of mental attitudes (Jacques Krynen's work on political thought, for instance);[13] to the prosopographical investigation of the men who gave the organs of government substance and weight (Alain Demurger's study of the holders of the office of *bailli–sénéchal* in the early fifteenth century, for example);[14] to the means of communicating authority through symbols and ceremony (such as the work of Guenée and Françoise Lehoux on royal entry ceremonies);[15] or to informal but fundamentally important processes of patronage and brokerage which permeated government at all levels (illuminated by Cazelles's research on political society under the first three Valois kings).[16] It has even become possible once again to envisage writing 'history as a series of events'. After all, a 'measure taken in 1400 does not have the same meaning as one taken in 1410.'[17] A number of studies by reign have appeared in recent decades which bear out this observation, notably Françoise Autrand's work on Charles V and Charles VI.[18] One of the key objectives of this book is to establish a narrative of events which students of the period can use, albeit a narrative suitably informed by a number of 'pregnant principle[s]'.[19]

With these introductory comments in mind, this book begins (Chapter 1, 'Ruling the French in the Late Middle Ages') with a discussion of the governing ideology and political culture of the kingdom, by which I mean the body of ideas reflecting prevalent political beliefs and interests, and the codes of conduct which shaped political action. Together, these factors reveal the unity of the kingdom as a political space, but this chapter will also say something about its diversity: not just the differences between north and south which are commonly pointed out, but also those which existed between east and west. As we shall see, long-term differences between continental and coastal France took on particular importance in our period.

In Chapter 2 ('Rural France, c. 1300–c. 1500'), we move from the king's concerns to look at the living conditions and preoccupations of the vast majority of his subjects, those who lived in the countryside. We pay particular attention to the demographic, social, economic and political impact of plague, famine and war and to forces for cohesion (as well as causes of migration) among the rural population. This chapter also considers the fortunes of those who owned the land rather than those who worked it, including ecclesiastical institutions and, increasingly, wealthy townsmen. By the end of the discussion it will be apparent that changing economic circumstances were not undermining the rural nobility's standing as the leading political class to the extent that some historians have argued; nor did they prevent the state's growing ability to tax the vast bulk of its subjects.

Chapters 3 and 4 use these points as the foundations of a political narrative for the period 1328–1461 ('Royal France, c. 1328–c. 1380 and c. 1380–c. 1461').[20] Although the royal familial community and the development of the Hundred Years' War loom large in our account, an important role is ascribed to the still-powerful nobility of the realm, grouped into regional networks which, in keeping with observations made in Chapter 1, can be broadly described as eastern and western in nature. The king's need for taxes drew other powers to the fore. To win approval for taxation and to hopefully speed up its collection, the royal administration began to consult assemblies of representatives from ecclesiastical institutions, the nobility and towns at the level of locality, region or kingdom. These gatherings, known as the estates (*états*), were intermittent and occurred in response to a summons from the king. How the estates fared was an important factor in determining the type of monarchy which would emerge from the conflict at the end of our period.

Finally, representative assemblies provided a forum for expressing the authority of another power at large in the realm, the municipalities. The importance of towns and townsfolk was such that they merit a chapter in their own right, not least because their action was mainly localised in nature and hard to present within a narrative account of the kingdom's history. We examine the demographic and economic factors which made the regional capital a key feature of our period, and, within the city walls, the political life of the urban community, played out around the ruling oligarchy, its rivals and its allies. This chapter also considers the role of municipal authorities within the political life of the realm – greater in our period than in the centuries immediately before or after.

No one believes any longer, with Augustin Thierry, author of a celebrated *Histoire du Tiers État* (first published 1853), that an all-conquering alliance of town and crown occurred in the late Middle Ages – not least because it has as its corollary the decline of the aristocracy, which is very far from the truth. But Thierry's emphasis on the importance of municipal government to its royal counterpart is entirely legitimate. The strength of the monarchy in late medieval France ultimately resided in its ability to assimilate and direct the energies of a plurality of powers, of which urban oligarchies were just one type. Churchmen of varying descriptions also played a key role, as servants, supporters and ideologues. Nobles remained the predominant military class with considerable power in the localities. To achieve its objectives, any royal administration would have to work through and with a plurality of such powers. In other words, if France was to be 'invented' around the monarchy in our period, it could not be on the king's terms alone.

Chapter 1: Ruling the French in the Late Middle Ages

Kings naturally sought to stand above all other forms of public authority in their realm, and in doing so the monarchy succeeded in establishing itself as a focal point of loyalty and identity among its subjects. In earlier centuries, churchmen such as Abbot Suger of Saint Denis (1081–1151) had played a key role in promoting the king's primacy by means of a 'royal religion' which claimed heavenly protection of the ruling line, and a special standing manifested, among other things, in the coronation ritual. Churchmen continued to have a close relationship with royal authority in the late Middle Ages as we shall see, despite the once-prevalent view that our period witnessed the birth of a 'lay spirit' and a declining role for the church in public life.

But reigning supreme was one thing, governing another. To give effect to royal authority, the monarchy had gradually developed administrative structures and a bureaucracy to attend to key matters such as justice and war. At first that administration was part of the king's household, but by the thirteenth century its various components were separating themselves out. How effective such an administration could be in communicating and enacting the will of the king depended on a number of things: not just the extent and nature of its own development, of course, but the diverse legal, linguistic, geographical and historical circumstances which prevailed across the kingdom.

With these points in mind, this chapter considers some of the key ideas which lay behind royal authority in late medieval France (**'Rex Christianissimus'** and **'Church and State'**), the means by which that authority was exercised (**'Rex Francorum'**), and the nature of the kingdom where that authority held sway (**'Regnum Franciae'**).

Rex Christianissimus

Of all the things a king of France could claim to be in the late Middle Ages, including lord, suzerain and sovereign, the title which truly set him apart from other rulers and magnified his powers within the realm was that of *Rex Christianissimus*, 'Most Christian King'. Lordship remained vital to the expression of a king's authority in France as elsewhere in Christendom, but even in its exalted form of suzerainty it retained a contractual quality. Lordship was renewed upon each succession, and undertakings were given on either side of the relationship when homage was performed. Notions of sovereignty which had re-emerged in France and England in the thirteenth century offered the prospect of unqualified obedience to the ruler, and it became increasingly difficult to contest the view, ultimately derived from Roman Law, that the French king was 'Emperor in his kingdom'. But even when it was understood as a gift from God, sovereignty, like lordship, was of this world not the next. By contrast, the legitimacy and authority of the Most Christian King were located between Heaven and Earth. When expressed in the royal pardon, as we see from the work of Claude Gauvard, the king's 'Special Grace' miraculously restored order to the world and contributed to the salvation of his people.

Components

The many elements that had become entangled in the central idea of 'Most Christian King' are usefully summarised by Étienne de Conty, a learned monk and judge in an ecclesiastical court who wrote in northern France in 1400. His views command our attention because he was not part of the inner royal circle of his day; indeed, as Philippe Contamine observes in his work on the author, it was on the king's orders in 1392 that he was passed over in the succession to the post of abbot at Corbie. Étienne tells us that of the five kings crowned and anointed in the west (those of France, England, Sicily, Scotland and Jerusalem), only the French king's divine right to rule came directly from God; it was not mediated by the papacy, which took tributes from the kings of Sicily and Jerusalem and homage from the king of England (a reference to England's status as a papal fief created in John's time). Of Christendom's 17 realms, the most richly endowed was that entrusted to the Most Christian King, 'the greatest, the most powerful, the most noble, the holiest and the most judicious' of all rulers.

Justifying each of these claims in turn, Étienne de Conty dwelled longest on the holiness of the Most Christian King. His coronation was superior because it entailed the use of a holy oil brought from Heaven by an angel for the coronation of Clovis, the first Christian king of France, by St Remi, archbishop of Reims. The Most Christian King could heal the scrofulous by his touch. The royal emblem of the lilies was another miraculous gift to Clovis after his victory at the Battle of Tolbiac (usually dated 496) and conversion to Christianity. In the subsequent history of Most Christian Kings, their special standing was exemplified by the refuge they had offered to popes and their defence of Holy Church against heretics within Christendom.

Étienne de Conty's views reflect a conception of sacerdotal kingship which was widely held and deeply layered by his lifetime. A tradition of royalist chronicle writing in the monastery of Saint-Denis dating back to the twelfth century was a rich source of such material. It was in this abbey that the royal war flag (*oriflamme*) and other insignia of kingship were kept from the twelfth century on. That the king was *Rex Dei gratia* was a fundamental tenet stretching back even further, to Carolingian times. The tale of the miraculous Holy oil used in Clovis's coronation was first recounted by Hincmar of Reims in the ninth century. By the late thirteenth century, as Joseph Strayer has shown, the link between France as a Holy Land, the French as a Chosen People and the Most Christian King could be found in a variety of texts, such as the sermons of the Dominican Guillaume de Sauqueville or the treatises of the jurist Pierre Dubois. Colette Beaune has demonstrated in her work on French royal ideology that the story of the lilies was a more recent development, one that gradually emerged in the course of the fourteenth century under the influence of monks at the Praemonstratensian abbey of Joyenval, and which attained wider circulation at the court of Charles V. Of all his attributes, however, it was probably the 'King's touch' which most tangibly demonstrated his sacred powers in the eyes of contemporaries. More than a century before Étienne was writing, as Marc Bloch established in his study of the thaumaturgical powers of kings, the sick were coming from regions as distant as Brittany, the Bordelais, Toulouse, Montpellier, Provence, Savoy and Lorraine to be healed.

At a time when the legitimacy of public authority was understood as a function of its antiquity as well as its sanctity, there were other ways in which Étienne de Conty could have chosen to emphasise the standing of the kingdom and its ruler within Christendom. Many French monastic chronicles contained versions of the story, first recounted in the seventh century by the chronicler Fredegar, of how Francio and his followers had fled from Troy and founded the Kingdom of France. The matter of Troy had gradually become linked to the later crusading exploits of Franks in the east and acquired a slightly less heathen character, with the result that it had emerged as an additional (rather than an alternative) vision of the kingdom's distant past. But the Trojan legend had its drawbacks too, notably the fact that other peoples had their own version of the story. The anonymous author of the *Débat des hérauts d'armes de France et d'Angleterre* (c. 1450) knew better than to adduce Trojan descent as grounds for French superiority over the English, because he was aware that Britain took its name from Brutus, descendant of the Trojan Aeneas, who had first conquered the isle of Albion from a race of giants.[1] By contrast, there was no need to debate whether there was more than one Most Christian King. Linked to the idea of France as a Holy Land and the French as a Chosen People, the concept demonstrated unequivocally the independence and the superiority of the ruler and the realm.

The evolution of an idea

Although its many strands were clearly very old, the idea of the 'Most Christian King' was a late medieval success in France, its propagation mainly the work of French churchmen. The title was originally accorded by popes to any monarch whose support was welcome or sought. In the course of Philip IV's struggles with Pope Boniface VIII over appointments, jurisdiction and taxation within the French church (1296–1302), it was royal apologists who began to use the title to justify the king's resistance to papal intrusion. In a sermon of the Dominican preacher Renaud d'Albignac (1302), a French audience was told that in his dispute with the papacy, 'what the king does, he does for the salvation of your souls.' The pope, by contrast, was a sinner (according to Guillaume Nogaret, one of the king's closest advisers and a leading protagonist in the disputes): Boniface VIII attacked 'the Gallic nation, a nation which is notoriously the most Christian.'[2]

The spread of the notion of Most Christian King in the first half of the fourteenth century is apparent in works such as the *Chronique des Quatre Premiers Valois*, but the strongest expressions of the idea emerged later, towards the end of the papacy's first residence at Avignon (1309–77) and during the Great Schism which followed (1378–1417). Even before the Schism began, Nicolas Oresme, highly respected theologian at the University of Paris and royal secretary, was arguing that it was the duty of the King of France – 'the most catholic and true son and champion of Holy Church and the most excellent of all the princes on earth' – to call for a council of the church to address the perceived abuses of the Avignon papacy.[3] In 1391, as solutions to the Schism were sought, the chancellor of the University of Paris, Jean Gerson, urged the Most Christian King to use his spiritual standing to help end the division of the church between Rome and Avignon. First conflict with the papacy, now division within the church itself greatly contributed to the moral authority of the Most Christian King.

Once the Schism was over, the French church passed a little further from papal control by its adoption of reform decrees of the conciliar movement under the terms of the Pragmatic Sanction of Bourges (1438). The notion of Most Christian King was more relevant than ever. Supporters of the Pragmatic could present the sanction as the natural culmination of centuries of royal protection of the church and of the faith generally, and of monarchs' personal devotion and generosity to both. Later in the fifteenth century, Pope Paul II made the title the standard formula of address to the King of France in papal correspondence.

The Most Christian King and his subjects

Although the title of *Rex Christianissimus* gave the king a certain moral authority in Christendom, it is the impact of the ideology within the boundaries of the kingdom which interests us here. Jacques Krynen argues that the concept effectively abolished

> any idea of a contract or constituent pact which might exist between the monarch and his people, an idea so characteristic of the medieval west, and which in other states . . . encouraged during the same period a veritable constitutionalism.[4]

To grasp the point, we need to note that the king's subjects – in common with many in the West – were commonly understood as belonging to different orders of society (also expressed as ranks or estates), or as different members of the same organic body (the nobles as the hands, the labourers and merchants the feet and so forth). Each estate or limb ideally performed its appointed task beneath a king whose primacy was divinely ordained, thereby assuring social harmony. The idea that the limbs of the body politic or the different ranks of society should ever control the head was, to use a

contemporary term, 'unnatural'. St Thomas Aquinas had taught in
the thirteenth century that God gave power to the people who then
invested it in a monarch, and this was a notion which excited intellec-
tual debate in other parts of Europe, such as Aragon. But in France,
the debate was passed over more or less awkwardly by commentators
in our period: the emphasis was firmly placed instead on notions of
political authority which were, in their nature, 'descending' (from
God) rather than 'ascending' (from the people). No wonder Krynen
considers the concept of Most Christian King as the key to the emergence of another idea, rule 'by absolute power'. Precisely this last
phrase can already be found in at least one source from the very end
of our period.[5]

In some key respects, of course, we should not exaggerate the
impact of the concept of Most Christian King. Among other things,
it was an idea which placed weighty restraints upon a ruler. The Most
Christian King, quite as much as his subjects, had a divinely appointed
role to fulfil, one he was personally bound to respect by his faith. The
Picard nobleman Philippe de Mézières – ardent publicist of crusading, and for a while an intimate counsellor and tutor of Charles VI –
thought that the sole purpose of the royal dignity was the good of
the king's subjects. Hence the following text from the prayer book of
Charles V, recorded by Jean de La Grange, bishop of Amiens, another
tutor of royal children:

> I protest I am unworthy of having received such an honour from
> you as to have become and been ordained king and leader of your
> Most Christian kingdom, and to have been entrusted with justice
> and government for its people. That is why I pray that you might
> give me sense, understanding and knowledge, so that I might con-
> duct myself wisely and justly enough to attain your grace, love,
> goodwill and paradise ...[6]

As Lydwine Scordia has argued, the 'superchristianization of the temporal power' embodied in the notion of Most Christian King could
even hamper rulers as they went about their business.[7] How, for
instance, could a Christ-like king justify raising taxes upon his subjects
for the purpose of carrying out his own divinely ordained obligation
to defend them? Many naturally concluded that the Most Christian
King should meet this expense himself: hence the longevity of the
notion that the king should 'live of his own', a major obstacle to the
growth of a fiscal state. While there may have been little sense of a
'constituent pact' between the Most Christian King and his people,

it was nonetheless expected that the ruler's responsibilities towards his subjects would be foremost in his mind – not least because his own salvation depended on it. Unjust wars and illegal claims to territory were among the other matters which gave late medieval kings pause for thought in their conversations with holy men and women, in confession, or in their daily prayers.

Nor was the practical reform of government alien to the towering construct of Most Christian King. On the contrary, reform was a moral imperative for all Christians and for the church. The archetypal *Rex Christianissimus* Louis IX set the tone for all of his successors when he promulgated the first of several reforming royal *ordonnances* upon his return from crusade in 1254. This act sent the *enquêteurs* – many of them mendicant friars and secular clerics, living embodiments, in Joseph Strayer's phrase, of the 'conscience of the king' – out into the realm on a more regular basis than before to reform abuses of government. Philip IV followed his grandfather's lead in March 1303 with a reforming *ordonnance* – the so-called 'great statute' – which sought to address the more common complaints of laymen and the church against his officials. Raymond Cazelles (in his work on reform of royal government) finds that the terms of the act were confirmed no fewer than 24 times in the remainder of the fourteenth century, notably in the crises periods of 1315–19 and 1355–7, although calls for reform appear to have tailed off in the fifteenth century as we shall see.

Whatever the aims and outcomes of reforming initiatives, their very existence comforted the belief that if the Most Christian King erred, he did so, not because of any personal failings, still less some inherent flaw in his divinely ordained office, but because he had been misled by evil counsel or was badly served. It follows that to challenge the Most Christian King directly must have struck contemporaries as a radical step to take. Anger, drink or madness led many royal subjects to make verbal attacks upon individual kings of France in the late Middle Ages, as Jacqueline Hoareau-Dodinau's work on letters of remission has recently shown in detail. But it was one thing to blurt out that Louis XI needed just a single horse to transport his council, quite another to reject the prevailing monarchical form of government altogether. And in pardoning the intemperate utterances of his subjects by letters of remission, the Most Christian King simply underlined the heaven-sent power to pardon. 'The state was founded more on forgiveness than on anger.'[8]

But how was one to deal with a Most Christian King whose government proved impervious to calls for reform, or whose conscience pricked him but little? The opposite of the *Rex Christianissimus* was the tyrant. As Peter Lewis has shown, this was not a charge which many intellectuals were willing to bandy about lightly in late medieval France. It is interesting to note that the theme of tyranny figured less and less in the writings of French commentators from the early fifteenth century onwards, around much the same time that the theme of a general reform of royal government was also beginning to dissipate. Worn down by the wars and political divisions of our period which are recounted in later pages, it seems that the king's subjects were gradually reconciling themselves to the need for strong kingship embodied in the notion of a *Rex Christianissimus*. Despite its limitations, the notion of Most Christian King was the core element of French political culture in the late Middle Ages.

Most Christian King and the royal blood

Yet it should not be thought that the notion of *Rex Christianissimus* placed monarchs beyond reach of all the challenges they might have to face. The king's primacy came from above rather than below, but it was also established over time by the holiness of the royal line. The point was made with some force in a widely disseminated defence of monarchical authority, the *Songe du Vergier* (1378). As Marion Schnerb and others have argued, this text was probably written on Charles V's command by Évrart de Trémaugon, formerly teacher of canon law at Paris and dean of Chartres cathedral. In it we learn that 'the sanctity of this blessed line' was proven 'first, by the deeds and miracles of My Lord Saint Charlemagne, of My Lord Saint Louis, king of France,[9] Saint Louis of Marseille,[10] saint Charles of Blois, formerly duke of Brittany,[11] and of several other saints.'[12] More than anywhere else, as André Vauchez has shown in his study of late medieval sainthood, the French royal familial community took a lead in promoting saints from among its own ranks. One can readily understand why, given the aura which saintly ancestors cast upon the royal line.

But the holiness of the line and its importance as a foundation for the notion of *Rex Christianissimus* were potentially problematic. Saintly predecessors set examples which were not easy to live up to. The charge of falling short when compared to one's Most Christian ancestors was laid before Philip IV by Pope Boniface VIII in 1302, before Charles VII by the princes who assembled at Nevers in 1442, and before the same king by those who objected to his refusals to revoke the Pragmatic Sanction of Bourges. The accusation was more than a calculated insult. Around the ruler were men of the royal blood who might be considered better representatives of the holy line. Members of the royal familial community certainly considered themselves a group apart in political society on account of the blood which flowed in their veins. In 1415, Jean, Duke of Berry, uncle of Charles VI, reportedly told a deputation of leading Parisians that

> you should not intervene in the affairs of my lord the king or of we who are of the royal blood, for we can be angry with one another when we want to, and we will make peace when it suits us.[13]

Duke Charles the Bold of Burgundy was not a popular man in the France of Louis XI, but nonetheless it was stated at the Estates-general of the realm in 1468 that because '[the duke] was of the royal line, . . . it was possible the crown could devolve upon him'.[14] Late in the reign of Charles VII, the perfectly loyal Norman priest Robert Blondel, tutor to the future duke of Brittany, François II (1458–88), warned the king that his kingdom (above all others) had been created 'by divine ordinance, not by human agency'; should it please God, He might 'transfer the government of it from anyone who is unsuitable to another who is more useful.'[15]

It is no accident that the strongest challenges to ruling kings in our period came from those who had the greatest claim, after the king, to be agents of the divine: his closest male relatives. The necessary relationship between holy bloodline and Most Christian King opened up the tiniest possibility of a 'pluralism of power' in late medieval France, even here, in the holiest of holies, the king's divine right to rule.

But in practice it could be asserted confidently that primacy within the blessed royal familial community still lay with the Lord's anointed. Christine de Pizan, one of the most successful authors of the period, daughter of Charles V's astrologer and widow of a royal secretary, thought the hierarchy could be understood arboreally. The princes of the blood were the sturdy branches of the royal tree, but the king himself was no appendage: he was the very root, his sons the fruit.[16] That Robert Blondel's fears were never realised suggests the processes by which one became Most Christian King had come to seem reasonably robust to the people that mattered.

The processes in question were initiated when one emerged as rightful heir from the blessed line – no longer by election (although that principle might still be invoked), but by dint of being the eldest male. The act of burying one's predecessor marked the official inception of a reign from the later thirteenth century on, when the *oriflamme* fell over the coffin and then rose again to the words 'Long live the King'. The mystery of the *sacre* (holy sanction of a king's coronation) saw the monarch anointed and receive communion in both kinds like a priest, before being crowned with the 12 peers of the realm or those chosen to represent them in attendance, characteristically divided into leading prelates and princes. It was on this occasion that the king swore the two coronation oaths, one to defend the church, the other to preserve peace, justice and orthodoxy in the kingdom. The coronation did not make the king, but it strengthened his power by associating it with God and the clergy, as Richard Jackson has noted in his study of the ceremony. So unnatural was the prospect of regicide to Frenchmen by the end of our period that however close some might have come to it, as Peter Lewis has demonstrated, the monstrous crime was imagined as a defining characteristic of English history, not of French.

In short, the Most Christian King was clearly superior. And yet equally clearly, the notion of a holy line incorporating a wider royal familial community cannot be neglected. Proximity by blood to the Most Christian King afforded the best means of obtaining access to his person, his council, the offices in his gift, the powers exercised under his authority, and the monies raised in his name. The greater the proximity to the king, the greater the expectations his relative might harbour. No wonder (as Jean-Philippe Genet observes) that 'this [royal] blood flows without fail...through the living tissue of the events of the closing centuries of the Middle Ages'.[17] When we come to our account of events in late medieval France, this point will become abundantly clear.

Most Christian King and other forms of public authority

Beyond the confines of the royal familial community, the notion of Most Christian King had the capacity to absorb, shape, override or undermine other visions of how public authority was exercised within the Kingdom of France. The king was not alone in offering protection, providing justice, granting liberties or taking levies, and so it was desirable to him that his legitimacy and primacy should be apparent and respected. Because a 'plurality of powers' existed in late medieval France, a plurality of ideologies existed too. But the sublime concept of Most Christian stood head and shoulders above the rest. The point may be demonstrated by a discussion of the two most significant forms of public authority other than the king, namely the leading princes of the realm and the municipalities.

Over the centuries, most princely dynasties of the realm had become related in one way or another to the royal line. It follows that to be the king's 'Fair Cousin' or his 'Good Uncle' was an important determinant of one's importance and power. To distance oneself from the Most Christian King by means of a distinct princely ideology was not an obvious course of action to take, at least for the majority. Some princes did have separate illustrious titles. René, Duke of Anjou (1434–80) inherited the title of king of Jerusalem, and vaunted it through the media of his seals and stained glass windows he gave to churches in his lands, as Christian de Mérindol has shown in his work on symbols of princely power. But René was also a cousin of Charles VI and brother-in-law of Charles VII, a prince of the blood and a vassal of the crown in France – an important but subordinate figure in the realm. The *éclat* of extra-regnal titles simply added lustre to the French royal line of which René was part, with the result that what might seem a competing ideology was in reality a complementary one. There could be many kings, but only one Most Christian King. In ideological matters, plurality here did not affect the one.

A similar logic affects how English rulers approached the question of royal ideology in a French kingdom which all of them, from 1340 onwards, claimed the right to rule. Most kings of England were more or less distantly related to their counterparts in France. (Hence, as Malcolm Vale observes in his study of the origins of the Hundred Years' War, Edward III's adoption from a young age of two fleur-de-lys in his seal.) It would have been misguided for Edward or his successors to project an ideology of kingship which was alien to established French practices. While some attempt was made to develop a distinctive face for the so-called 'dual monarchy' under Henry VI in the early 1430s, as John McKenna argued, it is possible to overstate its importance. For most of his time as regent in France from 1422 onwards, John Duke of Bedford, Henry VI's uncle, adhered closely to a French royal style of rule. Hence his willingness to bring out the *oriflamme* in times of crisis, or his devotion to St Denis, 'protector of all of France', discussed by Guy Thompson. It was only sensible to act like the king of France if one wanted to be taken as such.

But some princes clearly did wish to distinguish their dominion from that of the king, and had all the ideological trappings to match. The last two Valois dukes of Burgundy, Philip the Good (1419–67) and Charles the Bold (1467–77), are sometimes discussed in this connection, although in reality it was not until very late in our period that the umbilical cord between France and Burgundy was broken – a point we will return to in a later chapter. The Montfortist dukes of Brittany are a more striking and clear-cut case of a princely dynasty which distanced itself from French crown. The relative independence of Brittany which fuelled these ideological initiatives resulted from the duchy's geographical location within a wider Atlantic world, and the fact that the dynasty owed its position to military success rather than royal gift. From Jean IV's time onwards (1364–99), as Michael Jones has shown, the dukes claimed a number of regalian rights. Evidence for the crowning of Breton dukes emerges in 1401, although the practice was almost certainly older. By 1417, the dukes were styling themselves rulers 'by the grace of God', and by 1455, ducal servants were sometimes referred to in internal documents as 'royal officers belonging to the sovereign' (by which the duke, and not the king of France, was meant).[18] One Breton author even claimed the only difference between the coronations of Breton dukes and French kings was the unction used in the latter case.

That princes should imagine their authority in terms that consciously imitated royal authority was not a new development, as Geoffrey Kolziol has argued in his work on Capetian political culture. But in contrast to earlier centuries, French kings – now Most Christian Kings – were far less willing than their predecessors to permit even pale imitations of their authority. The few princes who affirmed they ruled by the grace of God in late medieval France generally found their supposed rights contested, such as Jean IV, Count of Armagnac (1418–50), who was forced to drop his claims by Charles VII's administration. Moreover, the gulf between princely and royal ideologies had widened significantly compared to Capetian times. Efforts were made to project the antiquity and sanctity of Breton ducal power into an imagined past by chroniclers linked to the dynasty, as Jean-Christophe Cassard and Jean Kerhervé have demonstrated. But the chronicles in question were comparatively few in number, late in redaction and less significant in terms of their reception than the French royal chronicles written at Saint Denis. As Bernard Guenée has shown, the French royal *Grandes Chroniques de France* from the monastery of Saint Denis were copied and owned across the northern half of the realm, including Brittany itself. Kings might have been irritated by Breton pretentions, as Louis XI was by the François II's adoption of the symbol of a crown with flowerets on ducal seals and banners and by his use of the title *Dei gratia*. But a duke by the grace of God was not a king *Dei gratia*, let alone a Most Christian King. And for all the ideological trappings of Breton ducal power, it remained possible, at the end of our period, to describe oneself as both a Good Breton and a Good Frenchman.[19]

Unlike the dukes of Brittany, and indeed unlike cities in some other parts of Europe (notably Italy), French municipal authorities did not seek to acquire a distinct ideology of power. This was not because towns were weak and insignificant (far from it, as we shall see). But the main characteristic of municipal ideologies is that they were either compatible with, or simply part of, the monarchy's. The term *bonne ville* which was used to define towns as political entities in late medieval France helps explain why municipal ideology was so oriented towards the crown. As Albert Rigaudière and others have shown, towns were considered 'good' because they were loyal to the king. Charters and privileges which defined towns as corporations were issued by the monarch. Understandably, urban origin legends tended to imagine glorious pasts which town and crown shared, preferably from as early a time as possible. At Reims, as Pierre Desportes has shown in his work on that city, the municipality's earliest privileges were attributed to Saint Remi, baptiser of Clovis, reputedly the first Christian king of France (a spiritual link that was natural for a city that hosted the king's coronation). Elsewhere, municipal ideology tended to emphasise antiquity rather than sanctity. At Chartres, as Claudine Billot notes, the author of that town's *Vieille Chronique* (1389) aligned the municipality with the Trojan legends of monarchy. Most authors (following the twelfth-century historian Rigord) considered Paris a Trojan foundation too. Perhaps it was just a southern sense of humour that led the Provençal Honoré Bouvet, in his wide-ranging treatise entitled *The Tree of Battles*, to claim the capital had been founded at the scandalously late date of 499 AD, by Saracens.

'The French monarchy retained a veritable monopoly over ideological processes of legitimation, against which no ideological production from a particular locality or social group could impose itself, other than at a purely local level.'[20] Princely ideology tended to imitate the royal, while municipal ideology tended to sublimate itself within it. The state relied on more than ideas: it also relied on its ability to raise money and men, or to provide justice. But ideas were of capital importance, and the notion of Most Christian King was supreme among them.

Church and State

But what of the clergy? It is apparent from what has gone before that secular power was imbued with the spiritual power in late medieval

France. Few historians would now agree with Joseph Strayer that the 'secular sovereign state' rose at the expense of the church, that a 'laicization of society' had occurred in the thirteenth century and the church had consequently become 'a private society with no public powers or duties.'[21] Most historians would now accept instead Jean-Louis Gazzaniga's observation that 'the state did not impose itself over the church, it imposed itself by means of the church' (albeit in ways which differed significantly from earlier periods of French history).[22] The relationship between church and state may be considered in human, material and spiritual terms.

Churchmen in the service of the state

Few French churchmen spent all or even most of their time in the service of the Most Christian King, but some clearly did. Kings of France and leading princes of the realm had a growing power to influence appointments to canonries and other ecclesiastical offices. As a result, the post of canon was a popular one among clerical princely servants. As Elizabeth Lalou has shown, 273 of 1884 officers who are known to have served Philip IV (14.5 per cent) held the post of canon in a cathedral or collegiate chapter.

It might seem that the state acquired servants on the cheap when it succeeded in placing men in the church, and that the spiritual duties of the cleric were compromised by his service of the state. As Louis XI ironically remarked of Jean V Héberge, bishop of Évreux, in 1475, 'he is a right devil of a bishop, because although it may not always be so, at present he is fully occupied by my affairs.'[23] Such was not necessarily the attitude of the clergy. Canon law taught that it was the duty of the church to assist those who held the secular power. To judge from the snapshot of the bishops of the realm presented by Vincent Tabbagh for the year 1438, nearly one-fifth must have believed that serving the ruler was entirely in keeping with their calling, for that is how they were occupying themselves.

Clerics no longer enjoyed a near monopoly of governmental positions as they had in smaller royal or princely administrations of earlier times, but they were still present in significant numbers, despite (and in some areas, because of) growing specialisation. The *Chambre des comptes* which emerged from the king's court early in the fourteenth century with responsibility for audits, records and appeals relating to crown revenues was, until well into the reign of Charles VII, a bastion of clerics in government (as Jean-François Lassalmonie's study of royal finances shows). It probably helped that clerics were far more likely than nobles and lawyers to have experience of administering large estates. Another body which began to emerge from the king's court at the start of our period, the *Parlement*, was divided on principle of parity between clerical and lay members. As Françoise Autrand has demonstrated, that principle was largely respected from 1350 to 1450. Clerics were less well represented in the king's council (judging from Pierre-Roger Gaussin's work on that body in the reigns of Charles VII and Louis XI), but among their number were some of the longest-serving and most regular attenders. Robert de Rouvres, bishop of Séez and later of Maguelone, sat for 30 years on Charles VII's council and was deputy keeper of the royal seal.

Resources of the church in the service of the state

The material resources of the Most Christian King were also greatly increased through his relationship with the church. Clerical tenths (levies of one-tenth of clerical income) were granted to French kings by popes long before our period began, ostensibly for a specific holy enterprise such as the crusade, but increasingly for a wider range of purposes too. These levies were a regular occurrence in the decades leading up to c. 1350, then again after c. 1420. Prior to the fiscal changes of the mid-fourteenth century, clerical tenths were in fact the single largest source of income after receipts from the main administrative units of *bailliages* and *sénéchaussées* across the realm, and in the 1320s alone they amounted to between 15 per cent and 30 per cent of treasury revenues.

In principle, the clergy enjoyed exemptions from the direct taxes which the crown began to raise with greater success from the second half of the fourteenth century on, but the widening fiscal net captured clerical income in many other ways. Indirect taxes affected clerics and ecclesiastical institutions, and kings permitted municipalities to demand contributions from local clergy towards the spiralling costs of defence. French kings also enjoyed a number of older rights over the property and income of the church, such as the right to levy a fine upon fiefs which were acquired by the church (the *amortissement*), or the role of guardian, with its attendant profits, over vacant bishoprics and monasteries (the *régale*).

In the long term, finally, ecclesiastical models and structures shaped the development of royal taxes directly in our period. The diocese formed the basis of many of the *élections* or administrative districts for the raising of taxes from the middle of the fourteenth century on. The parish became the basic unit for the apportionment of the direct tax burden of the state, a natural development given that it performed a similar function for a significant number of revenue sources for the church (including the tithe or payments for sacraments), and was used for administrative purposes by local lords (to announce dates for the holding of seigneurial tribunals and so forth). From 1355, the local parish priest advised on the selection of a panel of three of four worthy men who would visit heads of household, in principle in the priest's company, to establish how much taxation should be paid. Increasingly, the local worthies chosen were churchwardens already entrusted with collecting revenues for the upkeep of the church building, the focal point of the community.

Here we see that the work of the king's government had become the concern of another form of public authority, the church in its base unit of the parish. The capacity of the 'royal state' to develop depended on its ability to mobilise the support, resources and skills of other powers in society. While the point is made here with reference to the church, later we will extend the observation to other groups, notably the military classes and municipalities.

Church, state and nation

Last but not least, the authority of the Most Christian King was bound up with and advanced by the spiritual concerns of the church. When men of the church spoke to their flock, they did so in a language that emphasised hierarchy, order and obedience, all of which were necessary, since the Fall, to help attain salvation. When the Norman preacher Guillaume Pepin sought to explain the nature of God to his audience in the later fifteenth century, earthly comparisons were adduced:

> We see in all the heavens that one is supreme, who is called the first mover, just as among the seven planets only one has primacy. In addition, we see that in politics there is only one supreme monarch, who gives all the orders, and this is the most perfect form of rule. We find the same in the church, in which one pope rules alone. And from all these examples we can conclude that God is one.[24]

In the language of the mass, the conflation of kingship and the divine reinforced the themes of love and obedience which the audience was incited to offer unhesitatingly to the highest authorities, on earth as in Heaven. Jean Gerson's instructions to clerics are suggestive here:

> When the bells ring for mass you should think that it is a message from the King telling of the news of the King's arrival, and you should run to Our Lord as is fitting... When mass begins, you should know and think that the King is entering the door and you should go to welcome Him, and you should greet Him and say: welcome, My Fine Lord, and you should think how nobly He comes among you, and you should glory in His great beauty, in how great He is, how gracious, how glorious, how wise, how powerful, how graceful, how forgiving...[25]

Preachers did sometimes speak directly about political matters in late medieval France, as the southern Franciscan Olivier Maillard did in 1470 when he railed against royal taxes. But outright condemnation of public authorities risked provoking social unrest: it was exceptional and rarely went unpunished. At Châlons in Champagne, the town council obliged all clergy

> to counsel and exhort by preaching and in other manners... that everyone shall be good and true to our sovereign lord the king and to the good town of Châlons, to the honour and profit of the said king and his kingdom, and the public weal of the kingdom, and to My lord the duke of Burgundy.[26]

More commonly, then, the sermon sought to reinforce authority. Parish priests were less and less inclined to preach to their flock during mass, but the king still featured in this daily event by mentions of him in prayers. Instructions of the bishop of Autun to the priests of his diocese in the fifteenth century included the order to have daily

> prayers for the pope and the Holy Roman church; for all of the church, its unity and peace; for the kingdom and the king; and for the duke of Burgundy and Brabant.[27]

The sequence of the prayers is significant, as was the order of the public authorities mentioned in the earlier example by the town council of Châlons. Although Autun and, at the time, Châlons lay within the dominions of the duke of Burgundy, Burgundians' prayers still placed the king above the duke. That was the right order of the world from the church's perspective, a perspective which necessarily accorded primacy to the Most Christian King and a secondary place to the princes of the realm.

Religious processions became a notable feature of late medieval spirituality in France as elsewhere, and they too brought the king and the wider royal familial community to the forefront of people's minds. At Abbeville in 1414, the population was called to process (among other things) for 'the reverence of God, and to beseech and pray that He might grant health and a good life to our lord the king, to our lord of Guyenne [Louis, Charles VI's eldest surviving son, d. 1415] and all those of their blood and lineage.'[28] Processions were primarily located in urban milieux, but could also draw in rural populations from miles around. Divine intervention was sought by processants to alleviate a wide range of ills, including plague, famine or hazardous weather conditions. They were also increasingly held in the hope of bringing victory to the king or ending political crises in his realm. As Bernard Guenée has shown in his study of public opinion during the reign of Charles VI, more than one-quarter of over 100 recorded processions in Paris during that period sought peace in the conflict between the princes of the realm. In circumstances such as these, 'politics does not seem to "use" religion, [politics] still seems to be completely immersed within it.'[29] The remark is equally valid for public events surrounding proclamations of peace. As Nicolas Offenstadt has recently demonstrated, the various elements incorporated within the publication of peace treaties located the event in a deeply spiritual context: the prolonged ringing of church bells was accompanied by cries of 'Noel' (recalling the feast of the Nativity), and by the lighting of bonfires (associated with the Feast of St John). Unified celebrations and noise-making warded off evil, in this case the evil of war, and opened a new era of divinely ordained, miraculous peace.

That the Most Christian King could occupy a particular place within the spiritual lives of his subjects seems clear. That standing might be reinforced in other ways during our period. A traveller in the diocese of Poitiers in our period could chance upon the chapel of Our Lady of the Recovery, built around 1370 to commemorate Charles V's reconquest, or that of Our Lady of Grace, erected as a memorial of Charles VII's suppression of a princely revolt known as the Praguerie (discussed later in this book). Among the saints most commonly mentioned in vernacular prayers in French Books of Hours are figures closely associated with the kingdom and its ruling dynasty, such as Saint Denis and Saint Michel. In prayers to these saints (whose importance was underlined by Colette Beaune in her work on royal ideology), the kingdom and one's own salvation and safety might be mentioned in the same breath:

> O Lord Saint Denis, who from false credence,
> Converted to God the kingdom of France,
> In faith, in charity, in firm assurance
> Maintain my heart, and keep me from mischance.[30]

If, as Bernard Guenée suggested long ago, the state created the nation in late medieval France, then it is clear, as his own work on processions has subsequently shown, that the church and the Christian faith played a large part in that process.

Rex Francorum

Ruling the French in the late Middle Ages clearly involved more than ideologies and drawing upon the human, material, spiritual and institutional strengths of the church. According to one fourteenth-century source,

> the government of the kingdom of France resides in five things, in council and government relating to: war; justice; the expenditure of his household; in … matters relating to the *Domaine*; and the remission of misdeeds, crimes and misdemeanours.[31]

As Françoise Autrand notes, each of these areas was primarily the concern of a central body, although considerable overlap existed between them. The widest range of competence lay with the *Conseil* at the centre, which could intervene in virtually any area of government. The *Trésorerie des guerres* disbursed monies for the king's armies. Administering the king's justice was the primary concern of the *Parlement* in Paris, and later also of its regional counterparts at Poitiers (1418–36), Toulouse (1443–1790), Grenoble (1453–1790) and Bordeaux (1456–1790). The *Chambre des comptes* and the *Chambre du Trésor* were mainly occupied with the finances of the king's household and *domaine*, while royal correspondence (including documentation for remissions) was the concern of the king's notaries in the *chancellerie*. Together with the royal household and the wider court which assembled around the king's person, and his servants in the localities grouped around the post of *bailli/sénéchal*, this was the core of royal government.

Capetian origins, Valois development

Naturally, the origins of a good many of these organisations and offices can be traced before our period begins. The establishment of *baillis* and *sénéchaux* (equivalent offices in northern and southern parts of the realm) occurred at an early stage, during the reign of Philip II (1180–1223). The office was originally established to oversee the older and more numerous *prévôts*, who continued to provide a first level of royal justice in the locality. *Baillis/sénéchaux* had wide-ranging competence in justice, peace and finance in the region, much like English sheriffs. Gradually, many of their roles devolved upon specialised officers as their work became more complex and demanding in the later Capetian period. The most important of these specialists were financial receivers (reporting directly to the *Chambre des comptes* in Paris from 1305), lawyers (*Juges-mages* in the south, lieutenants, advocates and proctors elsewhere) and captains (established with a military role from 1317 in some of the *bonnes villes*).

To an older generation of historians which considered institutional developments to be of paramount importance in political history, it seemed that the thirteenth century witnessed an apogee in French government. Many of the major organs of the state emerged in that time. The *Parlement* developed from the king's court during the thirteenth century (its earliest independent records date to 1254), and the *Chambre des comptes* was just beginning to do so, acquiring its own locale in 1303–4 and a clearer definition of its role by royal *ordonnance* in 1320.

In reality, of course, a great many governmental developments occurred after 1328, some of which were of immense importance. Take the issue of how kings funded their wars, the very first item on the list mentioned above. Between the war treasurers who disbursed monies to the king's armies and the parish notables who, at the opposite end of the scale, apportioned taxation in the locality, a range of new offices and procedures evolved over the course of the second half of the fourteenth century. At the root of these developments was the office of *élu*. The *élus* were usually townsmen, less often clerics and nobles, originally 'chosen' (hence their name) by representative assemblies in the localities during the 1340s and 1350s to collect subsidies from the king's subjects. The *élus* were not, strictly speaking, royal officers in their first incarnation, but became so as the crown gradually absorbed the post during the first two or three decades of its existence. (In passing, we note once again how the royal state could simply be an extension of other forms of public authority.) The *élus* ultimately answered to a new post which emerged at the centre, the *général des finances*, whose task it was to audit and redirect the monies which had been raised to the war treasurers. Such was the weight of business generated by tax-raising in the localities that a body eventually emerged around the *généraux des finances* known as the *Cour des aides*. This was a court of appeal for cases already heard by the *élus* in matters such as exemptions, fraud, non-payment and the like. Sustained activity in the locality was therefore generating significant administrative change at the centre in late medieval France. The fiscal product of these procedures eventually dwarfed the resources of thirteenth-century kings, as we shall see later.

Limits of government

Despite the development of an apparatus for raising taxation and other late medieval developments in government, we should not be tempted simply to replace the notion of a Capetian Valois apogee in governmental matters with a Valois one. In reality, the reach of government remained limited in our period.

Royal government was a relatively small world in the fourteenth and fifteenth centuries. Setting aside the king's court and adding together the personnel of the *Parlement*, the *Chancellerie*, *Chambre des comptes* and the *Chambre du Trésor*, the masters of the mint and the other main services, Françoise Autrand calculates that there were no more than 200 men at the royal centre during the reign of Charles VI. That figure remained fairly stable to the end of our period. The number of personnel at the *Parlement* in Paris, the largest central body save the royal court, did not grow significantly between 1360 and 1515 (although provincial *parlements* did emerge as we have seen). As Robert-Henri Bautier showed, Philip VI's reign witnessed considerable expansion in the personnel of the chancellery; thereafter, there was relative stagnation until the second half of the fifteenth century. Even in the locality where change was perhaps most evident, we would do well not to exaggerate the presence of royal officers. The number of *baillis–sénéchaux* virtually tripled in our period, and with the creation of each new *bailliage* or *sénéchaussée* came an increase in the number of specialists and auxiliaries in their service. But the total number of *baillis/sénéchaux* was never much more than 100. Gustave Dupont-Ferrier thought that the *élus*, usually between one and three of them operating in administrative units known as *élections*, could be counted in the low hundreds across the realm. Reviewing studies of royal administration just after our period ends, David Potter notes that royal officers amounted to just over 4000 executive office-holders, rising to perhaps double that figure later in the sixteenth century. But even then, the number of royal office-holders and their dependents was around one-sixth of the size of that same group in the France of Louis XIV. Encounters between the king's men and the king's subjects were clearly increasing in our period, and were helping form attitudes towards the royal state, for good and for ill. But the number of such encounters, and the impact they might have had, remained necessarily limited.

Historians would now commonly point to a second limitation of government, what Robert Fawtier called 'administrative ignorance and distraction' in late medieval France. In the *Chambre des comptes* under Charles VII, as Henri Jassemin showed in his study of that body, the masters could not be sure if the regional receivers who answered to them were alive and in office, or indeed what their names were, for registers of nominations were not kept. The 1328 parish and hearth survey which the masters collated for the royal *domaine* was an impressive achievement, but Ferdinand Lot has shown that the surviving copies contain numerous errors, such as the underestimation of the number of parishes in Anjou by a factor of nearly 12. A manual made for the *Chambre*, first studied by Philippe Contamine, contains the imaginative claim that the kingdom was composed of 1,700,000 church bell towers (i.e. parishes). This is an entirely fabricated figure which probably appealed because of its sheer size, and because the number 17 generally had positive associations in Christian symbolism.

Given such evidence, it may well be true (as Fawtier argued in another article) that fourteenth-century kings would have found it impossible to imagine what their kingdom looked like – indeed, no map of France is known to have existed before 1472. The royal administration could, if it needed to, get a letter to the southern reaches of the kingdom in less than a week under Philip VI, and by the close of our period a relay system was established to permit news to travel from Tours to Bordeaux in a day under the best conditions. Officers of the *Parlement* in Paris had some understanding of the geographical extent of their jurisdiction, summoning plaintiffs and officers to hear cases and appeals from the *bailliages* and *sénéchaussées* in a clear order (as Françoise Autrand has shown). At the local level, the king's administrators usually knew the limits of their jurisdiction, to within a few hundred metres in the case of the *bailliage* of Senlis, studied by Bernard Guenée. But clear evidence of the limitations of administration at the centre cannot be ignored. However few external restrictions were placed upon the Most Christian King

by the ideologues, royal power, when expressed through the imper-
fect mechanism of an administration, was far less impressive in reality
than it was in theory.

It should be noted (although it rarely is) that the same point is
true of princely government. For those who consider the fourteenth
and fifteenth centuries as a new age of principalities in French history, a theme first articulated by Édouard Perroy and developed by
John Le Patourel, the emergence of princely administrations was a
serious threat to royal authority. But if the organs of princely government were modelled on those of the crown – indeed, were sometimes
run by the very same men – we are entitled to doubt their ability to
impose their master's will any more effectively. Princely administrations had smaller territories to govern than their royal counterparts,
but they were smaller themselves too. (The *Parlement* established by
Charles the Bold for all his territories in 1473 was modelled on that
of Paris, but with a core of around 30 it was roughly one-third the
size of its royal equivalent – without counting the personnel of the
new regional *parlements* mentioned above.) The mere existence of
the royal administration was a further problem for its princely counterparts. Appeals against outcomes in local courts could be directed
to the *Parlement*, and a growing number of crimes (*cas royaux*: royal
cases, such as coining) were reserved for the king's justice alone. It
is important not to exaggerate tensions between royal and princely
administration of justice, but the hierarchical relationship between
the two levels of jurisdiction was clear. In few cases could it really
be said that the king's administration was 'virtually excluded' from
the lands held by leading royal vassals or apanaged princes in our
period.[32]

Rather than construct an account of late medieval French history
around the principalities as separate administrative entities, it is helpful to think of the princes as important elements in that 'plurality
of powers' whose interplay governed the political events discussed in
later chapters of this book. More broadly, the limits of governmental powers discussed here show that the state in late medieval France
could not easily impose itself. In the words of Bernard Guenée, 'the
state was only able to develop because it was accepted and even
desired.'[33]

The importance of office-holding

So historians no longer consider the administrative achievements of
the thirteenth century as a highpoint of governmental efficiency, and

are wary of exaggerating the reach of royal (if not yet princely) government in the two centuries that followed. But in one key respect 'the creation of royal corps of officials and the *parlements* [did] constitute the political dynamic of that period.'[34]

The small governing elites mentioned above tended to solidify and perpetuate themselves from the early fourteenth century on, and a great deal of power became concentrated in their hands. By the close of the fifteenth century, a fluctuating oligarchy of a dozen or so men, the so-called masters of the kingdom of Charles VIII's reign, was said to be able to dominate royal government.[35] As Mikhaël Harsgor (who coined this term) acknowledges, governing oligarchies were a feature of earlier times too; and we might add that they existed as much within the localities as they did at the centre. Between these many powers the political life of the kingdom was made. The key to their emergence and influence was the acquisition and retention of office.

Royal office was very often acquired by soliciting it directly from the king. Werner Paravicini (in the context of a comparative history of governmental institutions) illustrates the phenomenon perfectly with the example of how the post of *élu* for the city of Reims was acquired from a newly crowned Louis XI (1461). The king was approached no fewer than three times (once out on the road between Reims and Château-Thierry, later in the royal gardens at Les Tourelles, then finally within his chambers around eight in the evening at the Bastille) to agree to give the post to a particular supplicant. The practice of impetration was not, of course, a free-for-all. Gaining access to the ruler meant acquiring supporters like the king's chamberlain, equerry or even barber, all of whom were important men because they were close to the prince. But the press of petitioners around a king generated confusion and could lead to the nomination of more than one man to a single office, thereby contributing to the 'ignorances and distractions' of government discussed above. Once again, the sublime concept of royal power present in the notion of 'Most Christian King' seems very far removed from the reality of the daily business of governance.

For the most important posts in government, election (rather than royal nomination) was preferred by reformers and was increasingly becoming the norm. At first 'election' entailed the selection of a candidate, not by poll, but by the deliberations of a suitable body of men deemed able to judge his qualities. Elections by poll began to take place under Charles V. Other trends were gradually developing which would be less popular with reformers. Venality (in the sense of the public sale of office) became more common in the early sixteenth century, but from the beginning of our period the private sale of office between individuals was sanctioned by the royal administration in lowly posts such as that of royal sergeant. Private sales began to spread up the hierarchy of royal office towards the end of the fourteenth century, affecting important local posts such as *bailli*, procurator and royal advocate. The purchase of office might be regarded as an investment, the office itself a property to be passed on by practices such as resignation of office *in favorem* (whereby the officer resigned in favour of a named successor). Hereditability of office was not yet widespread, but it too was beginning to emerge by the second half of the fifteenth century.

Once office was obtained, its bearers tended to bind themselves together in different ways, as a group and as factions within the group. Marriage alliances were one means of achieving this end, with the result that governmental bodies might come to resemble extended family networks. Among the personnel of the *Parlement* of Paris from 1345 to 1417, a group studied in great detail by Françoise Autrand, a gradually increasing proportion of officers were related to one another: just under one-third had at least one relative among their colleagues at the start of that period, but nearly three-quarters were in that same position by the end. Another marked trend was the rise of men on the coat tails of a great lord or royal servant to whom they were already tied by bonds of lordship and regional association. Raymond Cazelles has demonstrated how, in the household of Philip VI, vassals and near neighbours of the powerful Burgundian *bouteiller* of France, Mile de Noyers, acquired a good number of key posts, including master of the household, master of petitions to the king's household, master of the royal stable and master of the queen's household. These figures in turn had the possibility of introducing men (and women, in the queen's household) of their connection into royal service. Further down the scale, royal service might acquire a familial air as a result of generations of marriages: the Thibault family at Senlis, for instance, whose members and relatives included a considerable number of royal advocates and procurators in the *bailliage* during the fifteenth century.

The process of election by one's peers and the bonds that grew between the families could produce a certain *esprit de corps* among royal servants. The crown might strengthen this sense of incorporation by extending the royal safeguard to its officers while carrying out their duties, and by the second half of the fourteenth century the idea was emerging in the *Parlement* that to attack a man entrusted with the king's business was an act of treason. The special status of the

king's man might be identified visually to the population in a number of ways: in his costume, in royal banners placed over his house
by the *bailli* as a sign of the king's protection, or in the place he
was accorded in the rituals of monarchy. Members of the *Parlement*
processed through Paris in their robes of vermillion (for laymen) or
violet (for clerics) lined with ermine on a range of occasions, notably
in royal funerals during which their unchanged attire served as a
reminder that although one king was dead, royal justice was eternal.
But emerging notions of public service and an *esprit de corps* did not
change the fact that office was sought because it could bring considerable benefits to the occupant, his family and friends. Here we
begin to touch on the key dynamic of political life as it evolved in late
medieval France.

Patrons, brokers and clients

If one wanted something done – the level of a tax negotiated, a
privilege restored, the outcome of a case influenced – it helped considerably to know the right people in the right places. Office-holding
encouraged informal mechanisms of brokerage which are difficult to
follow in the historical record, but which clearly enhanced the importance of the king's administration to other forms of public authority
in the realm.

The most important of the governmental organs where brokerage
prevailed was the royal court, far larger numerically than all the other
services combined. Although Elizabeth Lalou has succeeded in recovering something of the history of the royal household which lay at the
core of the wider court for the early part of our period, important
sources that would have permitted direct observation of networks of
influence and favour at that level were lost to fire in the eighteenth
century. But evidence of clientage at court and its impact does begin
to emerge indirectly, in the writings of a new wave of court critics.
Literary figures in the *chancellerie* (notably the royal secretaries Jean
de Montreuil and, after him, Alain Chartier) were among the earliest figures in this phase of renewed court criticism which emerged in
the late fourteenth and early fifteenth centuries. For such writers, the
court seemed to be dominated by greedy petitioners whose demands
for office, gifts and pensions inevitably drove up taxes. The king's
men in the *Chambre des comptes* were just as bad as the courtiers, to
judge from the comments of Nicholas de Baye, scribe of the *Parlement*
in the early fifteenth century. Observing their interventions in the

Parlement on behalf of family and friends, Baye was reminded of the Parable of the Unjust Steward (Luke 16: 1–9).[36] Down in the *bailliages*, as Bernard Guenée demonstrated, plaintiffs sometimes claimed that their adversaries were unbeatable in court because they were related to the *bailli*'s lieutenant or the king's procurator or his advocate. At the centre of these multiple networks of influence and favour, peopled by patrons, clients and brokers, was the king – a figure whose authority was their lifeblood, but whose ability to get things done was often constricted by their actions. A few examples will help illustrate these points in a more tangible way.

Municipalities needed brokers at the centre whom they could count upon to achieve their ends. Acquiring powerful friends usually required the distribution of gifts, and in the case of towns it is possible to follow the process because municipal administrations made and preserved records (whereas many other elements of political society, especially nobles and noble networks, did not). Pierre Desportes finds that an entire rubric of Reims's accounts was given over to *courtoisies*, such as the 48 garlands of roses offered to the masters of the *chambre des comptes* in 1340 (a gift the latter had themselves specified), or the 1,000 local pears and 3 dozen cheeses presented to the wife of the president of the *Parlement* in Paris in 1353. Some municipalities retained a team of fixers and legal experts in the capital to look after the town's affairs. One member of such a team was the jurist Jacques Bachelier, procurator for the city of Tournai. Bachelier's letters back to the magistrates were read aloud before an assembly in the town, and included the name of the usher who let him into the room where Charles VI received him, 'lying on his bed'.[37] The use of intermediaries at court was another way of exercising influence. One such was Hélie de Papassol, notary, whose journal recording the money he distributed to servants and relatives of the great royal officers on behalf of the authorities of Périgueux in 1337 was studied by Arlette Higounet-Nadal. Such fixers were important to the king's counsellors too, for through them they received a proportion of the rewards of office. As Bernard Chevalier has noted in his work on relations between the king's council and the towns of the realm, royal advisers even worked out zones of influence across the realm so as to avoid conflicts of interest between them.

Great princes relied on the services of men in the higher echelons of royal government quite as much as municipalities. During the prolonged period of Charles VI's mental illness discussed below, the leading princes of the realm sought to establish control over the substantial tax revenues of the crown (as Maurice Rey has shown in his

study of the royal *domaine* under that king). The most effective way
to achieve influence was through the appointment of specialists who
could be relied upon to achieve favourable outcomes for the prince.
Gradually, the royal financial administration was peopled with experts
who were princely clients. Jean, Duke of Berry was one of the first
princes off the mark, placing his friend, Gonthier Col, royal secretary and celebrated humanist, among the *généraux des finances* who
managed income from taxation. Two years later, Berry managed to
place another of his men in high financial office, this time Martin
Gouge, a canon from Bourges who was also his own treasurer. Soon
the duke of Berry was followed by his nephew, Louis of Orléans,
who obtained posts for the Master of his own household, Guillaume
de Laire and several other Orleanist servants. By the second half of
1404 the Orleanist stranglehold over the king's finances which these
men achieved for their master was such that the new duke of Burgundy, John the Fearless, found that his revenues from the crown
were rapidly drying up. The consequences of increasing Orleanist
control over key offices were dire, as we shall see later.

For now, the example illustrates how the development of a corps of
royal officers at the centre could constitute the most important 'political dynamic' of the period – not because of the size and efficiency
of central institutions, but because of informal mechanisms of power
distribution which developed around individuals serving within such
bodies. Hence historians' gradual abandonment over the past generation of the study of 'institutions' per se, and their greater interest
in the men who held office in the main organs of royal government,
usually studied using prosopographical methods.

Ruling the French was a more complex business in 1500 than it
had been in 1300, involving more men in general and more specialists in particular, all of them serving across a greater number of organs
of government. But growth was uneven, more evident in the locality
than it was at the centre in our period, where (with the exception
of the court) the number of royal servants remained relatively small.
Princes had a role to play in ruling the French, but they too formed
part of a wider network of influence and favour which centred upon
the king, and which extended outwards from the small but disproportionately powerful royal centre through many patrons, brokers and
clients to men and bodies with greater purchase in the locality: to
barons and noble affinities, merchants and municipalities and bishops and other clerics. The kingdom over which these powers were
exercised may now be considered in greater detail.

Regnum Franciae

As late as the thirteenth century the kingdom was still referred to as *Francia*, a term that appeared in the early Middle Ages and could mean where the Franks lived generally, or a particular centre of Frankish power, the Parisian region. The use of the term *Regnum Franciae*, Kingdom of France, is first recorded in 1205, and by the start of our period it had become the norm in documents issued by the royal *chancellerie*. In the course of the thirteenth century the king himself became *Rex Franciae*, 'King of France', rather than *Rex francorum*, 'King of the Franks'.

The first detailed description of the kingdom was written by Gilles le Bouvier, usually known by his official title of Berry herald, in the context of his *Livre de la description des pays* (Book of the description of lands, c. 1450). There we learn that the realm extended from Sluis in Flanders in the north to Saint-Jean-Pied-de-Port in the Pyrenees in the south; from Lyon in the east to Finistère in Brittany in the west. It was 'closed' by natural boundaries on all sides save the east, where Le Bouvier described a looser frontier of four rivers: the Rhône, the Saône and the Meuse, thence one day's journey to the Escaut in the Cambrésis, and down that great river to the Channel. These were effectively the frontiers created by the Treaty of Verdun in 843 to fashion the West Frankish kingdom of Charles the Bald from the Carolingian Empire.

There were other boundaries which Le Bouvier might have mentioned, but only one of them entered his account – that attributed to Gaul, incorporating lands now in the Empire, but 'which used to belong to the Kingdom of France, and where they speak French coarsely'. These lands included some which were closely connected to the kingdom in our period: the county of Burgundy, purchased in 1295 but tied to the duchy of Burgundy thereafter; the counties of Valentinois and Diois, held from the crown from 1316; the Dauphiné, purchased in 1349 on the condition it would always be held by the heir to the French throne; and the county of Provence, ruled by Angevins from 1384, and absorbed into the kingdom in 1486. In all, 18 duchies, 94 cities and 10 archbishoprics made up this 'Kingdom of France, the most pleasant, most gracious and best proportioned of all the others'.[38]

In this last remark, we touch upon a key characteristic of all descriptions of the kingdom viewed from the political centre, its essential unity. Gilles Le Bouvier saw the realm as a harmonious whole, with an equal balance of summer and winter months and a losange shape, neither square nor long. Even the wine-producing regions of the kingdom were handily placed near those which did not have vines. A similar tone pervades the anonymous *Débat des hérauts de France et d'Angleterre*, which stated that it was the very absence of harmony in England's geography – too few rivers, an intemperate climate – which made it inferior to France. Although recent victory over the English had surely contributed to the vision of the Kingdom of France which these military men shared, the view from the royal centre was always likely to be a unitary one. Already in the reign of Philip II, royal advisers were imagining the kingdom as a single 'vast lordship' under the monarch.[39]

The reality, of course, was far more complex. The diversity which characterised the Kingdom of France can be illustrated by a discussion of law, language and geography, and by a brief overview of how the king's authority had extended across the realm by the start of our period.

Law

In the practice of law, the diversity of the kingdom seems most obvious in the differences between a northern half where customary law prevailed, and a southern half where written Roman law had made a strong reappearance in the course of the twelfth and thirteenth centuries. The line between the two ran southwards from (and including) the Lyonnais, Forez, parts of Auvergne and La Marche, southern Saintonge into most of the Bordelais and, above all, Languedoc. When the Dauphiné and the county of Provence were joined to the kingdom, Roman law increased its presence still further.

It would be misleading to lay too much emphasis on a north–south legal divide in the kingdom. Customary law did continue to operate in the south long after the influence of Justinian's Digest re-emerged there, and indeed in some areas, the co-existence of the two could cause considerable confusion. At the end of our period, as Robin Harris shows in his study of Valois Guyenne, it was possible for a royal proctor to refuse the introduction of new evidence in a case on the grounds that customary law forbad it, only to be flatly contradicted by an advocate who told him written law had always applied in that region, not customary. Roman law meanwhile had spread north from an early stage and was studied there, not least at Orléans. In the course of the later Middle Ages, the jurist learned in Roman law became a feature of municipal and royal government in the north quite as much as the south, and the notary recorded the transactions and arrangements of every day life in both halves of the realm. Finally, customary law was being set down in writing in the north in the period c. 1250–1400, rather than simply retained in the memories of lay judges and transmitted orally. The development tended to further reduce contrasts between different forms of law, as Roman and even Canon law influences shaped the process of redaction. Customals were set down during this time for Vermandois, Picardy, Beauvaisis, Normandy, Brittany, Anjou, Touraine and Poitou, often by royal practitioners of law who were acting, not in response to any known central initiative, but out of an apparent desire to make it easier for judges and plaintiffs to dispense and obtain good justice.

Despite signs of growing uniformity and some common characteristics north and south, diversity was still the main feature of legal practice across the realm. Between northern customary practices there existed considerable differences on points of law, so much so that in his *Coutumes du Beauvaisis* at the close of the thirteenth century, local *bailli* Philippe de Beaumanoir observed that 'customs are so diverse that one will not find two castellanies in the whole Kingdom of France which follow the same custom in all cases'.[40] A century later the Norman jurist Jacques d'Ableiges thought much the same: 'there are even local customs which exist in one small enclave among several others, [different] from the surrounding *pays*, and where the custom, which is totally contradictory to this small place, has no authority.'[41] In the south too, Roman law practices could be considerably modified from one jurisdiction to another by charters, privileges and statutes which had accreted over time, effectively giving each community its own law in fundamental matters such as the upkeep of highways. Northern customals accepted some aspects of Roman law but not others. As Paul Ourliac and Jean-Louis Gazzaniga note in their joint work, Roman law pertaining to property held in mortgage was not followed in Brittany and Anjou, but that relating to the guardianship of minors was.

And then there was the separate question of how the law, whatever its form, was applied (or indeed not applied) by judges in the very many jurisdictions that existed across the realm. If a plaintiff were unhappy with the decision of a seigneurial or municipal court, he could appeal, albeit at a cost, to a higher jurisdiction. If the case went (at even greater cost in money and time) to the *Parlement*, it came before legists who were increasingly interested in 'using such appeals in order to abrogate local customs that did not fit [their] own ideas of

jurisprudence'.[42] This last point suggests that if enough appeals had
wound up at the *Parlement* in Paris, greater uniformity would eventually have emerged. But the *Parlement* seems to have been quite happy
to accept the kingdom's diversity (for example, in the separation of
some of its business into cases from Languedoil and Languedoc), as
indeed were those fifteenth-century kings who created regional *parlements*, in which local practitioners mingled with men from Paris.
In any case, we may doubt whether the volume of business passing
through the *Parlement* was ever such that it could effect wholesale
change from the top down. As Romain Telliez notes in his study of
royal officers before the king's justice in the fourteenth century, cases
from regions badly affected by war are few and far between in the
judicial registers of the crown – and needless to say, there were many
such regions in that troubled period.

The king himself might decide to take steps to increase uniformity of practice, if only because of the number of complaints he
received from plaintiffs weary of having to prove which custom they
should be judged by. But this only happened very late in our period.
Charles VII issued an *ordonnance* at Montils-lès-Tours in 1454 instruct-
ing that 'the usages, styles and customs of each *pays* be written down,
in accordance with the customals and the people of each *pays*'.[43] The
resulting customals were to be brought before the *Parlement* of Paris
or the king's great council for approval. Such was the resistance of
local practitioners of law that very little was actually achieved, but
redactions did take place in Touraine, Anjou and Burgundy. A quarter of a century later, in an initiative studied by René Gandhilon,
Louis XI had the ambitious idea of amalgamating all the customals
into one 'new custom' applicable across the realm. In the end, Louis's
death put paid to the scheme. It was not until the middle of the six-
eenth century that the *Parlement* of Paris finally completed its review
of the redaction of customals ordered by Charles VII in 1454. In law,
diversity ruled.

Language

Law touched most people's lives at certain points, but language was
something they used everyday, certainly in oral form and (for a much
smaller proportion of the population, although how small is impossible to tell) in writing. Although diversity remains the overwhelming
characteristic here too, there were at least two broader trends in
the written language during the late Middle Ages which should be

mentioned: the spread of French in governmental matters, and its usage to express ideas which had hitherto been the preserve of Latin.

The shift from Latin to French as the language of government was a slow and uneven process, but important steps were taken in that direction during our period. Change was apparent earliest in locality and region rather than at the centre, with French becoming the language used in the administration of the *bailliages* of the north and in the *prévôté* of Paris already in the later thirteenth century, as Louis Carolus-Barré demonstrated. The reasons behind the development are suggested in Philippe de Beaumanoir's observation that lay plaintiffs found themselves at a disadvantage in courts where proceedings were conducted in a technical Latin. The same reasoning doubtless lay behind the adoption of French in administrative documents among certain northern and eastern municipalities in the thirteenth century, considerably earlier than the crown's use of the vernacular, particularly those where an emerging literary culture can also be discerned. Latin remained the main language used in the *Parlement* throughout our period, although already in the fourteenth century its members were advised to use a simple Latin close to French. From the second half of the fourteenth century onwards, French came to predominate in letters issued by the *chancellerie* to a wide range of individuals and corporations. In turn, it seems, the weight of administrative usage gradually began to exercise a normative effect upon the vernacular, as Serge Lusignan has argued, resulting in the emergence of a 'king's French' relatively devoid of the traits of regional written forms as early as the first half of the fourteenth century in some northern *bailliages*.

The crown would eventually try to impose the use of French in government by means of the *ordonnance* of Villers-Cotterêts (1539), but the halting acceptance of this measure in the south serves as a reminder of the limitations of central government's purchase – or even ambitions – in the area of linguistic change. While readers of Occitan could probably understand the king's French and vice versa, the illuminating eyewitness account of how, in 1443, the Dauphin Louis and his secretary failed to comprehend a letter handed to them by an envoy from the municipality of Millau suggests this was not necessarily the case (although as Auguste Brun reminds us, the Dauphin's clear irritation at receiving such a letter, and the fact that the municipality subsequently used a secretary who could write in French for its dealings with the crown, should also be mentioned). As Philippe Martel notes in his study of language in the south, Latin remained the primary language of written communication between royal government and urban communities into the fifteenth century. Regional forms of Occitan figured strongly in the greatly increased bureaucracy of municipalities, such as town council minutes and correspondence between southern municipalities. The example of Montferrand discussed by Tony Lodge, where Jean, Duke of Berry replaced a recalcitrant municipal administration with his own men in 1390, effecting in the process a sudden switch from Occitan to the king's French in the town's records, is interesting because it is exceptional.

In the course of the fourteenth and fifteenth centuries the vernacular developed considerably as a literary language, further enhancing the performative capacity of the written word. Lodge estimates that around 23 per cent of the vocabulary of modern French was first coined in our period, a notable proportion given that literacy levels in the late Middle Ages almost certainly did not match those of a more populous France in later centuries. The lexical creativity of the period and its contribution to a more uniform written vernacular may be explained in a number of ways, but perhaps above all by the growing number of learned northerners who were prepared to use French prose as a medium of communication. The trend had emerged first in the thirteenth century in the writing of history, as chronicle writing moved from its monastic and latinate background into aristocratic households (a phenomenon illuminated by the work of Gabrielle Spiegel). The translation and impact of classical histories, sometimes in compilation such as *Li Faits des Romains*, is one example of the growing creativity of the vernacular in that earlier period. Through history-writing the vernacular was coming to be seen as a language capable and worthy of mediating authoritative texts. The trend was not much enhanced by religious beliefs in the late Middle Ages, for clerics encouraged devotion over knowledge among layfolk, as Geneviève Hasenohr has shown. Some theologians, like Jean Gerson, did not even want the laity reading the Bible directly, although Guyart des Moulins rendered it partially with glosses in 1295, and Raoul de Presles produced a translation for Charles V in 1377. But in law, as we have seen, customals were being written in the vernacular in the fourteenth century; and under Charles V, political thinkers began to express their complex ideas in French. Nicolas Oresme's translation of Aristotle's *Ethics* even provided a glossary of the many unfamiliar terms and neologisms he had coined (including such fundamental concepts as *aristocratie, monarchie, oligarchie* and *définition*). Albert Menut estimates that this writer alone enriched the French language with more than 1000 words which he used for the first time.

Factionalism and troubles from Charles VI's reign onwards saw the growth of a polemical literature in the vernacular in treatise and verse forms. Public exchanges between poets in the service of competing figures in the French polity sharpened an awareness of the art of rhetoric and its application to the vernacular. The writing of French verse and prose came to be seen as appropriate pastimes for authority figures, as Duke René of Anjou (1434–80) (author of *Le livre du coeur d'amour épris*) and Duke Charles of Orléans (1407–65), a celebrated poet, demonstrated in their different ways. The spread of a more uniform literary French, less marked by regional traits and enhanced by neologisms, was resulting from these late medieval developments, and this is the language which the printing press would later adopt and spread. Presses existed as early as 1470 in Paris, but their influence is mostly a later story which can be followed in the work of Peter Rickard, among others.

It is important not to exaggerate the impact of literary developments upon linguistic change. Diversity was apparent here too, not least between north and south. Occitan was the language of town chronicles at Millau, Cahors and Montpellier, and texts originally written in Latin and French were translated into Occitan in our period, including a Latin encyclopaedia for Gaston III Phoebus, Count of Foix (1343–91) and the *Doctrinal de Sapience*, written by an anonymous Cluniac monk in the fourteenth century. Occitan grammars continued to appear in the late Middle Ages, such as the *Leys d'Amor*. While some famous southerners wrote in northern literary French, such as Honoré Bouvet and Gaston Pheobus himself, author of a successful treatise on the art of hunting, they were exceptional.

A second obvious limitation to note is that access to literary French affected but a small part of the population in the north itself. There have been optimistic evaluations of the extent of literacy among the rural and urban populations of Picardy, Champagne and Burgundy in our period, but the mention of schoolmasters established at the initiative of local church, municipality or lord sheds little light on what literacy actually meant in such instances. What we can say for certain is that book production was still dominated by Latin, and that book ownership was uncommon due to the costs involved. The evidence of surviving datable manuscripts studied by Carla Bozzolo and Ezio Ornato indicates that vernacular works amounted to between 20 per cent and 30 per cent of books made in France in our period. Twenty per cent of surviving wills from Tournai mention books, compared to just 3 per cent of those which still exist for St Omer.

The greater spread of literacy from the sixteenth century permitted norms of writing to have some impact upon the spoken language, but diversity was even more profound in the field of speech during our period than it was in written forms. Flemish, Breton and Basque (in that order) were spoken by relatively few, while English domination in large parts of France had little discernible impact upon linguistic norms, save perhaps in terms of abuse (*dogue*) and domination (*milord*). English residents had to learn to speak French, and did so with more or less success (less in the case of the English travellers in France recounted in the *Fabliau des deux Anglois et l'anel*, whose linguistic incompetence resulted, not in a meal of lamb, but of donkey flesh). But even setting aside these obvious areas of diversity in speech, subjects of the French king spoke in ways that could seem utterly different to their compatriots, ranging from ugly to humorous to incomprehensible.

One story may be suggestive here. It comes from a letter of remission studied by Jacques Monfrin for a fight which broke out between two workmen who were mimicking each other's accents in a Paris street in 1388. One of the workers was Parisian, Jean de Chastillon, the other Picard, Thomas Castel. Between northern speakers there was clearly a measure of mutual comprehensibility. The geographical mobility of the period was contributing to an increasing number of encounters between different language groups. Small-group language speakers like the Picard in Paris tend to assimilate more easily to the large group they move among, in the long-term contributing to greater uniformity, but that process was clearly not far advanced in this case. The fact that it was the Parisian who first mimicked his interlocutor suggests he thought his accent superior to the Picard's, a sentiment with which some contemporaries (and not just Parisians) would certainly have concurred.

Paris was still a vibrant capital in 1388, but the upheavals of Charles VII's reign would see a shift of the political centre of Valois France to the Loire (where, perhaps not coincidentally, the best French was subsequently deemed to be spoken). It is far from certain that the capital retained the same power to effect linguistic change two generations after the date of our story. Moreover, periods of upheaval could lead, not only to geographical mobility typified by the Picard in Paris, Thomas Castel, but also to a closing of ranks and a strengthening of rural communities. Denser social networks slowed the pace of linguistic change. Castel was a skilled male, a social type more likely than most to migrate in search of work and settle away from the family network. Female migration into cities seems to have been less common, at least judging by data cited in a later chapter. The finding has significant linguistic ramifications given that language acquisition was shaped in important ways within the domestic environment, and through maternal influence. The story of Thomas Castel and Jean de Chastillon therefore does not easily lend itself to a straightforward picture of growing uniformity of speech in France in our period. No wonder it was still possible for later writers to complain about France's linguistic diversity, as Christiane Marchello-Nizia notes in her history of the French language: Racine, for example, who wrote to his friend La Fontaine that once he had passed Lyon in his travels, he was in as much need of an interpreter as a Muscovite would be in Paris.

In such circumstances bilingualism, at least among certain groups, was desirable. Historians have sometimes assumed bilingualism was widespread among the elites of late medieval France, but the assumption may be misplaced. Jacques Rossiaud has shown that notable townsmen of Lyon did tend to know French but their bilingualism was superficial. Examples cited by Auguste Brun in his study of the spread of French in the south of France reveal that some people were clearly comfortable dealing with complex transactions in both French and Occitan. But others were less at ease with the northern tongue, such as the counsellor of Count Jean IV of Armagnac, a future bishop of Montauban, who claimed to his English interlocutors that he found it easier to negotiate with them in Latin rather than French. Nor was speaking French popular with all regional elites, such as the bishop of Viviers who demanded in his will in 1303 that his heirs should speak Occitan, not French. All of these examples raise complex and interesting questions, but they tend to demonstrate that bilingualism among elites should not be taken for granted. And below the elite, of course, there were many for whom French was difficult or impossible to follow. Dauphiné bishops instructed their priests, in French, to conduct key parts of the ceremony of exorcism in *romans* so that their flock knew for sure the task had been performed.

Arguably, of course, it did not matter to the king which language his subjects spoke, so long as his authority was recognised within the *Regnum Franciae*. Nor did speaking differently from the king mean that his subjects were necessarily any less loyal. But the linguistic diversity of the kingdom did pose practical problems, and encouraged reliance upon narrow social groups with the requisite skills.

Geography

Few would argue that the kingdom's linguistic diversity promoted unity in the late Middle Ages, but there were once scholars who thought that France's geography did precisely that, such as the great nineteenth-century historian Jules Michelet, or Paul Vidal de La Blache, an historical geographer of a later generation. The geography of the kingdom is more likely to be seen today as one more reason why France should not exist.

Then as now, the land mass of France contained four distinct fluvial basins which led in quite distinct directions: the Seine linking Burgundy, Paris and ultimately Normandy; the Loire draining the waters of a wide region through Anjou and the *pays de Rays*; the Garonne, stretching from the western edge of Languedoc to the Atlantic beyond Bordeaux; and the Rhône-Saône corridor which royal France straddled only occasionally. Together these basins account for over half of the surface of the territory of modern France, more so in the case of the late medieval kingdom. In Berry Herald's description the major navigable rivers figure prominently, creating natural links between towns situated along their length. He does not consider the corollary of his statement: at a time when the easiest means of communication was by water, France's main river systems also created divisions within the land mass of the kingdom.

Where rivers meet the sea there lies a coastal France which is different again, as Marc Russon's recent study of the 'warrior coasts' reminds us. The vast western and northern shoreline faced a sea which Berry Herald (thinking like a typical man of the geographical and political centre) believed led only to the land of the mythical Prester John. In reality, of course, those seas led to other maritime communities, not least across the Channel (a stretch of water that was still known in the fifteenth century as the English sea). England was also at the end of the wine route from Gascony up the western seaboard, past Brittany and the Channel Islands (which remained in English possession after the loss of Normandy in 1204). Along this maritime flank (as Michel Mollat has shown in his study of Atlantic France), people used English and Celtic words for certain navigational terms, borrowings from Dutch for aspects of ship construction, and Spanish and Portuguese loanwords for juridical features of seafaring. These linguistic realities are symptomatic of the fact that in Western France, the 'preoccupations, interests, adventures and vital terrain would virtually never be those of the capital and the great landmass of the French interior'. As a result 'the seaward periphery was a ready focus for dissidence.'[44] By contrast, the Mediterranean seaboard in our period was short and far removed from the political centres of the north. Lucien Musset's belief that it was the Mediterranean façade above all which made France is certainly applicable to Roman Gaul and some other periods of French history, but is of limited relevance to the late Middle Ages.

Looking inwards from the western seaboard with Maurice Le Lannou (in his study of the physical geography of France), we find that the terrain rarely exceeds 200 m in height in a line from Bayonne on the Bay of Biscay to Rethel on the edge of the Ardennes. To the East of that line lay more hilly or mountainous terrain, where forestation was denser. But even the lower landscapes of the west gradually changed in complexion away from the sea. A rolling west marked by open fields and, increasingly, hedgerows, gave way to vaster plains with narrow fields in the north and east. This was the richer land which had encouraged the Carolingians to form a capital there, as Edward Fox notes in his historical geography of France. Continental France looked to a landlocked capital rather than to the sea, especially in eastern regions such as Burgundy. Paris itself looked for sustenance – in grain, livestock and wine – through river networks which led north, east and south. In certain basic respects the capital looked everywhere but west.

The contrasts between east and west are further apparent in terms of habitation. Large towns and cities were a feature of eastern France, especially the north-eastern corner on the edge of Flanders and into Artois (where cities such as Tournai, Amiens, Lille and Arras were to be found), and the south-eastern corner in Languedoc, where Montpellier, Narbonne and Toulouse were prominent. Atlantic France, by comparison, knew only limited urban development. Charters for urban communities were a late development here. Bordeaux and La Rochelle were by far the largest ports on the coast. Inland, with the exception of the corridor of Loire towns and Poitiers, western France was markedly more rural than the north east and south east.

Whereas language and law tend to emphasise differences between the northern and the southern halves of the kingdom, geography therefore highlights contrasts between maritime and continental France. The result is an impression of even greater diversity. France lay at the westernmost tip of the central landmass of the European continent, and concentrated within its boundaries was all the diversity of that vast area. According to Bernard de Rosier (1400–75), a southern bishop trained in law, the kingdom contained different languages and peoples, but it was united by its adhesion to a single church and, above all, by the government of a line of 'Most Christian Kings' assisted by 'the heavenly angels of the Lord'.[45] As we shall see in our closing section, the king's authority over the geographical kingdom in 1300 could not be described in such terms.

The Kingdom in 1300

As a lord, the king directly ruled those lands which, along with a great variety of rights, constituted his *domaine*. These lands and rights were scattered across the geographical kingdom and are not easily represented on a map, but they had grown in number and scale from the closing decades of the twelfth century onwards. It was during this time that the core of royal possessions around Paris and Orléans was extended by the acquisition of Artois and the Amienois to the north, and then spectacularly by the collapse of two extensive princely empires of earlier times. The great increase in the size of the royal *domaine* massively augmented the financial resources of the Capetians, bringing as it did more payments of dues, tolls and other levies from the populations which lived under the king's direct lordship.

The first princely empire to fall was that of the Plantagenet counts of Anjou, when King John lost Normandy, Anjou, Maine, Touraine and Saintonge to Philip II (1204–6). The Angevin empire that once straddled the Channel and extended down the western seaboard of France was now reduced essentially to its northernmost and southernmost elements, respectively the kingdom of England and the duchy of Aquitaine or Guyenne. The formerly Angevin territories extended the French *domaine* enormously, leading the chronicler Rigord to dub Philip II 'Augustus'. By the terms of the Treaty of Paris in 1259, John's son Henry III accepted the losses that had been suffered, and agreed that he and his heirs would perform homage for the lands they still held in the Kingdom of France.

Guyenne, like all the great fiefs, did not form part of the *domaine*, but it did belong to the kingdom and was held of the king by his vassal the duke. Although the king had limited financial rights in the great fiefs, his justice was sovereign there. By the late thirteenth century, the Plantagenet administration in Guyenne had devised several expedients for limiting the number and impact of appeals from the duchy to the king's *Parlement* in Paris, but they could never be eradicated completely. The powerful idea that 'the king is emperor in his kingdom,' articulated among others by Roman lawyers such as Jean de Blanot and Jacques de Révigny in the second half of the thirteenth century, was finding practical expression in the exercise of royal sovereignty over Guyenne.

The king's authority over his vassals outside the *domaine* naturally depended a great deal on the number of contentious issues and the *rapport de force* between them. Relations between the dukes of

Guyenne/kings of England and the rulers of France were inevitably the most fraught in these respects. Emerging notions of sovereignty on both sides of the Channel aggravated other tensions, such as growing hostility towards the Plantagenets among some elements of the French royal familial community, or the Franco-Scottish alliance of 1296. Twice the duchy of Guyenne was declared confiscate by its French suzerain and war ensued, first in 1294 when Edward I was deemed to have failed in his duties as a vassal, then again in 1324, over a dispute concerning the royal enclave of Saint-Sardos.

Plantagenet awareness of the vulnerability of Aquitaine increased as a result of these conflicts, leading successive dukes to seek alliances elsewhere in the realm or on its periphery. Alliances were at first made with rulers in the Low Countries and down the eastern flank of the kingdom, as Henry Lucas's work on the Low Countries and the Hundred Years' War showed in great detail. Henry III, Count of Bar (1291–1302) was one eastern lord prepared to consider an alliance with Edward I, a decision which resulted in him having to perform homage to the French crown for his lands on the left bank of the Meuse in 1301, thereafter known as the *Barrois mouvant*. It was the naturally dissident western seaboard of the realm, and not the landlocked east oriented towards the capital, which eventually provided the most willing allies of the Plantagenets in their struggles with French kings.

But for now, marriage alliances were contracted to bring the king/duke and his French royal overlord more firmly together. The second wife of Edward I (1272–1307) was Philip IV's sister, Margaret. Edward's son by his first marriage, Edward II (1307–27), took Philip IV's daughter Isabelle as his bride. When Edward III (1327–77), the grandson of a French king, married Philippa of Hainaut, herself the niece of King Philip VI, in 1327, he thus had even better Capetian credentials than his wife. The gradual entangling of the Capetian and Plantagenet royal lines could help settle differences, but in the long term they created further potential for trouble, not least the fact that Edward III, under the right circumstances, might have a claim to the throne of France.

As for the other leading vassals of the French king, the *rapport de force* on the eve of our period was more obviously in the crown's favour. In the county of Flanders, Philip IV was able to rely on support from the governing classes of some Flemish cities (especially Ghent) against the threat of an Anglo-Flemish alliance. For a time, the establishment of direct royal rule in the county seemed a distinct possibility, particularly when French forces occupied Flanders in 1297 and 1300. Popular revolt and a resounding defeat for the French in 1302 at Kortrijk (Courtrai) prevented this outcome, but Philip IV was still able to impose a demanding peace in 1305, and in 1312 the towns of Lille, Douai, Orchies and Béthune were made over to the king by Count Robert (1305–22).

In Brittany, meanwhile, royal influence was such on the eve of our period that it looked as though the county might wind up sharing the fate of its neighbours, Normandy and Anjou, by being absorbed within the Kingdom of France. In 1297, Brittany was raised to the status of a duchy (a standing which some Breton rulers had felt entitled to since the tenth century), and Jean II (1286–1305) was made a peer of the realm. At no point was a sense of the autonomous rights of the dukes of Brittany ever lost, and indeed Jean III (1312–41) sought confirmation of Breton privileges in 1314–15 from the French crown. Nonetheless, the *Parlement* in Paris became the court of appeal for cases from its Breton counterpart, much as had happened in Gascony two generations earlier.

Last but not least, the dukes of Burgundy were among the most reliable of leading royal vassals, attending the king's court and providing spouses for the royal line. Robert II (1272–1306) was a trusted member of the royal familial community, serving as lieutenant in Languedoc and governor of the county of Burgundy after its purchase in 1295. Ducal loyalty did not prevent royal penetration into the duchy by means of agreements with lesser lords and the protection of church lands, but as Jean Richard's work on the history of Burgundy demonstrates, royal gains were limited. For their part, the dukes of Burgundy acquired a measure of influence over French kings which was not given to many of their contemporaries among the princes of France, and influence over a king was potentially a firmer basis for power than extensive territorial possessions. In his work on French political society in the early fourteenth century, Raymond Cazelles has noted that 'men of the east' were an established feature of Capetian government some time before they became trusted servants of the Valois kings, such as the chancellor Gui Baudet and the president of the *Parlement* Pierre de Chalon under the sons of Philip IV. In contrast to the west, where Guyenne was a frequent source of concern, kings of France could look to the east with greater confidence. Ancient geopolitical realities – a dissident west and an east which looked to Paris – thus manifested themselves in France around 1300.

The second princely empire to collapse to the monarchy's benefit in the thirteenth century had been in the south, that of the Raymondine counts of Toulouse. The process began with the invasion of Languedoc by northern crusaders in 1209 and was effectively settled by the treaty of Paris (1229), but it was not until 1271 that these lands were wholly absorbed into the royal *domaine*. By the end of the thirteenth century, the spread of royal government was extensive. The demise of the leading princely houses during the region's absorption into the kingdom removed a potential for conflict that was present elsewhere in the kingdom. The large towns of Languedoc, which once looked as though they might acquire liberties and powers to compare with their counterparts in Italy, now accepted the rule of a powerful but usually distant king whose support could be useful to them. As Paul Dognon emphasised in his study of the political institutions of Languedoc, this mutually beneficial relationship made the region one of the most consistently loyal in the kingdom – despite the legal and linguistic differences which separated it from the North.

The absorption of Languedoc into the kingdom was facilitated when this region was attached by marriage to the lands of Alphonse of Poitiers, brother of Louis IX. Several such grants were made in the thirteenth century by French kings to their younger brothers or sons to provide a living, and they were known as apanages (from the Latin *appanare*, to provide for). The apanage was perhaps the most tangible manifestation of the role and rights of the royal familial community in the government of the realm which we discussed above, and could help enforce royal authority. In Alphonse's case, his defeat of rebellion in Poitou and the administrative measures he took in Languedoc created a strong presence in the south, and served to remind restive local lords, notably the counts of Foix and Armagnac, of the growing reach of the crown. Lands granted in apanage were held in return for homage, and it came to be expected that the apanage would revert to the crown in the absence of a direct heir. Within the apanages kings retained ultimate jurisdiction, but in other respects – such as raising revenue – the apanagist enjoyed a fair measure of autonomy. By the start of the fourteenth century just a few lands were still held as apanages, notably Anjou, Maine, Bourbon, Artois and the county of Clermont. Further important grants would be made under John II with far greater consequences, as we shall see.

To the east, finally, the royal *domaine* was extended by the acquisition of the counties of Champagne and Brie, a vast complex of lands extending from the outskirts of Paris towards the Empire. The process began with the marriage of Philip IV to the heiress, Jeanne of Navarre, in 1284, but was not finally secure until the crown had succeeded in fending off competing claims in 1328. Along with

homages received for Bar and Valentinois-Diois and the purchase of
the Dauphiné, the acquisition of Champagne contributed to a period
of marked expansion towards the Empire on the eve of our period.
Royal rights were extended in other ways too, such as the agreements struck with the archbishop of Lyon and the bishops of Cahors,
Mende, Le Puy and Viviers early in the fourteenth century, whereby
the king came to share jurisdiction and revenues in substantial parts
of the Cahorsin, Gévaudan, Velay, Vivarais and the Lyonnais. This last
region included the great southern city itself.

Elsewhere in the east, the protection extended to leading churchmen by the Most Christian King of France soon translated into greater
power over their temporal affairs. In the north, the large city of
Tournai and the extensive Tournaisis were reunited to the crown in
an agreement between Philip V and the bishop in 1320. Combined
with purchases, confiscations and escheats (land which passed to the
crown by default of an heir), these smaller acquisitions were a valuable means of extending royal power within the realm under the last
Capetians. The trend was undoubtedly facilitated in the east by dynastic weakness in the Empire, although Capetian attempts to secure
election to the German crown itself (in 1272, 1308 and 1324) met
with little success, and the rumour that the Emperor had allowed the
King of France to extend his lands to the Rhine (1299) turned out to
have no substance.

The extent of royal authority under the last Capetians and the
fate of princely empires of earlier centuries might suggest that an
apogee had been attained around 1300. Such a conclusion would be
no more convincing than the belief that 1300 marked a highpoint
in the development of royal government. Recent Capetian expansion into the east and south of the kingdom had certainly bolstered
the monarchy, and would remain important in the fourteenth century as we shall see. But along the northern and western shores,
where Capetian expansion was a little older, the crown's difficulties
had grown significantly. The conflicts in Flanders and Guyenne from
the 1290s demonstrated that whatever the extent of the lands under
their rule, kings were never very far from the limits of their resources.
Even gradual amelioration would require significant development of
the governmental structures the last Capetians had inherited. Such
change came about in response to the events faced by the dynasty that
posterity has called the Valois kings of France, the subject of chapters
three and four below.

*   *   *

We have seen in this chapter that the notion of 'Most Christian King' was a powerful ideology in late medieval France, one which built on older notions of sacerdotal kingship, and prefigured the belief that 'absolute power' resided in the figure of the monarch. The Most Christian King had clear responsibilities, but he also stood head and shoulders above other forms of public authority, notably the great fief-holders and 'good towns'. Through the late medieval phenomena of mass processions and peace celebrations, the monarchy became a focus for loyalty and identity among a wider section of the population than ever before, particularly in an urban context. Only the princes of the blood came close to the king's authority. The king was clearly different from his closest male relatives, but their rights and expectations could not be neglected, as we shall see in later chapters.

If the legitimacy and authority of the Most Christian King were well established, the means at his disposal to govern the kingdom lagged some way behind. Royal government remained (numerically at least) a small thing, and any attempt to explain the development of French history in our period based on the growth of royal 'institutions' (or, for that matter, their princely equivalents) soon runs up against the fact that the purview of administrators at all levels was limited.

This does not mean, of course, that the organs of royal government were unimportant. On the contrary, office-holders were at the centre of informal networks of 'power distribution' which led outwards to a highly pluralistic political society made up of princes and lesser nobles, townsmen and churchmen of varying descriptions.[46] Such networks determined political action and placed the king's authority at the centre of French political culture. Although a king might wind up trapped in the web of brokerage which was spun around him by patrons and clients, it also gave him the means to draw in the many powers in political society whose support, skills and resources he needed to govern. As in earlier times, 'the success of familiar collaboration with the right people was the secret of French government'.[47]

That some unity, however loose, was afforded by the governing ideology and political culture of the kingdom was important, for otherwise that political space was characterised by enormous diversity arising from legal, linguistic, geographical and historical circumstances. Historians commonly point out the differences between north and south, especially in terms of law and language, and that emphasis is surely justified. But from the king's perspective, how people spoke or were judged in Languedoc was ultimately less important than the fact that it became a remarkably loyal region. Indeed, perhaps the most important geographical contrasts from the king's perspective in 1300 lay between West and East. Dispersed along the seaboard were populations with maritime horizons and a tradition of dissidence. This was the region where the crown's most powerful and troublesome vassals held their lands. In the East, by contrast, there were fewer great lords of note and a larger number of urban communities which had yet to find a strong political role in the kingdom. The greatest vassal in the East was a loyal supporter of the crown, his men a reliable source of royal servants at the highest level under the last Capetians.

Differences between east and west, the role of the royal familial community and the importance of relations between the king and the plurality of powers within his realm will feature strongly in subsequent chapters. But for now we turn to rural France, where as many as nine in ten inhabitants of the kingdom lived. As Alain Chartier put it in his *Quadrilogue invectif*, a lament on France's dire circumstances at the end of Charles VI's reign, 'the people are indeed a notable member of the kingdom, without whom the nobles and the clergy cannot govern, nor maintain themselves and their standing.'[48]

Chapter 2: Rural France, c. 1300–c. 1500

The impression left by an English visitor to the French countryside towards the end of our period, Sir John Fortescue, is one of considerable poverty and hardship, with peasants reduced to eating apples, rough bread and offal in contrast to their better-fed English counterparts who ate meat and fish to their heart's content. But Fortescue's testimony is open to question on a number of grounds, not least his desire to show the French as a less happy people than the English because some of them lived under Roman law. The great many regional studies of the rural history of late medieval France which have appeared in recent generations paint a different picture of peasant fortunes. These same studies also consider afresh the supposed decline of the lay aristocracy and the church as landowners, and the reported rise of the bourgoisie as landowners, with their supposed interest in farming for profit.

This chapter begins with a discussion of demographic change in rural France, considering not only population decline, but also the important question of geographical mobility (**'Demographic Change'**). Once we have looked at the status of peasants in the countryside (which was different in significant ways from England: **'Peasant Status'**), it will be possible to discuss in more detail the question of peasant fortunes (**'Peasant Fortunes'**), and whether changing economic circumstances had a particular bearing on the increased incidence of revolt in the countryside (**'Rural Revolt'**). The chapter then moves on to consider those who owned the land and their changing circumstances in the period: first, the lay aristocracy (**'A Crisis of Seigneurial Revenues?'**), then the church and townsmen (**'Landowners – Old and New'**). The last section looks at church and religion in the countryside, and suggests a number of ways in which rural and urban life were becoming increasingly distinct in our period – a theme we will pick up at a later stage in this book.

Demographic Change

After at least two centuries of remarkable growth, the population of late medieval France experienced dramatic decline. The main depressants of population levels were famine, plague and war. Recovery only became apparent in many regions from the middle of the fifteenth century onwards. While the respective weight of the three causes of population change is hard to assess, it is apparent that they produced rather different responses from the population of rural France when compared to those of England and the Empire, particularly with regard to geographical mobility.

Famine

The onset of demographic decline in the late Middle Ages is usually traced to the early fourteenth century, when poor weather contributed to widespread famine, particularly in the second and third decades. But as the work of William Chester Jordan has shown, the 'crisis of the early fourteenth century' was a northern phenomenon in European history. Stagnation then decline has been traced by Guy Bois in eastern Normandy as early as the late thirteenth century. But in southern parts of the kingdom – the Lyonnais in the east, studied by Marie-Thérèse Lorcin, Bigorre in the west, considered by Maurice Berthe – there was little sign of change before the 1330s or 1340s. Even as far north as Bar-sur-Seine, Michel Belotte finds that the famine of 1315–17 had little discernible impact.

Perhaps more important than any widespread crisis of the early fourteenth century in French history is the fact that agrarian structures were fragile throughout our period. Famine could still have a marked effect in the later fourteenth and fifteenth centuries, even though there were far fewer mouths to feed. The years 1408 and 1426 were years of dearth in the Bourbonnais (as studied by René Germain), while across much of France 1438 witnessed poor harvests and food shortages. Robert Boutruche finds rural famine at work in the Bordelais in 1457. By this last date, gradually recovering population levels may have had a part to play in food shortages, as certainly happened later in the fifteenth century. In Anjou, Michel Le Mené finds that the early 1480s witnessed the worst famines of the century. Scarcity was also severe in the east of the kingdom in the period 1476–83, although here it was war (resulting from the collapse of Burgundian power) rather than climate which tipped the fragile equilibrium between food supply and demand.

The periodic failure of peasant fields and gardens to meet demand was not simply the result of poor climatic conditions or war; more fundamentally, it arose from limited agricultural techniques. There were some interesting late medieval innovations, such as the increased application of alternate periods of crop cultivation and controlled flooding for fish-farming studied by Catherine Benoît, apparent in the Dombes region north of Lyons, the county of Burgundy and in Sologne to the north of Orléans. But on the whole the late Middle Ages was not a time of widespread or radical agricultural innovation in France. Particularly severe at the start of our period in the north, famine therefore remained a significant threat to the recovery of population levels throughout.

Plague

French historians of the late Middle Ages have devoted less time to detailed studies of the plague than their Anglophone and German counterparts, perhaps because the prolonged experience of war distinguished rural life in France from some other parts of Europe, and has consequently received greater attention. But there can be little doubt that plague was the main agent of demographic decline, spreading northwards through the realm in the pandemic of 1348–9, and recurring endemically thereafter.

The severity of the disease's impact varied considerably across the kingdom. Le Mené finds that although Anjou was badly affected in 1348, neighbouring Maine and Brittany suffered less. Around Bar-sur-Seine studied by Belotte, it was the second wave of plague in 1361 which caused the greatest mortality. Localised outbreaks followed different patterns: in the Bourbonnais studied by Germain, for instance, the initial pandemic was followed by repeated outbreaks in later years, especially marked in the periods 1361–84, 1400–16 and 1420–39. Recurrences of plague after the first pandemic were often described as killers of children and men in particular. The resulting gender imbalance and generational gaps may have sapped the population's residual fecundity, holding back recovery for longer. There are signs the latter was well underway in the second half of the fifteenth century as subsequent outbreaks killed fewer people, perhaps due to the growing immunity of the population, as Sam Cohn as shown. But it is likely that pre-1300 levels of population density were not attained again until the eighteenth or nineteenth centuries in many parts of France.

Calculating the part of plague in causing mortality and emigration, as distinct from factors such as war and famine, is nigh on impossible. To further complicate the picture, other diseases had a drastic impact at certain points too, such as the whooping cough epidemic noted in regions as distant from one another as Paris, the Bordelais and Forez in 1414. But evidence of population decline driven primarily by plague and greatly aggravated by other factors is undeniable. In the hills of upper Auvergne, Pierre Charbonnier's comparisons of hearth tax registers from 1328 and 1357 (useful sources for assessing the impact of the initial pandemic) indicate a thinning of households from 7.63 per sq. km. to 3.3. In one *prévôté* of the duchy of Bar, a region more noted for labour-intensive arable farming, Alain Girardot finds that hearths per sq. km declined in the longer term from around 37 in 1321 to around 10 in 1437. Mortality rates thus appear far higher than the one-in-three figure favoured in older studies, with many surpassing 50 per cent in the worst years.

In principle, survivors of plague should have found that their living conditions improved. But in the French countryside, more than any other part of Europe, warfare was a further source of misery.

War

Registers of letters conserved by the Avignon papacy for the period 1362–70 contain many complaints from churchmen in different parts of Europe about war damage to church property, notably Italy and the Anglo-Scottish border. But Anne-Marie Hayez has shown that the great majority of the correspondence the papacy received at that time came from churchmen in the Kingdom of France, despite the fact that the years 1360–9 were ostensibly covered by official peace treaty. Some contemporaries understandably believed they lived in an age of perpetual conflict. One priest from the Cahors region famously testified late in the fourteenth century that 'for the whole period of his life he had only seen war in the *pays* and diocese of Cahors, nor had he ever seen peace in those said parts.'[1]

How far we should follow the picture of desolation painted in contemporary documents is a perennial topic for debate. Clerics reporting to their superiors on the damage to their church obviously had good reasons to portray their suffering in stark terms. It is nonetheless striking how closely, in every regional history of the king-dom, the cycle of crisis and recovery is linked to the varying intensity of conflict. A period of respite, and in some areas of population growth, can be discerned from roughly 1370 to 1410; another, more durable, begins to emerge after 1450, but is noticeably slower to develop in those areas which were affected by the king's wars with leading princes of the realm. War damage was greatest along the main routes taken by armed bands through any given area. Warfare did not follow a cycle, like famine or plague, and could last for years in strategically important spots. Although dearth and disease were the main causes of mortality among non-combatants, war was therefore the principal impediment to the natural recovery of population levels in the French countryside.

But large-scale organised warfare was not omnipresent by any means, and it is important to emphasise this point lest a picture of utter and unmitigated devastation is conveyed. Records for the lands of the hospital of St John of Angers (studied by Le Mené) demon-strate that although the rural population did melt away from zones of intense conflict, just a few miles distant lay properties which were virtually unaffected. Gérard Sivéry's work on the rural economy of Hainaut has shown that misery in one region could contribute con-siderably to prosperity among its neighbours. Comparisons over time reveal that the conflicts which wracked later medieval France were also less disruptive of rural life than those of the sixteenth and sev-enteenth centuries – a finding made for the region of Quercy by Robert Latouche, and the Cambrésis by Hugues Neveux. In this last region the difference can be quantified. Compared to figures for grain production around 1300, the worst of the late medieval con-flicts witnessed a decline of around 25 per cent. But a fall of between 35 per cent and 50 per cent occurred in the periods 1580–1600 and 1635–59, when there were even more mouths to feed.

War compounded and extended the misery of famine and plague, but it did so unevenly; with less drastic effect than in later centuries; and with potential benefits for neighbouring regions unaffected directly by hostilities. These points are worth bearing in mind when it comes to matters such as the ability of kings to raise finance from subjects who were much reduced in number, or lords to make a living from their lands.

Geographical mobility

It is no surprise to find, with Arlette Higounet-Nadal, that geographical mobility was the key note of the demographic history
of the period. Despite the continuing protection offered by castle
walls and other rural fortifications, the local town or city offered
greater security and the possibility of advancement. The later Middle Ages was, as we shall see, a period of considerable immigration
into towns, most of it from surrounding rural areas. But population movement did not only benefit towns. The chance of bettering
one's conditions caused population movement within rural regions,
revealed in the appearance of new family names in successive *censiers*. Berthe finds evidence of migration from hill settlements to
the more densely populated plain in Bigorre, for instance, where
the land was more productive and there was greater safety in numbers. In the fertile countryside around Paris, Guy Fourquin finds
evidence of long-distance immigration, most of it from the north
(notably Picardy and Valois), but some of it from poorer regions further afield (especially Brittany and Auvergne). The traditional image
of the French countryside as a bewildering mosaic of small worlds
only rarely in touch with one another, 'an aggregate . . . of cells which
are simply juxtaposed', is challenged by late medieval evidence of
the growing pulling power of the town, and more frequent and sustained encounters between rural dwellers from different parts of the
kingdom.[2]

But we should not take the point too far. The upheavals of the
period also encouraged rural populations to stay put. Michel Le Mené
considers Anjou a net exporter of migrants, but there is little evidence
of mass abandonment even here. Lands vacated in the multiple crises
which affected Anjou from 1363 to 1375 were reoccupied to within 10
per cent of previous levels by the early fifteenth century. Emmanuel
Le Roy Ladurie finds that the complete abandonment of villages was
less common in France than in Germany or England in our period.
The peculiarly French experience of prolonged warfare thus appears
to have had two, quite distinct effects. On the one hand, a part of the
rural population became detached from its roots and was prepared to
move, whether to towns or to other rural areas; on the other hand, a
large proportion responded to the dangers of the period by entrench-
ment. As we shall now see, relative immobility was also a consequence
of the ways in which many peasants had come, over the thirteenth
century, to hold their land.

Peasant Status

It is impossible to calculate the number of peasants in France who still owned lands free of any obligation to a local lord. The survival of free peasant tenure in the kingdom depended in large measure on the strength and predatory instincts of local lords in earlier times. In the twelfth and thirteenth centuries, landowners had extended their possessions to such an extent in some parts of the kingdom that there was 'no land without a lord', such as the Bourbonnais studied by Germain. In southern regions such as Bigorre, Comminges and the Bordelais, Berthe thinks the proportion of free peasants may have been as high as 10 per cent. But even in these southern parts it is clear that the majority of agriculturists in later medieval France lived and worked as serfs, tenants or sharecroppers. The first of these three groups was declining in numbers in our period, although it had certainly not disappeared by any means; the second had become preponderant; and the third, although important in the long-term history of the French countryside, was only gradually emerging.

Serfs

Serfs were in theory unfree from the crown of their heads to the toes of their feet. The most characteristic rights of the lord over the serf were restrictions placed on marriage, the servile tax which serfs paid (known by various terms, such as the *queste*), and the lord's right to dispose of a serf's property after death in the absence of an appropriate heir. Serfdom expressed in these stark terms had acquired pejorative connotations by our period, partly because it had disappeared from so many parts of the realm. Historians have found serfdom to be rare in Roussillon, Armagnac, Bas-Quercy and Anjou by the start of our period; in Brittany it was limited to a few western lordships, while in Normandy its absence was a long-established fact.

The early disappearance of serfdom in large areas of the kingdom distinguishes French rural history from that of some other parts of Europe. In England, to take an obvious point of comparison, as much as three-fifths of the rural population remained unfree in the late thirteenth century, and serfdom remained present for much of the fourteenth century. The reasons for the disappearance of serfdom were doubtless practical. The sale of charters to individuals or communities could be lucrative for landowners, and for the recipients of charters their economic prospects and status were enhanced. Where serfdom survived, this was doubtless because it suited the financial interests of landowners. In Bigorre, Berthe has shown that the comital family still derived around 20 per cent of its income in 1300 from payments from serfs.

Although the decline of serfdom generally suited a majority of those who worked the land and those who leased it to them, it is important to note, with Guy Fourquin and others, that the Capetian kings of France took a lead in promoting the development, especially from the time of Louis IX onwards. In 1250–1 and in 1278 in particular, the crown extended its protection to peasants who were seeking to be freed from serfdom, and among the grievances of discontented landowners in 1314 was the crown's intervention to end the rights of lords to the property of serfs who died without an heir. The areas where serfdom remained strongest at the start of our period were those which had most recently become part of the kingdom, notably Champagne and Brie. Robert Boutruche finds that some lords in the Bordelais freed serfs as a pious act, making their serfs, in the words of one notary trained in Roman law, 'free, liberated and like Roman citizens' (1425).[3] Clearly it was appropriate that the king, greatest of all lords and closest to God, should set an example in this area as in others. This was one of the few areas in which kings intervened more or less directly in French rural life.

Tenants

The majority of those deriving a living from the land were free tenants who obtained a holding in return for dues which they owed to a landlord, who in turn remained the legal owner. Peasant holdings usually constituted a large part of seigneurial estates, with a smaller proportion, the reserve, retained for the lord. Peasant tenures were most often *à cens*, requiring a fixed payment to the lord which was often made in cash, but which might also (or only) be made in kind. In Sologne (studied by Isabelle Guérin), payments were almost exclusively in monetary form; in eastern Normandy (studied by Bois) primarily so. But in the Lyonnais, Lorcin finds that payment in kind was as widespread as the alternative, while in Auvergne or Quercy it predominated. Payment uniquely in services was rare by our period, which suited tenants who needed family labour to exploit their holdings. At the same time, the ability to make payments with produce suited landlords and tenants alike during times of monetary instability, which were a recurring feature from the time of Philip IV on. In this respect, lords and tenants could avoid some of the effects of price rises which periodically afflicted the inhabitants of towns.

A second, less widespread form of tenure was *à champart*, in which the tenant gave a fixed proportion of his harvest as payment to the lord (commonly one-twelfth of the crop, but sometimes as much as one-quarter). *Champart* was less appealing to peasants in times of plenty and to lords in times of dearth. Fourquin finds that tenure *à champart* was becoming uncommon in the grain-growing Parisian countryside at the start of our period, but in the less-developed Limousin Jean Tricard does not detect its decline until the fifteenth century.

By the beginning of our period peasant tenures *à cens* and *à champart* were tending to become hereditary, a significant characteristic of French rural history which must be underlined. From the landlords' perspective, hereditary tenure afforded them a measure of stability and status. Income from the tenancy was maintained, the inconvenience of finding new tenants was avoided, and the number of able-bodied men on the land was unlikely to vary greatly. For their part, tenants acquired an important stake in the land. In more prosperous or densely populated regions, the subletting of tenures (where it was permitted) offered further benefit. An entry-fine would commonly have to be paid to obtain use of the tenure, but the possibility of selling it on (also often subject to the payment of a tax to the lord) existed in Anjou and other regions by the thirteenth century.

Tenants might therefore acquire a fair measure of control over their holdings. Where the value of the *cens* had been fixed early, the cost to tenants had become low relative to the potential income of the tenure. No wonder historians of the French countryside in the later Middle Ages equate peasant tenure with peasant ownership, a feature of rural life in the kingdom which stands in sharp contrast to English circumstances. The attachment of peasant families to tenures over a number of generations helps explain the lesser incidence of abandoned villages in the French record evidence and the willingness of rural populations to stay put in the face of economic hardship and war. In similar fashion, the mobility of a smaller element of the rural population may be explained by the existence of men who had found it harder to establish themselves where hereditary tenure was widespread. Although convincing evidence is hard to find, one suspects that it was a younger, male population which was on the move in late medieval France.

Despite having greater control over the land they worked, tenants were nonetheless subject to the authority of the landowner in many respects. Marc Bloch considered the extent of seigneurial rights over the tenantry to be a distinguishing characteristic of French rural history, at least when compared with lordship in England or the Empire. These rights could compensate for the lord's diminishing hold over peasant tenures. Seigneurial monopolies included the right to charge tenants for the use of the lord's mills to grind grain and his ovens to cook bread. A lord might demand food and lodging (*droit de gîte*), ban the sale of wine other than his own during the hottest months of the year (*droit de banvin*), levy tithes (especially but not exclusively in ecclesiastical lordships) and demand military service or payment for exemptions from it (particularly the watch, or *droit de guet*).

The exercise of justice was another seigneurial prerogative of great importance. Not all lords had jurisdictional rights, of course, and the extent of the latter varied according to the category of crime to be judged. But even in the lowest jurisdictions, matters such as boundary disputes might receive their one and only airing in the lord's court. Pierre Charbonnier finds that seigneurial justice was popular because it was generally quick and cheap – on average, a settlement cost as little as 2 days' wages for a labourer in Auvergne around 1450. Seigneurial justice across the Kingdom of France left fewer and far more scattered documentary traces than its royal counterpart, but it would be wrong to underestimate its importance. Where it obtained, the exercise of seigneurial justice emphasised the authority of the noble lord within his locality, placing him and his officers at the centre of a wide range of transactions and settlements involving tenants. The lord remained a force to be reckoned with in the French countryside, and any narrative of the kingdom's political history must try to take account of that fact.

Massive population decline after 1348 left its mark on peasant tenure and seigneurial rights, but both proved sufficiently flexible to weather the storm. Payment of dues dried up in the worst affected areas, sometimes spectacularly so: in Quercy, Jean Lartigaut finds no fewer than 166 lordships without a single household in 1440. But when recovery came, the *censier* and the terms of tenure it recorded provided a framework for replenishing the countryside with tenants. Landlords might propose attractive terms to encourage the restoration of abandoned lands. As dues were moderated, it is possible that the extent of seigneurial rights over their tenants decreased, at least by comparison with the early fourteenth century. When population levels began to rise once more, the need for landlords to make concessions diminished. What French rural historians have called a 'seigneurial reaction' began to emerge in the second half of the fifteenth century, characterised by increased rents, enforcement of rights and the expansion of the lord's reserve through the appropriation of existing peasant tenures. Lordship that was once under threat could flourish again.

Sharecropping

In one major respect the late Middle Ages did witness a significant change in peasant status, and we should mention it because of its long-term importance: the spread of sharecropping. Notarial acts from the Toulousain studied by Germain Sicard record how the relationship worked. For a temporary period (most commonly 4 years), the lessor would provide the land, the lessee the labour, usually in the form of the family unit supplemented by hired help during busy periods. The cost of hired help was normally shared. Investment in seed, livestock or vines was usually shared too, except in the common case of new sharecroppers unable to meet the start-up costs of the arrangement; here, the lessor paid up front. The harvest was divided between landlord and occupant in proportions set down in the contract, the lessee usually doing rather better than the landlord.

On the face of it, sharecropping created a more equal relationship between landholder and agriculturist, and might suggest a weakening of seigneurial rights over those who worked the land, in contrast to the experience of tenants discussed above. The ancient customal of Brittany described the lessor and lessee as companions, the former having no jurisdiction over the latter. But in contrast to other forms of tenure which tended towards a greater measure of peasant ownership, possession of the land remained in the hands of the lessor, not the sharecropper. Moreover, once landlords began to farm out supervision of sharecroppers to middlemen, the conditions under which sharecroppers worked could become more demanding. The arrangement nonetheless suited peasants in a period of expanding population, because it afforded access to land and reduced the costs of starting up. It follows that the spread of sharecropping was most marked towards the end of our period, when pressure on land began to increase once again.

René Germain finds examples of sharecropping contracts in the Bourbonnais as early as the thirteenth century, but the practice did not become widespread there until the second half of the fifteenth

century. In the countryside south of Paris after 1450 studied by
Yvonne Bézard, sharecropping contracts were still very rare. In other
words, sharecropping had not yet greatly altered the status of peasant
tenants in France, who generally enjoyed more legal freedom than
their counterparts in some other kingdoms and had acquired a significant measure of control over their holdings, but who remained
subject to a wide variety of seigneurial rights which underlined the
continuing importance of the lord in rural society.

Peasant Fortunes

Within the framework just described, how did rural dwellers fare
in the changing economic circumstances of the late Middle Ages?
As we have hinted, the picture is less clear-cut than contemporary
stereotypical commiserations with the peasants' lot would suggest.

A golden age of waged labour?

In theory, at least, the demographic impact of plague should have
brought increased prosperity to anyone who sold his or her labour.
A significant proportion of rural dwellers belonged to this category
at different points in their lives. Jean-Pierre Leguay and Hervé Martin find that more than one-third of a sample of 180 or so Breton
rural workers in 1475 possessed little or no land, and lived primarily from wages. Arguing from a limited set of data in 1956, Édouard
Perroy doubted that the late Middle Ages was 'a golden age of
waged labour' in France (as Thorold Rogers famously said it was in
England). Subsequent generations of French rural historians have
reached more optimistic conclusions. At Hadonville in the Verdunois,
Girardot finds that mowers (a relatively skilled group of the working
population) enjoyed an increase of around 50 per cent in their daily
wages in the decade following the pandemic. Rising wage demands
encouraged the introduction of labour legislation which was comparable – in intention, at least – to the English Statute of Labourers,
notably in the region of Paris in 1351, or around Metz in 1355. In the
longer term, when the effect of monetary fluctuations and short-term
crises even out, sustained increases in wages nonetheless became the
norm. Boutruche finds that specialised vineyard workers in the pay of
the archbishops of Bordeaux enjoyed twice the salary in 1430 which
their predecessors had received in 1350. Guy Bois thinks agricultural
labourers' wages in eastern Normandy may even have tripled over
roughly the same period.

But the picture of growing prosperity for waged labour must be qualified in a number of significant ways. The higher wages commanded in some sectors have to be set against the lesser rates of daily pay given to women, who commonly received half the wages or less paid out to their male co-workers. Similarly reduced rates were offered to younger males hired to serve single or multiple households as shepherds or labourers. As the fifteenth century wore on, the upward trend ceased and salaries tended to stabilise, even to decline. In his work on the lands owned by the Périgord College of the University of Toulouse, Philippe Wolff finds that wages remained fairly constant in the first half of the fifteenth century, but were detrimentally affected by renewed demographic growth after 1450.

Finally, gains made through the sale of labour might be mitigated by other developments. Relatively few rural dwellers derived all of their income from wages alone. To a greater or lesser extent, everyone was subject to the wider economic forces dictated by the prices of grain, wine and beasts in later medieval France. Here, conditions were less clearly to the advantage of the producer.

Agricultural prices

Although there were inevitably great fluctuations in the immediate aftermath of plague or in famine years like 1438, grain prices on the whole stagnated after 1350 due to greatly decreased demand. Guy Bois's study of wheat prices at Rouen certainly bears out this overall conclusion. At Douai, where the aldermen publicly announced grain prices on the feast day of Saint Remi outside the town hall, Monique Mestayer finds that prices did gradually begin to rise through the fifteenth century. But setting aside the exceptional 1430s (marked by famine) and 1480s (affected by war), the average price for a measure of wheat was only around 8 per cent higher in the period 1400–50 than it had been from 1350 to 1400, and only 19 per cent higher in the period 1450–1500 than it had been in the first half-century following the plague pandemic of 1348. The benefits of lower grain prices included some improvement in diet, including the use of wheat rather than rye for bread as Lorcin finds in the Lyonnais. But on the whole grain production did not provide a route to prosperity for those who lived from the land.

Other agricultural sectors were more promising, so long as rural dwellers could afford the investments involved. The raising of livestock was lucrative in times of reduced population, exploiting the greater availability of grazing land and the less labour-intensive nature of the work for much of the year. Records for the Norman barony of Le Neubourg studied by André Plaisse suggest that hus-bandry of cattle and pigs was the principal ingredient in the recovery there. In the Angevin lordship of Buron studied by Le Mené, returns on investment in sharecropping contracts for rearing of livestock were commonly around 20 per cent–30 per cent. But the economic benefits of pastoral farming were felt unevenly in the French country-side. Heavy investment in herds and flocks brought the best returns, but also the greatest risks. Not surprisingly, notarial acts from the Limousin analysed by Tricard indicate that butchers and bourgeois investors were the major agents in the cattle market, while the more numerous smallholders who appear in his documents were involved in smaller and less frequent transactions. Growing evidence of com-mercialisation in pastoral farming is apparent, but it seems that the trend had a limited impact on peasant fortunes.

Viticulture was potentially more rewarding. Boutruche has shown there were relatively high and stable profits to be made from the sale of barrels of claret at Bordeaux from 1385 to 1457, one barrel then commanding roughly three times the amount paid at the start of the fourteenth century. Fourquin finds that barrels from the estates of the monastery of Saint-Denis more than doubled in price over a sim-ilar period. The cost of labour made viticulture a risky business for large proprietors, and this was something the small producer, with the help of family and neighbours, might exploit. Importantly too, all of the crop could be sold without the need to retain a portion for reseeding, as happened in arable farming. In Anjou, where small peasant producers played an increasing role in viticulture and greater landholders leased out their vines to save labour costs, Le Mené finds that the profits of even a minor holding could be substantial. As ever, of course, conditions varied considerably. But so long as the weather was kind, the landowner not too demanding and the soldiery kept at arm's length, viticulture offered good prospects of peasant prosperity in many regions.

The secondary cultivation of industrial crops and some involve-ment in low-intensity rural cloth production provided useful addi-tional sources of income for agriculturists. The planting of tow, hemp or linen was a feature of the countryside in many parts of France, cul-tivated in small quantities for domestic purposes in or near peasant gardens. In some areas industrial crops were destined for commer-cialisation on a significant scale. Linen figures prominently in the accounts of the barony of Le Neubourg in the early fifteenth cen-tury, examined by Plaisse. Increased consumption of luxury materials encouraged the planting of crops used in the process of dying cloth, such as madder and woad, the latter figuring in sharecropping contracts from the Toulousain (albeit much more rarely than cereals, as Sicard notes). Linen production in the countryside south of Laval acquired something of a reputation in the later Middle Ages, adding to the area's known expertise in making wool which André Bouton has studied.

But the production of woollen cloth itself was mostly an urban activity. Small rural producers benefited from the larger urban industry by selling on surplus raw materials, with dealers collecting the pelts once the shearing was done. Such cloth as was made in the countryside might be prevented from reaching urban markets, not least because merchants sought to avoid competition by legislation, as Le Mené finds at Angers. Bézard notes that in the countryside south of Paris after 1450, rural cloth production suffered as skilled workers migrated to the capital in search of more lucrative employment. There were industries in the countryside which clearly benefited rural dwellers: iron production in the Châtillonnais (as Belotte notes), employing lumberjacks, charcoal burners and smiths; or the paper industry which first began to emerge in the late Middle Ages, particularly marked in Champagne. But often this was specialized work, and the impact of rural industry was consequently limited.

It is nonetheless clear that Fortescue's image of a downtrodden and ruined French peasantry was wide of the mark. Guy Fourquin's study of the property of Garges shows that within the context of a broadly stable number of tenures from 1315 to 1405, the number of peasants owning only one or two plots dropped by around one-third, a finding which suggests a gradual improvement in the fortunes of the less well-off. Demographic decline created opportunities for a much smaller proportion of the rural population to seize, such as renting the farm of a seigneurial reserve, or buying up tenures from those less fortunate than themselves. Few studies of the French countryside in our period fail to mention the *coqs de village* who seized the chance to improve their fortunes. Antoine Mondiat from the village of Sallèles near Narbonne was one such peasant, studied by Gilbert Larguier: Mondiat owned 3 houses and exploited 30 plots of land (including fields, meadows and vines) with his 7 horses, 175 sheep and 1 cart. In one Angevin village studied by Michel Le Mené towards the close of our period, the apportionment of taxes by parishioners reveals that while three-quarters of the population were asked to pay less than 40 *sous* to meet the communal tax burden, around one-quarter were considered good for between two and three times that amount. A single very wealthy peasant household accounted for 7 per cent of the total receipt, paying more than seven times the sum owed by most villagers. The existence of a growing peasant elite with relatively conspicuous immovable wealth helps to explain why a much decreased rural population in late medieval France was able to bear the increasing financial burdens placed upon it.

Fiscal and parafiscal demands

The burden of state taxation began to make itself felt in a sustained and regular fashion from the middle of the fourteenth century onwards. In addition to taxes, monies had to be raised to meet what Philippe Contamine calls the parafiscal demands of the soldiery, particularly in the form of protection money (*appatis*) paid by agreement between communities and nearby garrisons. In principle, both fiscal and parafiscal commitments protected rural dwellers from a third level of exaction, robbery and pillage, although clearly this was not always the case.

How heavy was the new burden of state taxation on peasant income? There is no easy answer to this question. Pierre Charbonnier finds that direct royal taxation in Auvergne represented a very small proportion of the estimated value of land in the early fourteenth century, perhaps one-twentieth in hill communities, far less in the more profitable plains. In the Angevin parish of Rest studied at the close of the fifteenth century, Le Mené has calculated that royal taxes amounted to between 7.5 per cent and 10 per cent of a share-cropper's annual revenue, a little less in the case of a labourer's. It therefore seems safe to say that the fiscal intrusion of the state grew considerably in the French countryside from a relatively low base at the start of our period, but even at the end the sums involved were not ruinous.

Guy Fourquin has shown that by the close of our period in the countryside around Paris, levies paid to the state in taxation amounted to more than double the sums which tenants paid to their lords in the form of dues. We should remember, however, that tenants' dues were often fixed for a long period of time by contract, and lords might gather a large part of their income from tenants by the enforcement of seigneurial rights and monopolies, not just dues. Closer examination of the subject has made it abundantly clear that royal taxation was not overtaking seigneurial demands as the principle drain on peasant income. On the basis of material from parishes in Auvergne between 1438 and 1468, Charbonnier has shown that royal taxation amounted to less than half the amount paid from the peasant purse to the aristocracy (in the form of dues and seigneurial rights) and the church (in the form of tithes, collections and other gifts). So although the burden of royal taxation was clearly growing in the countryside, it did not deny the rural aristocracy or the church their share of peasant income.

In the case of protection money, villagers probably suffered more, albeit on a temporary basis. During periods of intense conflict rural dwellers were more likely to be subjected to *appatis* than townsmen, so long as the latter could remain safely behind their walls. In Brittany between 1342 and 1359, Nick Wright finds that just three English garrisons were able to exact protection money from over 120 local parishes. The profits could be considerable. In the chronicles of Jean Froissart, a Gascon squire known as the Bascot de Mauléon boasts how, even in 1388, a time of peace for much of the kingdom, the castle of Thurie in the Tarn region brought him so much protection money that he would not have swapped it even for the town of Orthez. As a result of the actions of men like the Bascot, the demands of the soldiery must often have been the biggest drain on the peasant purse, particularly in periods such as the 1360s and 1430s. No wonder rural dwellers were increasingly prepared to shoulder the lesser burden of taxes if these could reduce the unpredictable demands of the soldiery.

Fiscal and parafiscal pressures could have a galvanising and even empowering effect on rural communities. Chronic insecurity, labour shortages and the sharing out or avoidance of tax burdens encouraged kin groups, friends and locals to draw together to improve or maintain their fortunes. In the Lyonnais, René Fédou observes, peasants held assemblies and conducted inquiries into bourgeois ownership of rural property with the intention of reducing the proportion of taxation they had to pay. The growing number of inquiries into the status of men claiming nobility (and hence exemption from direct taxes) was driven forward by villagers acting together to prevent what they perceived to be an unjustified evasion of the communal tax burden by some local upstart. Moreover, the village community could extend its powers without entering into potentially damaging conflict with the local lord. Villages were not necessarily co-terminous with lordships, and landowners rarely played a role in the potentially contentious issue of the allocation of state taxes. The growing role of laymen in the upkeep and management of the village church (*fabrique de l'église*) from the thirteenth century was another way in which communal needs were gradually being addressed in the countryside. Parish accounts were among the first documents generated by rural dwellers, such as those of the parish of Marck near Calais which date to 1309, discussed by Antoine Follain in his work on the use of money in the countryside. Sources which reveal village organisation are often external to that community, such as the town council minutes from Provence in which Michel Hébert finds mentions of peasant assemblies, or the commissions given to procurators by rural communities to act on their behalf in legal or other matters, as Fredric Cheyette has shown. Village organisation was nonetheless clearly developing, and it was one means by which peasant fortunes could be protected.

More than that, as Douglas Aiton has demonstrated, village assemblies could also play an active role in the political life of the kingdom at the local level. There is frequent mention of village assemblies in legal documents relating to the widespread peasants' revolt known as the Jacquerie. And rural revolt, as we shall now see, was a more marked feature of our period than of earlier times.

Rural Revolt

Organised contestation by agriculturists of some attribute of lordship certainly featured in French rural life before our period, such as the rising which took place on the Orly lands of the chapter of Notre-Dame in 1251, where serfs gathered in their hundreds from the surrounding countryside to protest at the exactions placed upon them. But reports of revolt in France increase in number during the later Middle Ages, and the countryside witnessed at least four large-scale risings in particular.

The Jacquerie was a short but intense explosion of peasant discontent mainly to the north of the capital in May–June 1358. The *Tuchinat* took a very different form, that of a series of guerrilla wars and insurrectionary acts in three longer phases. The first two phases occurred in upper Auvergne and further south in Languedoc from the later 1360s to the early 1380s. There was a third, open rising in upper Auvergne (1384) which displayed wider animosity towards nobles, clerics and wealthier townsmen. Different again were the uprisings of peasants which took place in the Caux region of Normandy during the Lancastrian occupation of the duchy (1435–6). These Norman revolts are sometimes portrayed (although not uncontroversially) as a resistance movement. Finally, a later

Tuchinat, located to the east in Forez, the Beaujolais, Lyonnais and Velay, flared up in May 1422 and smouldered on until its bloody suppression in 1431. Rural protests were thus very different in character from one another, and historians' interpretations of their causes vary considerably.

Revolt and crime

From one perspective rural revolts were simply the high watermarks of disorder and violence which were inherent in rural life. The fifteenth-century letters of remission from villages in Artois studied by Robert Muchembled suggest a pattern of rural crime which was replicated in the main revolts of the period. Murders and maimings were committed in the vast majority by males, often young, frequently in the context of feuding and the consumption of alcohol, mainly in the spring months of April, May and June. It is unlikely to have been a coincidence that the Jacquerie and rebellion in Forez in 1422 also began in the second half of May. Longer days, increased association outdoors and the lull before the busy harvest time of July are just some of the factors which explain why the late spring and early summer tended to witness 'the familiar rhythm of peasant criminality developing into insurrection'.[4] The preponderance of males and the relative absence of women from late medieval revolts, demonstrated by Sam Cohn, is another area which parallels the evidence of the criminal material studied by Muchembled.

The high degree of mobility in the rural population further contributed to the climate of violence, uprooting men for whom social reintegration became difficult. The ranks of those living out in the woods or squatting in ill-gotten lodgings were swollen by the perennial figure of the landless peasant with few prospects: men such as Jehan le Petit, a Norman who found employ in the early 1370s with an English garrison and used his new-found power to lord it over his 'betters' in the village community. Such men were to be found in England too, but to a lesser extent and in fewer regions, most of them probably northerners dislodged by occasional Scottish raids.

Revolt and the soldiery

Above all, however, it was the presence of the soldiery which made for violent and rebellious times in the French countryside. Resistance to the soldiery led to a degree of militarisation of peasant society similar to that found in frontier communities elsewhere in medieval Europe. Michel Pintoin (the chronicler formerly known as the anonymous Monk of Saint-Denis) records how villagers in the countryside around Paris sought permission to arm themselves against the troops on both sides of the Burgundian–Armagnac conflict in the early 1410s. Soon these forces became a significant problem in their own right, resorting to acts of brigandage which rendered unsafe the very regions north of Paris where the Jacquerie had burned hardest two generations earlier. Around 1429, the Bourbon servant and *bailli* of the County of Montpensier, Pierre de Nesson, wrote a poem which characterised war as a diabolical figure with the power to transform ordinary labourers into cut-throats and robbers. Like every caricature, it has a basis in fact. Popular revolt in the French countryside of the later Middle Ages was often a reaction to, or simply an extension of, brigandage perpetrated by the soldiery of all descriptions.

It is tempting to describe the peasants who rose up in the *pays* of Caux in 1435 against their English rulers as something different – that is to say, as patriots – but in some respects theirs was also a rising of the peasantry against the soldiery. Rural brigandage had been a significant problem before the Lancastrian occupation of Normandy, and to this extent attacks on the soldiery were not new in the region. A later group of Norman rebels was known as the *Galants de la feuillée* (companions of the woods) because of the nature of the hit-and-run attacks such men carried out against the Breton soldiery returning from raids into Normandy in 1466–7. In central and southern France the *Tuchins* led a similar existence. They were sworn associates who emerged from the woods (*touche*, the root of the name, means wooded land) to exact retribution on groups of *routiers* living off the land. Soon, of course, many of these men were condemned as brigands themselves, such as the *Tuchins* under the Luzers brothers who terrorized the region of Bonnac in 1366–7.

It is rare to find reports of a coherent programme of action in the rural uprisings of our period. The third phase of the first *Tuchinat* (1384) witnessed attacks on socially privileged groups such as nobles and monks, and this might suggest that elements of the leadership were motivated by egalitarian ideals. But the activity of the rebels was limited to a few short months, and no document directly conveys their views. The evidence is more substantial for the later *Tuchins* in South-Eastern France (1422–31), one of whose leaders was credited with the revolutionary objective of destroying the nobility, priests, bourgeoisie, merchants and town governors (in that order). A similar sentiment was attributed to contemporary insurgents in the Maconnais and Forez, where rebels are reported to have announced that all men were condemned with Adam to live by the sweat of their brow, including the nobility, and that no more than two priests should be needed for their entire region. But our only source for these sentiments is a history printed fully 150 years after the suppression of the rising, so it is hard to know what weight to place on such statements.

Indeed, it was perhaps the very absence of a clear set of goals among many bands of insurgents which helped perpetuate their activities. When they did associate in larger numbers to further their aims by force, rebels were at their most vulnerable to the soldiery they had come to resemble. The *Tuchins* in Auvergne were routed near Saint-Flour by local nobles under the viscount of Polignac in June 1384. Those of Forez were defeated by troops under the command of the mercenary captain Rodrigo de Villandrando in the spring of 1431. As in Normandy, where the Caux rebels were crushed by Talbot in January 1436, the affected regions returned to the low-intensity brigandage which had constituted much earlier rural revolt in the period.

Revolt and lordship? The Jacquerie

But the Jacquerie of May–June 1358 stands out by comparison with the other rural revolts of the period, at least according to several of the studies of it published thus far. No commentator has failed to notice the recurring sentiment in contemporary documents that this was a primarily a revolt of peasants against nobles. Violent acts against noblemen, their families and their property are reported across a wide area from the Vexin to the north-west of the capital, through the Beauvaisis where the Jacques were probably most active, and on to the regions in the east between Oise and Marne, all within an intense period from the first outbreak at Saint-Leu-d'Esserent on 28 May to the destruction of the rural insurgents at Mello by Charles of Navarre and his men just 11 days later. Church lands, although extensive in the region, did not suffer at the hands of the Jacques to the same extent as lay possessions, suggesting a particular conflict of lay landlords and peasants. Small wonder the Jacquerie has been seen as a class war fought by oppressed peasants against the land-owning aristocracy. The word 'Jacquerie' itself derives from a contemporary identifier for a peasant, 'Jacques Bonhomme,' so called because of the short tunic or *jacque* sometimes worn by agriculturists.

One school of thought has rejected the notion that peasant concerns were at the root of the Jacquerie at all. Raymond Cazelles
examined letters of remission issued to men accused of participat-
ing in the rebellion and concluded that the participants were a far
more mixed group, including rural artisans and even a few nobles,
clerics and royal officials, rather than simply agriculturists. David
Bessen built on these findings to suggest the Jacquerie was a 'co-
opted rebellion', manipulated by one political party, that of Charles
of Navarre, against the Valois dynasty. The Navarrese party are said
to have encouraged the Jacques until it became too dangerous to
be associated with their excesses, at which point they turned against
the rebels. But neither Bessen nor Cazelles really brings us closer to
understanding why the revolt originated in a rural context, drew wide
support from the rural population, and was directed overwhelmingly
against the lay aristocracy. Both interpretations fail to take account of
the abundant evidence from chronicles which state that the participants were *rustici* (peasants). Moreover, surviving letters of remission
for men who wished to distance themselves from the uprising tell us
little or nothing about the background of the vast majority of the
rustici who were slaughtered at Mello.

But in one respect Raymond Cazelles's reading of the Jacquerie
does seem convincing. The rising is not easily characterised as a
rebellion arising from the economic difficulties of the peasantry. The
revolt was most intense in the relatively prosperous grain-growing
regions to the north and east of Paris, where the better-off parishes
were to be found – and not the poorer areas to the south of the
capital, such as Hurepoix. Guy Fourquin made a similar observation,
and suggested that the rebellion arose from frustration among more
prosperous peasants at long-term price fluctuations which were holding them back. But as Sam Cohn points out, it is unclear why this
extended experience of price fluctuations dating back to the crises of
the early fourteenth century did not spark rebellion sooner – or for
that matter, why that discontent should have been directed primarily
against the nobility.

But in another respect Guy Fourquin does provide important findings which illuminate the causes of the Jacquerie. Lordship in the
Parisian region was weak. From the thirteenth century on, Fourquin
shows that noble landownership around Paris was faring badly compared to the stable or improving fortunes of the church and the
growing presence of bourgeois landholders. Succession practices had
contributed to the 'pulverisation' of fiefs, the tenure of 'rump lordships' and the emergence of a 'plebian nobility' which was now forced

to 'live from something other than its lands'. In a statement that sums up a classic view of the aristocratic landholder to which we shall return, Fourquin writes that 'the lesser noble had to make himself a mercenary of the king, try to find himself a bourgeois marriage, or enter the royal administration'.[5] The relationship between lord and tenant, already weakened in this economically advanced region by the growing rights of peasants over their tenancies, was slackening still further.

Even the traditional seigneurial role of protector of his tenants was diminished by the apparent decline of the castle in the Parisian region, replaced increasingly by simpler and smaller country houses. Seigneurial residences could pose a threat to rural dwellers when they became the focal point of military operations. On 14 May 1358, a meeting of the estates at Compiègne ordered the destruction of residences in poor repair, and the supplying and garrisoning of those that were serviceable. It was over the restocking of one such residence that the Jacquerie began. This revolt was indeed a war of peasants against nobles, but only to the extent that it was a contestation of what noble lordship had become in the Parisian region. At one and the same time, the lay aristocracy was less relevant to agriculturists as landowners and natural protectors, but more threatening to them as members of a military class which was beginning to seriously damage their fortunes.

It is ironic that while the term 'Jacquerie' has enjoyed a long posterity as a byword in French for rural revolt, the rebellion had no obvious successors in our period. Organised peasant resistance to the military classes did persist after 1358, but was most effective when it was conducted from the relative safety of the woods. The severity of the Counter-Jacquerie launched by the supporters of Charles of Navarre was no doubt sufficiently exemplary to discourage emulation of the mass action of 1358. Moreover, the presence of experienced soldiery on a war footing in the countryside for some of our period must have been a fair disincentive to would-be rebels. In both respects France in 1358 differed from England in 1381, where suppression of the rebellion was moderate by comparison, and where the countryside was largely spared the presence of the soldiery.

But lordship was not challenged again in France as it was in the Parisian region by the Jacquerie of 1358. Emmanuel Le Roy Ladurie has suggested that the more archaic the form of the lordship, the less likely it is to be contested. And traditional lordship, despite the view that the aristocracy experienced a major crisis in the later Middle Ages, was not faring as badly as was once thought.

A Crisis of Seigneurial Revenues?

Sources of seigneurial income

Since by definition nobles did not work or engage in trade, their land was worked by others: on the one hand there was the reserve, culti-vated for the lord's sole profit by full-time or temporary waged labour, by those fulfilling labour services or, more rarely, by serfs. On the other hand there were peasant tenures, leased out in the manners described above, that is to say to tenants paying in cash, kind or both, and to sharecroppers.

More seigneurial income came from peasant tenures than from the reserve. In the castellany of Souvigny in the Bourbonnais stud-ied by René Germain, a total of 29 per cent of the lord's revenue in 1411 derived from the seigneurial reserve, the majority of it in the form of profits from the woods, with just a little raised from the prof-its of arable and pastoral. The bulk of the income of the lordship, amounting to 53 per cent of the receipt, was raised from tenants in the form of dues paid for use of their tenures and in other charges. The lesser value of the seigneurial reserve was common elsewhere in later medieval France. In the region south of Paris studied by Yvonne Bézard, up to two-thirds of seigneurial lands were usually leased out. Marie-Thérèse Lorcin finds that some lords retained no reserve what-soever in the Lyonnais, preferring to let their estates out in their entirety.

In an age where serfdom had all but disappeared from many parts of the realm, the reduction in size of the seigneurial reserve made sense. Labour costs were minimised and a more-or-less fixed flow of income was secured. In the Île-de-France (studied by Fourquin) or eastern Normandy (examined by Bois), the seigneurial reserve itself was often placed in the hands of farmers by the middle of the fifteenth century. These middlemen, commonly from a peasant back-ground so far as we can tell, leased the right to manage the lord's estates for a fixed period and an agreed sum, and emerged in the early modern period as a new group of rural bosses with their own aspirations. Among them no doubts were to be found the *coqs de village* discussed above.

The predominance of peasant tenures over the reserve was already far advanced in some regions by the thirteenth century. The phe-nomenon led Marc Bloch to describe the lay aristocracy of the later Middle Ages as *rentiers du sol* – a class which lived from levies and dues paid by agriculturists, rather than from the exploitation of the soil under its own direct management. This reliance on peasant tenures and monopolies has been seen as a key ingredient of an economic crisis of the aristocracy in later medieval France.

Revenues under threat

Fixed dues paid by tenants declined in real value over time due to monetary erosion. In the Angevin lordship of Mestré, Michel Le Mené finds that devaluation brought the value of the *cens* paid by tenants down from 81 grammes of gold in 1400 to just 43 grammes in 1485. Plague had a more direct impact on the payment of peasant dues, dramatically cutting the number of tenants in the short-term and suppressing it for decades thereafter. Plague also reduced the willingness of new tenants to subject themselves to the rates which their predecessors had been prepared to accept. In eastern Normandy, Guy Bois finds that seigneurial income from peasant dues decreased in nominal value by as much as two-thirds or even three-quarters during the period from c. 1300 to c. 1450.

On top of the declining value of the *cens*, income from the reserve was subject to the same economic forces which were affecting peasant incomes. Where the reserve was exploited directly and not farmed out, the lord's administration was exposed to the rising cost of industrial goods and skilled labour, rather more so indeed than his tenants were, since they might at least rely on their own labour and that of their family. Seigneurial monopolies, another source of income, required skilled labour and costly equipment to be exploited profitably. Moreover, the property which was required to make money from monopolies – mills, barns, ovens and the like – was just as vulnerable to military action as peasant goods, and often more expensive to replace.

Finally, the varying seigneurial right to exercise justice provided little compensation for declining revenues elsewhere. It is possible to cite examples of profits in middling lordships arising through fines (such as Souvigny, cited above, where the income from justice amounted to 18 per cent of total revenues in 1411). More commonly, the expense of holding assizes and the salaries of personnel outweighed revenues. In the lordship of Bécon in Anjou, studied by Le Mené, the cost of exercising justice outweighed income by a proportion of more than two-to-one in the years 1464–86. The fact that lords were prepared to lose money to uphold their jurisdiction suggests that the latter was a valued seigneurial prerogative, but it was also a financial burden.

From this analysis it emerges that the core of seigneurial revenue was under threat in many parts of France in the later Middle Ages, even without taking into account the economic consequences of the way nobles traditionally aspired to live their lives: in appropriate noble style, which was increasingly expensive due to the consumption of luxury goods, or in pursuit of arms, which was affected by rising industrial prices.

Evidence of seigneurial decline

It is no surprise to find that evidence of declining noble fortunes is frequently cited in regional histories of rural France in the late Middle Ages. Particularly striking are the fate of small lordships of minimal value, and the inability of lesser nobles to maintain the lifestyle expected of their social standing.

Because of succession practices in different parts of France, there were often a large number of smaller lordships in the countryside. In the Bourbonnais, where remarkable records of the rental value of more than one thousand lordships survive from the fourteenth through to the early sixteenth centuries, René Germain finds that the number of fiefs estimated at less than 5 *l.t.* in annual income constituted between 30 per cent and 47 per cent of the total. In the small Vannetais region of southern Brittany, Jean Gallet has shown that modest lordships known as *sieuries* with no jurisdiction and only limited resources constituted an entire category of landholders numbering between 300 and 350 in 1450.

It is not possible to tell exactly how many of these very minor lordships were owned by nobles, or if this land was the only source of income for the noble owner. But we may be certain that incomes from minor lordships consisting of a tiny reserve and just a few peasant tenures were very low indeed. In Bigorre around 1300 Maurice Berthe finds a large number of minor lords with revenues estimated at between 5 *l.t.* and 10 *l.t.* per annum. These figures are thrown into stark relief by the fact that in the same year, 1 *l.t.* bought 120 chickens or 48 lambs at market. In the small Breton *sieurie* of Kerabrahan in Séné, 84 per cent of revenue derived from a single sharecropping contract in the period 1461–82.

Given such potentially precarious circumstances, it is unsurprising that examples of the sale of lands are commonplace. Lesser holdings were more readily alienated by their proprietors than larger, flourishing patrimonies In the Verdunois studied by Alain Girardot, sales of lordships increase in number from 1364 on, with nobles figuring much more regularly among vendors than purchasers in the sources from the region. In the Limousin studied by Jean Tricard, notarial records show the shift in the fortunes of noble families such as the Larons, Jauberts or Daniels, from lenders in the fourteenth century to borrowers and debtors in the fifteenth century.

The increasing inability of some nobles to equip themselves for military service, and the rise in instances of voluntary renunciation of noble status (*dérogeance*), may be taken as further signs of hard times for noble landowners. Lesser nobles and second or third sons of poorer noble families had every incentive to seek their fortune as best they could away from the family lands, and this group inevitably contributed to the growing ranks of the soldiery which plagued the countryside of late medieval France.

Alternative sources of income

And yet even the most ardent proponents of a 'crisis of the aristocracy' in late medieval France believe that the problem was not entirely without remedy.

Guy Bois, who considers the decline of aristocratic revenue as part of a broader 'crisis of feudalism', is a case in point. In his view, the product of the seigneurial levy was bound to diminish once thirteenth-century growth ceased, and in this sense the crisis of the later Middle Ages was the result of an inherent flaw in the system rather than the sudden product of external factors like plague or climate change. The crisis was eventually alleviated by the state. As their own revenues declined, the aristocracy saw an opportunity in the rising fortunes of the ruler, the latter propelled ever upwards by soaring taxation which, in this scenario, was gradually supplanting the seigneurial levy as the main burden on agriculturists. The surplus product of the countryside creamed off in taxation now found its way back into noble pockets through the medium of the princely paymaster. A service nobility was gradually being created from the ranks of an older landed aristocracy, occupying itself with the business of its princely or royal patrons in war, at court or in the ruler's administration. In short, the 'crisis of feudalism' advanced the process of state-building, by funnelling the landed aristocracy into the paid service of the ruler. The lord, meanwhile, became a more distant figure on his own estates.

Elements of this picture of changing aristocratic fortunes may be picked out in the story of the Salers family from upper Auvergne, analysed by James Goldsmith. The family estates in this case were badly affected by external circumstances, pillaged first by brigands in 1357 and again in 1429 by Villandrando's men. Attempts to restore the declining value of the land through the issuing of favourable terms to tenants and by the expansion of the seigneurial reserve do not appear to have halted the decline in the fifteenth century. Locally, the family faced competition from noble rivals, mercantile wealth and even its own vassals, resulting in at least two costly cases before the *Parlement*. Although his mother worked hard to retain the family lands, Charles de Salers opted for princely service at the close of the fifteenth century, making his way at the Bourbon court and finally selling some of the family lands to maintain his lifestyle there.

Our schematic picture of declining seigneurial income is subject to important qualifications, however. Every author who has chronicled waning aristocratic fortunes in the later Middle Ages has noted that the phenomenon was very far from being universal. In many regions where there is evidence of lesser lords suffering under prevailing conditions, larger noble landowners can be found extending their lands as less fortunate lords sold up, or expanding the reserve within their existing lordships as peasant tenures fell vacant. Such activity may explain why, according to Germain, the number of Bourbonnais lordships worth less than 10 *l.t.* per annum in rents fell from around 60 per cent of the total surveyed in the fifteenth century to around 35 per cent by 1503. Meanwhile, the number of lords owning fiefs worth more than 50 *l.t.* increased from 12 per cent to 17 per cent. The rich were getting richer, the poor were becoming less numerous.

It was possible for many nobles, perhaps especially those owning estates in which seigneurial income derived from a range of activities, to respond directly to worsening conditions. In such circumstances lords had a number of options, from the more flexible management of tenants and reserves to the simple enforcement of all seigneurial rights. Louis Merle has shown that in the Gâtine of Poitou, seigneurial fortunes were enhanced by a policy of gathering lands and re-leasing them to sharecroppers. Since the nobility – rather than some external agency, like the crown – took a leading role in the restoration of their lands, it is hard to believe (as Pierre Charbonnier has pointed out) that they did not try to shape the process to their own advantage. The *censier* of the lesser noble Jean Jossard from the Lyonnais suggests that far from being a distant figure, this lord was closely involved with those who worked his estates. Jossard personally attended 61 of the 99 appointments made with tenants to record the terms of their relationship, mostly in his castle but on some occasions out in the fields.[6]

'Another France': The durability of lordship

In addition to these causes for scepticism, the thesis of a later medieval 'crisis of feudalism' is demonstrably open to fundamental criticism.

Fraudulent estimates of the rental values of fiefs are known to have existed, raising the distinct possibility that the decline in seigneurial revenues has been overstated. In the Bourbonnais, where it is possible to compare seigneurial estimates of revenues submitted to the feudal lord with surviving receipts for the income of the fief, Germain finds that the vassal commonly declared less than 30 per cent of the real value of his holding. Declining income from peasant dues had a particularly detrimental impact on seigneurial fortunes in regions where payment in cash was the norm, but payment in kind still existed and sustained noble families in many regions as we have seen. Lords themselves might use goods received to make payment in kind, such as the Poitevin lord (noted by Joseph Salvini) who contracted with three Limousin stonemasons in 1438 to rebuild the choir of the local parish church, incorporating a vault bearing his family's arms. The work was done in return for substantial amounts of wheat, white wine, ham and olive oil (which were presumably consumed or bartered during the weeks the men were working) and the sum of 8 *l* 10 *s* in cash (which could be easily taken home or to the next job).

Evidence for seigneurial indebtedness is easy to find in later medieval France, but debt should not be equated with ruin. Debt may in fact have been a normal state of affairs for members of an aristocracy to whom saving was supposedly, in any case, anathema. The disappearance of noble lineages did sometimes result from impecunity, but it could result in landed wealth being concentrated in fewer hands. In such cases, the real problem of the period might have been how to manage several estates, rather than how to live on the limited revenue produced by one. Citing Guy Bois's evidence of a decline in seigneurial revenues by as much as 70 per cent in Normandy between 1300 and 1450, Charbonnier points out that these same monies were shared out among noble families which had themselves decreased in number by as much as 75 per cent. There was no need in such conditions to rush into the service of a ruler whose share of the income of ordinary agriculturists, as we saw above, did not yet match (let alone supplant) the seigneurial levy.

Several of these challenges to the thesis of seigneurial economic decline are exemplified in the journals of the fifteenth-century lesser nobleman Guillaume de Murol, from Auvergne.[7] Here was a lesser noble whose *censier* was well-stocked with tenants. By far the greater part of the dues paid to Guillaume were received in kind, protecting him from monetary erosion. The product of the Murol estates was diverse, so the modest needs of the lord's table and household could be met. If Guillaume was slow to pay some of his bills, this did not necessarily mean he was in debt; rather, he was holding back reserves to make territorial acquisitions. The image of a dispendious and impecunious nobility is countered by the careful calculations on every page of Murol's journals, but also in similar material, such as the *terrier* of the Norman lord Georges d'Orbec, which carefully listed the dues his tenants owed him and their obligations to other lords and peasants.[8] Charbonnier thus presents the image of 'another France', one in which the nobility as a whole was not the victim of debilitating crisis at all.

He is not the only historian to have taken this view. Hard times affected some lords, especially those with minor holdings who did not inherit more land. But in Anjou, 'the landed aristocracy was never called into question' (Michel Le Mené), while in the Limousin, 'the nobility still had a firm hold on the countryside' (Jean Tricard).[9] The seemingly perpetual decline of the nobility must be viewed with considerable caution.

Noble power in rural France

The French rural nobility which emerges from this discussion does not seem so very different from its English counterpart, described by Christopher Dyer as 'a remarkably resilient and flexible class, able to adapt to new circumstances and thus to maintain their social position'.[10] We are entitled to wonder if the same might be true of the political power of the aristocracy in the French countryside, which is rarely accorded much weight in narrative histories of the period.

True, many lesser nobles must have succumbed to economic difficulties and renounced noble status or drifted into the soldiery. But the numerous noble families which clearly managed to sustain themselves remained an important force. Nobles found themselves bypassed by the ruler's mechanisms for raising taxes from villages, and village communities grew in autonomy and authority as a result. But the proportion of peasant income taken by the lord remained significant thanks to his rights and monopolies, not to mention the payment of peasant dues. The lord's share of peasant income could be far higher than anything the crown took in taxes. The ruler's justice was available to many in late medieval France and was an important means for the crown to extend its authority, but seigneurial justice was much cheaper and more easily accessible. Lords still valued the status which this often costly service afforded them. The rural castle had become a less prominent feature of the landscape in the countryside around the capital, but castle-building was still the focus of much effort in other regions. In Auvergne and Normandy, Charbonnier finds villagers prepared to pay for temporary lodgings in the castle courtyard and contribute to the watch during times of chronic insecurity. Finally the local noble often remained an active military figure, such as the petty Norman lord Étienne le Bis, studied by Gareth Prosser, who turned out fully armed for all the king's summonses from the 1460s to the 1490s, and fought in a number of important engagements.

Beyond the level of lordships where their authority was manifest in all these ways, the local nobility belonged to a wider political society in which kinship, lordship and other forms of alliance governed political interests. Ties of blood were significant in determining the action of the nobility within the locality, as Bertrand Schnerb's study of the Bournonville family in northern France demonstrates. Any contentious matter involving a branch of the Bournonvilles – a legal case, a loss suffered, a sleight received – was likely to see members of a widely extended family network rally together to achieve common ends. French vassals and their lords were still bound to one another by mutual obligations of service and protection in the late Middle Ages. As Marie-Thérèse Caron has shown in her work on Burgundy, the military duties of vassals were still taken very seriously in our period, and any vassal who refused to serve his lord faced confiscation of his lands in that region.

In addition to visible hierarchies established by family and feudal ties, newer, more flexible and often less visible forms of alliance were beginning to emerge in our period, as Peter Lewis has shown. In such 'decayed and non-feudal' agreements, one party usually promised service and loyalty in return for money from the other. A great lord could use such agreements to establish a firm but highly flexible base for himself among the local nobility, as Gaston Phoebus, Count of

Foix managed to do in the south-west thanks to a network of alliances spread across his own lands and those of his regional rivals in the later fourteenth century.

In all of these ways, the nobility remained 'the political class *par excellence*'.[11] The actions resulting from the many bonds between powerful local noble families can be hard to follow within the locality, let alone the region, still less the kingdom. In England, the study of politics 'from below' is made possible by a number of factors, including a more detailed knowledge of the numerically smaller nobility within the localities, and the greater survival of royal records at the centre. There is sadly nothing in France to compare with the correspondence of the Paston family in fifteenth-century Norfolk, which allows the historian to explore how events at the local, regional and regnal levels related to one another. But some scholars, notably Raymond Cazelles and John Henneman, have shown it is possible to trace the role and influence of regional noble groupings in the political life of the kingdom, and we will attempt to build on their work in the next two chapters of this book.

Landowners – Old and New

In the meantime, what of other landowners in late medieval France? The two main groups we have not yet considered were ecclesiastical institutions and wealthy townsmen. The decline of the former and rise of the latter were for a long time accepted truths in studies of our period, but such views now appear overstated in the light of the findings of a plethora of regional studies of the French countryside.

Church landownership

Pious donations, careful management and a policy of territorial acquisition had, over the centuries, made prelates, cathedral chapters, priories and monastic orders the owners of a good deal of the French countryside. In the fertile region of the Parisian basin studied by Fourquin, the cathedral chapter of the bishopric of Paris and the monasteries of Saint-Denis and Saint-Germain-des-Prés were by far the biggest landowners. In Quercy, Latouche finds that the most extensive estates belonged to the bishop of Cahors, while in the Cambrésis, Neveux estimates that the church owned over 40 per cent of the countryside. Given such circumstances, as Marie-Thérèse Lorcin reminds us, it was not uncommon for agriculturists in later medieval

France to find themselves the parishioners, tenants, tithe-payers and recipients of justice of the same ecclesiastical lord.

Judging from the evidence gathered by Henri Denifle of the devastation of churches, monasteries and hospitals during the Hundred Years' War, the economic conditions affecting peasant fortunes and lay lordship clearly took their toll on church lands as well. Guy Fourquin finds that the purchasing power of the revenues of the monastery of Saint-Denis was effectively halved by monetary devaluation between 1334 and 1342, and this despite no significant change in the product of its estates. The cartulary of the Cistercian abbey of the Vaux-de-Cernay records that at one undated point in our period the monastery was so much reduced that its only inhabitant was a 'poor old monk who lived all alone for 12 years in great difficulty and misery without an abbot or any brothers at all'.[12]

In many regions, however, it is apparent that the church's holdings remained much the same from the late Middle Ages down to the Revolution. Compared to lay estates, there was remarkable continuity of ownership and exploitation. The only significant change in church ownership of land which Berthe detects in Bigorre over a hundred-year period was the abandonment of two small communities owned by the Hospitallers. The sixteenth century would witness the abuses of lay administration of church property and a greater incidence of alienation. But it is the relative stability of church landownership in the later medieval period – and with it, sustained or even increased prosperity in some cases – which has struck many observers of French rural history.

Part of the explanation lies in the solidity and indivisibility which characterised church ownership of land. The decline of donations and bequests by laymen to ecclesiastical institutions was a tendency across much of France in the late Middle Ages, at least compared to the great foundations of the twelfth or thirteenth centuries. But grants did not dry up altogether, and they might still be generous, such as the gift of a residence at Bicêtre with its lands and vines which Jean, Duke of Berry gave his to the canons of the cathedral chapter of Paris in 1416. Once church property had been acquired, canon law discouraged its alienation. Girardot has shown that the bishops of Verdun were particularly assiduous in respecting mortmain on their lands, a legal right which ensured that a fief held of the church reverted to the ecclesiastical lord on the vassal's death. By contrast with the lay landowner, of course, the church did not have to confront the additional problems of partible inheritance or the absence of direct heirs.

A second advantage lay in the fact that the larger ecclesiastical institutions often enjoyed a more diverse and therefore more reliable
economic base than lay lordship. Belotte finds that the many estates
of the great monastery of Molesmes in Burgundy were spread over
90 villages in the region of Bar-sur-Seine by the sixteenth century.
Where urban property featured among the lands held by an ecclesiastical institution, rents could provide additional protection from any
decline in rural revenues. Michel Le Mené has shown that 75 per cent
of the temporal revenues of the bishop of Angers came from property
and rights within the regional capital itself or its immediate surround-
ings. In some parts of France the lay nobility also owned a significant
amount of urban property, such as Flanders or Quercy, but it was the
church which generally achieved a better balance of income from
town and country, and with it greater stability of income in the long
term.

More stable and varied sources of income enabled the larger ecclesiastical institutions to benefit from such economic opportunities
as presented themselves. Thanks to their generally greater liquidity,
churchmen might benefit from the cash-flow problems of the aristocracy. Cash reserves also facilitated the making of loans. Given the
church's teachings on usury it is not surprising to find that loans were
made without interest, but profits accrued through agreed penalties
for late payment.

Thanks to the significant advantages enjoyed by larger ecclesiastical
institutions, the biggest threat they faced as landowners was the mal-
administration of their property. The Lyonnais chapter of Saint-Just
is a case in point, as Lorcin has shown. The internal disorganisa-
tion of the chapter was such that the bell-ringer resigned because
he simply did not know who was in charge. The canons also landed
themselves with considerable expenses, such as costly arrangements
for providing justice to those under their jurisdiction, and their failure to lease out some of their more distant possessions which resulted
in frequent and expensive travel for their personnel. Where leading
churchmen were called to serve the king or the church, it was always
possible that their estates might suffer as a consequence. Saint-Just
was nonetheless the only ecclesiastical institution in the Lyonnais to
experience effective bankruptcy, and its plight seems largely to have
been self-inflicted.

Broadly speaking, then, the larger ecclesiastical institutions were
in a better position than many landowners to weather the economic
difficulties of the late Middle Ages. The servants of the state who
emerged from the ranks of the clergy could thus be very well-provided
for indeed.

Townsmen in the countryside

While urban wealth was helping maintain or enhance the revenues of ecclesiastical institutions, it was also preparing the way for what is sometimes claimed to have been a marked transformation in the countryside during the late Middle Ages: the increased acquisition of rural land by wealthy townsmen.

Among the first to emphasise the importance of bourgeois landownership was Marc Bloch, for whom the development did not simply represent the replacement of one type of proprietor by another, but rather the injection into the French countryside of a capitalist mentality promoted by men who were used to calculating profits and losses. By the start of our period, wealthy townsmen had already acquired rural property in some parts of France, notably the Île-de-France studied by Fourquin. Comparison of bourgeois owner-ship of rural land in the Lyonnais between 1388 and 1493 by Lorcin reveals not only a considerable increase in the number of holdings, but a wider geographical spread across the region. In the Limousin studied by Jean Tricard, townsmen granted loans and invested in joint ventures with agriculturists, particularly in pastoral farming.

But the penetration of bourgeois ownership into the French coun-tryside and its ability to effect change can be overestimated. In Sologne, Isabelle Guérin thinks rural poverty led urban investors to place their money elsewhere. In the Verdunois, Girardot finds that the church's firm hold over its extensive lands discouraged bourgeois acquisition on any meaningful scale, while in Auvergne, Charbonnier thinks the aristocracy was not selling up to acquisitive townsmen – either because it did not need to, or because bourgeois purchasers were simply insignificant in the rural landmarket.

It is true that none of these regions was particularly urbanised, but even in areas which were, we must be wary of declaring the dis-placement of the old landed nobility by urban wealth. No region was more urbanised in later medieval France than the Parisian basin. Here, as Guy Fourquin notes, a study of the lands held in fief from the great monastery of Saint-Denis around 1400 reveals the continu-ing solidity of noble ownership, save in villages which were closest to Paris. The corollary of rising bourgeois landholding, namely declin-ing noble fortunes in the countryside, is once again thrown into doubt.

Moreover, it is far from certain that bourgeois ownership (where it figured) transformed the way the land was farmed and managed. It was no easy matter to guarantee a consistent profit from the owner-ship of arable land, herds or vines in later medieval France. We may suspect that more than one urban fortune disappeared into a black hole of rural landownership. The emerging wealthy peasant elite discussed above, implanted for far longer in the countryside, was in a better position to exploit such opportunities as presented themselves.

In any case, rural property might have been acquired for other reasons by bourgeois owners. Bloch's vision of the townsman happily receiving the fruit of his land, delivered cap in hand by his sharecropper, destined to be consumed at his table, may not have been so far from the truth – for some at least. In difficult times this might not simply have been an issue of status, but of necessity, especially when prices rocketed under the pressure of war. For other, perhaps wealthier, townsmen, the acquisition of noble lordships confirmed social ascension achieved through mercantile wealth or public office. Among the many examples which could be cited is Hugues Jossard, father of Jean, who made his name as a lawyer. Hugues's acquisition of several lordships in the Lyonnais and his ennoblement in 1398 confirmed his rise in the world. To be someone important in the countryside, it was better to be a lord.

The Church and Religion

Bourgeois ownership of rural property serves as a reminder that contrasts between the urban and the rural worlds should not be exaggerated, but clearly they did exist. This last point was increasingly apparent in the sphere of religion, in matters such as the background of the rural clergy or the role of the church in rural society. Some of the differences which were emerging in our period help explain why, at its close, reforming ideas were to win greater support in urban milieux than in the countryside of early modern France.

The rural clergy

Rural priests were primarily recruited in the countryside and tended to live close to their flock. Around Nogaro in Gascony, Gilbert Loubès finds from notarial records that most of the 150 or so rural clergy who can be identified had peasant origins. In the wills of clergy from the villages of Forez studied by Marguerite Gonon, it is apparent that priests often dressed like their parishioners, dined with them, pruned vines in their company and so forth.

Some historians are understandably keen to point out that for all their similarities to their parishioners, clerics were part of a wider vocational group with different powers, standing and training. Yves Grava finds that rural priests living near Montpellier or Avignon included graduates who owned books. Around Strasbourg, Francis Rapp thinks the country priests were outsiders in the village community, usually better educated than their parishioners, and far richer than them because of income from the tithe.

But examples from eastern regions relatively close to large towns cannot be allowed to stand for the whole of rural France. Vincent Tabbagh's discussion of registers of ordinations of priests for 14 dioceses across the kingdom at the end of our period finds that in 'Atlantic France', the clergy were far more numerous, closer to their families and even resident with them. Here, the rural clergy provided religious services locally whilst still forming a valued part of the labour force. In the east, by contrast, Tabbagh finds that priests were fewer in number and more often immigrants from other regions. Tabbagh explains the difference in the following terms: in the west, 'salvation is always assured by a community which takes financial responsibility for its priests, those specialized intermediaries between heaven and earth'; in the east, salvation 'was generally conceived of as the consequence of a purified and clean conscience, and of behaviour in keeping with the teaching of scripture, the reward of a personal journey modelled on Christ'. But the interesting contrast he finds is surely linked more prosaically to the fact that the west was the most rural part of the kingdom. The priesthood was more firmly integrated in rural societies where community bonds were closer. The east, by contrast, was more urbanised. Urban societies were relatively fragmented, peopled in large part by relative newcomers partially or wholly detached from their communities of origin. Thus what appears to be a religious difference between eastern and western France is really one between a part of the kingdom which had few large cities (the Atlantic) and another where they were more common (the east).

Clerical inadequacy: Myth or reality?

The proximity of the rural clergy to their flock was once seen as symptom and cause of the many failings of the priesthood attested in records of episcopal visitations of French dioceses which (as Noël Coulet has shown) survive from the later thirteenth century on. These documents certainly crackle with examples of slack morals and ignorance among parish priests, to which stories of clerical

misbehaviour gleaned from letters of remission were added by scholars persuaded of narratives of late medieval clerical decline, especially
in the countryside.

But a more recent generation of historians avoids the uncritical
acceptance of the picture emerging in the records of episcopal visitations. These records are far from complete, both in terms of their
scope (some concerned only church property) and survival rate (just
two sets of visitation records survive for the diocese of Lyon). They
were also usually the result of inspections of very large numbers of
parishes carried out in a relatively short period of time, seven or ten
parishes a day being a not uncommon rate of progress. While episcopal visitation records mention many clerics who were fined, those
whose conduct and church were found to be perfectly satisfactory
should not be overlooked.

Moreover, as Sylvette Guilbert points out, the growing number of
rural clergy fined for misdemeanours says as much about attempts at
episcopal control and reform as it does about clerical failings. In the
south-west, Fabrice Ryckebusch has shown that episcopal reform of
the rural clergy was based on three related elements: the diocesan
synod, to which local priests were regularly summoned; the diocesan statutes, which the clergy were issued with and were expected to
know and promulgate as required; and the episcopal visitation itself,
which was the means of checking up on the implementation of measures specified at the synod and in the statutes. The extent to which
such measures were effective is hard to judge, but their very existence
undermines the well-worn image of uncorrected clerical inadequacy
in the countryside.

Roles of the clergy and church in rural life

Rather than being locked in a spiral of decline, the rural clergy and
the church in the countryside often emerge as forces for cohesion
and stability.

The problem of absenteeism among the rural clergy now appears
far less marked than once was thought, more likely to occur in rich
benefices located in or near large towns rather than deep in the
countryside (a fact which further distinguished religious life in each,
of course). Where parish priests were absent, they were very often
replaced by salaried members of the numerous clerical proletariat
produced by the period, men who were likely to be closer in origins
and lifestyle to their flock than the absent holder of the benefice.

Whatever his limitations, the parish priest fulfilled a number of roles above and beyond his religious duties which placed him at the centre of community life. Charitable assistance did not generally figure here, for the indigent were often the concern of family and neighbours in the rural environment, in growing contrast to the towns. But the care of children was one area where synodal statutes certainly placed expectations on priests, to the extent of recommending mothers to place babies in cots rather than in the parental bed for safety's sake, or ordering the sealing of wells in close proximity to houses to prevent children falling in (as Paul Adam notes in statutes from the bishopric of Nantes). In the parish of Orvault in Brittany studied by Henri Martin, the cost of raising abandoned children fell to the parish under its priest. Schooling, where it existed, usually fell to the parish priest too, although in the wake of plague the Carmelite friar Jean de Venette complained that insufficient clerics could be found 'to instruct children in the rudiments of grammar'.[13]

And then there was the role of the church building itself, central in medieval life at any time, but undoubtedly more so in later medieval France due to its widespread defensive role. Philippe Contamine finds that fortified parish churches in one 50 sq. km region south of Fontainebleu were 28 in number in 1357, and this 15 years before Charles V issued general instructions on the matter. Reports of fortified churches sheltering up to 300 refugees are not uncommon in the material studied by Henri Denifle, and diocesan statutes permitted peasants to keep bags and chests containing their precious possessions in the church during times of danger.

The upkeep of the parish church gave rise to another core element of parish life, the *fabrique de l'église*. The laymen who formed this body had to raise levies from their fellow parishioners to pay for repairs to the church where all were expected to worship, and often they carried out their tasks without the involvement of the priest. The *fabrique* came to undertake other communal work, some of it of considerable value to the local community such as the repair of roads, bridges and wells within the parish. The management of communal affairs was coming to be seen as the duty of a small peasant elite, men such as Symmonet Thomassin, a labourer from the village of Solers whom Gustave Prévost has found auditing the accounts of the parish church in the company of the priest and rural dean in 1367. In the town, where the clergy were more numerous, there was less need to involve laymen in key affairs of the church. And as we saw in Chapter 1, the parish was coming to occupy a central role in other public spheres, such as the levying of taxes.

The growing importance of the rural parish could only be strengthened by the fact that rural religious confraternities tended to include
the vast majority of the inhabitants of a single parish, unlike those
of the town which might be grouped around a trade, a particular
cult or holy purpose rather than a parish, and where membership
of more than one confraternity was possible. Rural confraternities
could heighten cohesion by resolving disputes and promoting socia-
bility through their annual feast, processions and other religious
duties, and membership of them might include nobles as well as
non-nobles, as was the case of the *Charité* of Surville-en-Auge (studied by Catherine Vincent in her work on Norman confraternities). In
many important ways the church was coming to occupy a central role
in the French countryside in the late Middle Ages, more so than in
the town.

Religious belief

Despite the presence of many clerics of varying types in the countryside and the efforts of the higher clergy to extend its control there,
religious beliefs retained features which barely seemed Christian to
educated contemporaries – a finding emphasised by Jacques Le Goff
and Jean Delumeau. In the *Évangiles des Quenouilles*, a text probably
written in the circle of Philip the Good, Duke of Burgundy (1419–67),
tales attributed to old peasant women describe how husbands could
be bent to their wives' will by placing their shirts under the altar on
Good Friday. In the region of Toulouse, Marie-Claude Marandet still
finds 'a mix of superstition and magic' close to the surface of religious
beliefs in the fifteenth century.[14]

But there was orthodoxy in the countryside as well. When the peasant girl Joan of Arc was asked by her inquisitors whether she was in a
state of grace, her reply was assured: 'If I am not, may the Lord put
me there; if I am, may He keep me there.'[15] Louis Carolus-Barré has
shown that this precise response was in fact a phrase which figured
in fifteenth-century collections of prayers said in parish churches on
Sundays. It is a relatively simple spiritual world which emerges from
Joan's testimony, one in which immediate family, the parish priest
and the passing mendicant were the important figures – a fact all the
more impressive given the close and prolonged questioning of Joan's
inquisitors, whose fear of heretical beliefs in the end far outweighed
her espousal of them. Jean Gerson, chancellor of the University of
Paris, mentions in several of his letters his peasant background in

Champagne within a deeply pious community. Religious instruction was supplied by his father, a tenant on the lands of a Benedictine priory, and by one of his brothers, in training for the priesthood.

There were certainly dissident religious groups in the country-side, such as the Turlupins who roamed western France in the late fourteenth century preaching polygamy and the equal distribution of wealth (at least until the authorities caught up with them). But catharism, still present in the countryside at the start of our period as the registers of Jacques Fournier famously demonstrated, faded from view, perhaps finding a last hiding place among some southern con-fraternities. The Vaudois (as Gabriel Audisio has shown) migrated from west to east, the last remaining groups in Gascony dwindling away as centres in the Luberon and Dauphiné became the most prominent. It was with some justification that Erasmus could observe, in 1517, that France was the only land without heresy.

*   *   *

All forms of public authority depended on the resources they extracted in dues, rights and taxes from a predominantly rural pop-ulation. That population was greatly reduced in number from the middle of the fourteenth century on, a development that began a lit-tle earlier in the north due to famine. But the economic conditions of the period were less deleterious to peasant fortunes than some con-temporaries suggested. Waged labour, viticulture and inheritances all provided some relief. Under the right conditions, indeed, it was possible to improve one's circumstances, and a small proportion of rural dwellers grasped the opportunity to do so. The catastrophes of the late medieval period are well documented, but there was indeed 'considerable vitality beneath the pall'.[16]

Landowners and other forms of public authority were not, there-fore, ruined from below. Seigneurial rights over tenants were exten-sive and flexible, and payments taken by a lord could still be the single largest external burden on peasant income. Churchmen faced declining revenues, but compared to lay estates, larger ecclesiastical institutions were well placed to weather the storm and provide a living for leading prelates. The state's share of peasant income increased considerably from 1350 on, but the peasant garden and a barter econ-omy could lessen the impact of fiscal pressure on rural dwellers when compared to people in towns.

As a consequence of these developments, rural society was made up of a 'plurality of powers', quite as much as any another cross section of the French population. The powers we know least about are the village communities, records for which are rare before the sixteenth century. Village assemblies met and took concerted action over matters such as tax exemptions, and the church and religious organisations added further potential for cohesion. But only once does the village assembly seem to erupt onto the stage of regnal politics, during the Jacquerie. Such bodies were doubtless present in the many small actions taken to defend villages against the soldiery, fortifying churches or keeping the watch. The limited success of these measures helps explain why the rural population was prepared to shoulder the growing fiscal burden of the state. Unlike the mass of the urban population, which was admittedly more exposed to fiscal pressure as we shall see, rural dwellers did not generally rebel over taxes in late medieval France.

Among the developments of political consequence in rural France in our period, the financial difficulties of the landed aristocracy have attracted greater comment than the role of the village community. The decline of seigneurial revenues pushed the ambitious in the direction of princely and royal service, the bellicose into the ranks of the forces for disorder, and the destitute into renouncing their noble status. But although many nobles and noble families must have had such experiences, historians of rural France now tend to reject the once-widespread narrative of seigneurial decline. Lordship remained important in the locality, where justice was exercised and dues were taken; and in the region, where the still powerful forces of kingroup, vassalage and alliance shaped political action. Tracing the impact on the regnal stage of noble political action at such 'grass roots' levels is no easy matter. But it would be a good start to recognise that rulers needed the support of local and regional noble networks, and to seek patterns in the political behaviour of these groupings. As we have seen, such patterns were already beginning to emerge under the last Capetians, when eastern nobles were coming to occupy privileged places in the brokerage networks around the king. This observation can be carried into a narrative of events, the subject of the next two chapters.

Chapter 3: Royal France, c. 1328–c. 1380

A narrative of events in late medieval France necessarily takes as its central focus individual rulers and the fate of the monarchy. But around the ruler, as we have seen, there was a plurality of powers. An extended royal familial community with its own hierarchy, rights and expectations contained the most important of these elements, and linked to that community were the great fief-holders of the realm. The king and the leading figures around him expressed their authority through administrative structures and a bureaucracy which were becoming more significant in public life, mainly because they provided a forum for interaction with the plurality of powers that existed abroad in the realm. Foremost among this last group, despite frequent reports of their demise, were the nobles of the kingdom, whose revenues, local authority, military training and networks made them a force to be reckoned with.

Overlaying relations between kings, princes and nobles were geopolitical considerations of long standing, in particular marked differences between western and eastern France. The restive west was least amenable to royal authority on the eve of our period, and that problem merged into the series of conflicts known as the Hundred Years' War. The conflicts concerned, not just the king of France's relations with the leading fief-holder in the west, but others of that region who were prepared to exploit the monarchy's difficulties to achieve their own ends. How these geopolitical considerations played out will be a prominent feature in what follows.

To secure support and suppress opposition in the midst of these struggles, French kings needed to generate revenues in increasing quantities. The spectacular growth of royal finances must be a key part of the narrative that follows. Because the right to raise taxes was far from automatic, the king was led to seek the cooperation of other forms of public authority in his realm. Negotiation with leading lords, ecclesiastical institutions and municipalities to raise subsidies from populations under their jurisdiction took place in one of two ways, and often both: directly, in consultations with royal officers; or in assemblies of the representatives of the clergy, nobility and towns, these gatherings held at local, regional or regnal level. Representative assemblies, known as the *états* (estates), were first consulted at the level of the kingdom by Philip IV to seek support against the papacy, notably in 1302 and 1303. In 1314, representatives were called from across the kingdom for the first time to consent to the payment of taxes, and Philip IV's sons also resorted intermittently to the same tactic, albeit with very limited success. The crown's need for revenues therefore had the potential to add one more power to the plurality which already existed. How the estates fared will naturally be a concern in the pages that follow.

Philip VI (1328–50)

The succession crisis

All royal successions have the potential to be problematic, but Philip VI's had more than most. The count of Valois was the natural choice to succeed his cousin Charles IV, first as regent then as monarch, when the latter fell ill and died without male heir (February 1328). Son of Charles of Valois (Philip IV's brother, and a dominant figure in previous reigns), the 35-year-old count was a core part of the royal familial community. Alternatives to Philip could not be sought among the many Capetian daughters who survived Charles IV, for it had effectively been established in 1316 that women could not accede to the throne. But could Capetian women transmit claims to their male children?

Edward III, the son of Philip IV's daughter, was one such child, and in 1328 his representatives were understandably present at the assembly of notables which met to resolve the succession. Edward's rights were doubtless disregarded on that occasion for obvious reasons, foremost among them the fact that he was not 'born of the kingdom'. But the exclusion of a candidate whose claim was based on female transmission had something else to commend it. Upholding Edward's case might mean entertaining the claims of any son born to a female of the Capetian line, of whom there were several, at a later stage. That such an eventuality might occur was borne out in 1332, when Louis X's daughter Jeanne, the wife of Philip, Count of Évreux (1319–43), gave birth to Charles of Navarre. The effects of uncertain successions were there for all to see in recent upheavals in the Empire, where Lewis of Bavaria had had to defeat his cousin and rival Frederick 'the Fair' of Habsburg in 1322, or indeed in England itself, where Edward II was deposed in 1327, and where Edward III was only truly secure once Roger Mortimer had been executed.

Edward III did not formally renounce his claim to the throne of France after 1328, nor could he ever be accused of taking it lightly, as Craig Taylor has pointed out. But by performing homage for his lands in the kingdom to Philip VI in 1329, and by acknowledging its liege status in 1331, he nonetheless appeared to have accepted the magnates' decision in favour of Philip. At this juncture Edward III's primary concern beyond the Channel was his lordship in the duchy of Gascony, which had been left in a diminished state by the settlement of the war of Saint-Sardos in 1324–7.

Pillars of early Valois kingship

The new king came to enjoy significant support from influential quarters at an early stage in his reign, not least within the royal familial community and among the highest nobility. Odo IV of Burgundy (1315–49), already the king's brother-in-law of 17 years' standing, became a mainstay during the reign. Other brothers-in-law included Jean III, Duke of Brittany (1312–41), Robert of Artois (d. 1342) and the heir to the newly erected duchy of Bourbon, Pierre I (1342–56). Louis II of Nevers, Count of Flanders (1322–46) would soon have cause to be grateful to Philip as we shall see. Some direct Capetians certainly wavered in their support for the first Valois, but recalcitrants were placated by suitable concessions. It is sometimes said that the manner of Philip VI's accession to the throne compromised his authority, but the point can be overstated. Claimants might seek territorial compensation for what they had relinquished or lost, but to attempt to replace a fit and able Most Christian King after his coronation, not to mention his selection and likely election by the barons and peers of the realm, would be highly problematic.

Philip was further strengthened by noble support on both sides of the realm. The Burgundians were an important source of Capetian advisers as we have seen in an earlier chapter, and as Raymond Cazelles first noted in his study of political society under the first

Valois kings, Philip continued the royal tradition of recruiting among the men of the east. Prominent around the king and within the relatively small world of the royal administration were Burgundians such as the chancellor Gui Baudet, formerly a servant of Charles IV; Hugues de Pommard, master of the *Chambre des comptes*; and above all the leading councillor Mile de Noyers, royal *bouteiller* from 1336. The presence of these men reflected the influence of Philip's wife Jeanne of Burgundy and her brother, Duke Odo IV. Burgundian noble networks thus had privileged access to people who were close to the king, both within his family and in the highest reaches of his administration.

Although less well represented at court, a recognisable community of noble families linked by ties of kinship and property along the seaboard of France or its immediate periphery also lent its support to Philip VI in the first years of his reign. Cazelles called them 'men of the west', a phrase which has acquired Tolkeinesque connotations in English, but which we may adopt for convenience's sake. Among these prominent western nobles were the Harcourts, whose main holdings lay in Normandy, but who also had lands in the Loire region to the south and in Hainaut to the north. This was a family which commanded a potentially wide base of noble support along the maritime flank. Philip courted the Harcourts by erecting the patrimony of its main branch to the status of a county in 1339, and Count Jean IV would die in his service with other westerners at the battle of Crécy in 1346. Another important man of the west was the constable of France, Raoul I of Brienne, Count of Guines (d. 1344) on the northern seaboard, of Eu in Normandy, and holder of substantial lordships in lower Poitou: clearly a figure with influence over widespread noble networks at regional and local level. Support for Philip in these western regions was strengthened by the fact that his family's lordships were extensive there. The main possessions passed either to him (the duchy of Anjou and the counties of Maine and Chartres) or to his brother Charles (Count of Alençon (1326–46)). Servants from these mainly western territories remained with Philip VI after he became king. The financial cost of retaining followers from previous regimes, and from among one's own supporters and servants, was certainly significant. At the same time, a measure of continuity was assured by such precautions, and the potential dangers of a purge, always marked at the start of any reign, were avoided.

The new king further secured his position by tapping into the charismatic power of his Most Christian ancestors. Although not obviously destined to rule, Philip nonetheless belonged to that royal familial community from whose ranks all kings emerged. By commissioning a manual of royal history from the monastery of Saint Denis soon after he became next-in-line to the throne, as Camille Couderc has shown, Philip of Valois demonstrated his sensitivity to the examples set by royal ancestors. In measures he took to regulate coinage, persecute heretics and organise his household, Philip VI followed in the footsteps of his great-grandfather Louis IX. Pursuit of the unifying ideal of crusade along with his vassals – including Edward III, who initially envisaged joining the expedition – marked Philip out as the worthy descendant of Capetian kings who had died under the sign of the cross. The king's willingness to go to the aid of the Holy Land with no firmer assurance than oaths of loyalty sworn to his son John (October 1332) indicates that he had some confidence in the acceptance of his line by the regents, leading barons and churchmen who were to protect France during his absence. Some might say that the self-conscious upholding of royal precedent betrayed a certain insecurity on the part of the elected king, but the truth of that claim is less easy to demonstrate than the fact that Philip VI, the foremost member of the royal familial community, behaved as contemporaries thought a monarch should.

Growing Anglo-French tensions

The collapse of the crusading plans in 1336 was one of several factors which contributed to a worsening of relations between Philip VI and Edward III in the course of the 1330s. The performance of homage in 1329 raised the possibility that tensions might diminish, and the fact that a joint crusade was envisaged at all, albeit briefly, is proof enough that they did. But Edward had backed away from the crusading plan to assist his candidate to the Scottish throne, Edward Balliol. Since Philip maintained his predecessors' alliance with the Scots, the French king eventually threatened to turn his crusading fleet against England.

Within the Kingdom of France, two further zones of conflict along the maritime flank had a more direct bearing on relations. In English Gascony, jurisdictional grievances arising from the terms of the Treaty of Paris of 1259 continued to be intractable, and hardened the dangerous (and ultimately durable) view among Plantagenet servants, first discernible in the 1290s, that the lands of the duke-king in the south-west were allods, by which it was meant that they were held from God alone. In the county of Artois, meanwhile, Philip VI's adjudication of a succession dispute led the losing party, Robert, to seek exile in England, probably in 1334. Although he had strongly supported Philip's coronation, Robert of Artois became an isolated figure in the royal familial community and had neither the personal resources nor wider support to pursue his grievance. Robert resolved to seek help across the Channel. This was a natural response for a member of the military classes of north-western France during a period of growing tension. Only a small minority of north-westerners still held lands in England, such as the Briennes and the Harcourts, but ease of communication and the possibility of aid from the most substantial landholder in the west meant that their political horizons were necessarily broad. Robert of Artois did not bring a large network of regional and local noble support to Edward III's cause, but the welcome which the English king extended to the count was nonetheless taken as a contravention of his duties as a vassal in his French possessions, and Philip VI's instruction to confiscate Edward's lands in May 1337 was officially based on these grounds. This, the third such confiscation after those of 1294 and 1324, was an act which underscored the importance of the 1259 Treaty of Paris, and is commonly taken to mark the start of the Hundred Years' War.

Throughout these events, the matter of Edward's claim to the throne played no apparent role. Now it re-emerged, and in circumstances which suggest it was the product, rather than a cause, of the war.

In Flanders, where a prolonged revolt had dominated western regions of the county, Philip VI restored Count Louis of Nevers to power by his victory over the rebel army at Cassel (1328). The count had been brought up at the French royal court; this fact, and his reliance upon the crown's support, ensured he did not follow his predecessor Guy of Dampierre (1278–1305) into an English alliance. Philip VI was thus spared many of the difficulties in Flanders which had dogged his predecessors and stretched Capetian resources to breaking point. Thereafter, the king's greatest problem in the north lay in the extensive diplomatic alliances which Edward III contracted in the imperial territories of the Low Countries following his marriage to Isabelle of Hainaut in 1328.

But in 1339, Count Louis was forced into French exile once more by prolonged rebellion under the wealthy weaver Jacob van Artevelde. Edward took this opportunity to distract his adversary from English Gascony and went to Van Artevelde's assistance. Just before entering Ghent in January 1340, the Plantagenet declared himself king of France. Whether the step was suggested to Edward by his Flemish allies is impossible to say, just as one cannot know what role Robert of Artois might have had in goading Edward into laying his claim (a story that circulated in northern France soon after in a verse romance, the *Vow of the Heron*). It is nonetheless certain that Edward's declaration comforted acts of rebellion against Philip. So far these rebellions had not drawn in substantial bodies of noble support, for Robert of Artois was an isolated figure and the rebellions in Flanders were primarily urban in nature. But rebellions now increased in number and magnitude, nowhere more so than along the maritime flank of the kingdom, that traditional focus for dissidence in French history.

The monarchy and the men of the West (I)

In the face of Plantagenet willingness to exploit royal difficulties, Philip VI naturally sought supporters among the leading barons of the realm, for these were the men who could command the support of noble networks at regional and local level. Normandy was of great strategic importance under the circumstances. Philip VI had already called on Norman help in his efforts to succour his Scottish ally David Bruce in 1334, and Normans assisted in military preparations on the frontiers of English Gascony in 1337. In 1339, the king renewed the charter of Norman privileges secured in 1315, and agreed to an ambitious Norman plan to attack England itself. In a revealing indication of the kind of support noble networks might mobilise, Raoul I of Brienne, Jean IV of Harcourt and around fifty of the duchy's lords deemed themselves capable of forming an army of 4,000 horse and 20,000 foot (including 5,000 crossbowmen). Men and money were raised in the duchy, and shipping was assembled along the seaboard from Cherbourg to Calais for the first invasion of England since that of Louis the Lion (later Louis VIII) in 1216–17. The division of the spoils of the conquest of England was even worked out in some detail, to the benefit of the king's son (as duke of Normandy), as well as the nobility of the duchy. In the end, plans for a second Norman conquest were brought to nothing by the first major engagement of the Hundred Years' War, the important English naval victory at Sluis off the Flemish coast in June 1340. The chronicler Jean Le Bel recorded the drowning of a great number of 'French, Normans, Gascons, Bretons and Genoese'.[1]

How serious was French defeat at Sluis? In some respects the consequences were limited. The 'fatal corridor' of the Low Countries through which French enemies in other ages have passed was not carved open on this occasion. Mounting debts and the failure to take the key city of Tournai in the autumn forced an English withdrawal from Flanders (January 1341), leaving Van Artevelde exposed to his enemies grouped around Count Louis of Nevers. The Flemish leader was eventually killed in 1345, and Louis of Nevers himself died in the French cause at Crécy. The accession of his son, Louis of Male (1346–84), inaugurated a period of comital expansion in the Low Countries during which the new count sought to maintain stable relations with both the French and the English crowns. The threat of an English foothold in the Low Countries diminished correspondingly, as indeed it did elsewhere in the Low Countries for other reasons, notably in Brabant as Serge Boffa has shown in his work on that duchy.

More of a concern now was the western seaboard of the realm. In this context, as Cazelles notes, Sluis was 'one of the most significant events of [Philip's] reign'.[2] According to the (Norman) chronicler Pierre Cochon, 'those who were jealous of the Normans, like the Burgundians and others, and especially [Mile] de Noyers' warned the king against the Norman invasion plan in 1339: should they succeed in their wars against the English, '[the Normans] will never obey you again because of the great honour they will have won'.[3] The cross-Channel ambitions of leading Normans and the noble support they commanded were nonetheless encouraged, then thwarted. These developments occurred against a backdrop of residual Norman wariness of the crown's administration. Combined with aggravating circumstances in neighbouring Brittany which are discussed below, it is possible to see why there was increasing Norman disaffection from the Valois cause in the years 1340–50.

Foremost among discontented Norman lords were men who had figured prominently in the invasion plan of 1339, notably Godefroy of Harcourt, lord of Saint-Sauveur, brother of Count Jean IV. Godefroy's acts of disobedience increased in the years 1340–2. Finally condemned for treason, he fled to England in 1344 (just as Robert of Artois had done before him), there to seek Edward III's help. Although one must not underestimate the loyalty which many leading Norman nobles and their affinities continued to display towards Philip VI, cracks had begun to emerge in the relationship between the monarchy and the western military classes after Sluis. These were dangerous developments which would mark French history for the next decade at least.

The war of the Breton succession

Within months of the sea battle at Sluis, royal adjudication of a second succession dispute created further opportunities for Plantagenet intervention along the seaboard. In the duchy of Brittany, Jeanne of Penthièvre and her husband Charles of Blois, nephew of Philip VI, were deemed by royal commission to be the rightful heirs to Duke Jean III (1312–41). The rejected party was Jean, Count of Montfort to the west of Paris, the late duke's brother, and he enjoyed little support from noble networks in the duchy at first. Edward III's willingness to back Montfort was certainly an important factor in the emergence of a prolonged contest between the claimants. Despite the capture and detention of Montfort by Philip VI (1341–5), and of Blois by Edward III (1347–56), the struggle for succession in Brittany developed into an internecine war during which the Anglo-Bretons and their noble allies tended to control the western and the northern coasts, the Penthièvres and their supporters the eastern regions of the duchy.

In the course of the Breton conflict, as Simon Cuttler has shown in his work on treason trials, Philip VI was more willing than any of his Capetian predecessors to accuse and prosecute nobles for treason, resulting in the execution of prominent Bretons such as Olivier IV of Clisson and the Malestroits (1343). This was one area in which the king's authority could cut through the 'plurality of powers' around him. But among those prosecuted that same year for having served the Montfortist cause in Brittany were several Norman barons, suggesting a potentially dangerous merging of Breton and Norman noble dissidence. Concerted opposition of this kind could not be easily addressed by legal means, and the discovery of common ground between noble networks in different regions was a worrying sign.

Equally ominous was the fact that the prolonged conflict in Brittany was beginning to generate and attract a professional soldiery dependent on continued warfare for its livelihood. In the Breton arena, such men included Raoul de Caours, a captain who served first the English then the French in Brittany; or Bertrand du Guesclin, whose rise from lowly Breton soldier to constable of France was later lauded in verse by the poet Cuvelier, and in prose by the chronicler Jean Froissart. Warlords recruited among the men of their connection, often lesser nobles on the make, creating in the process a body of experienced soldiers ready and willing to involve themselves in all kinds of conflict, so long as there was money in it. The king's peace was becoming increasingly hard to keep as Norman and Breton affinities started to spiral out of the Valois orbit, all the while drawing to them other forces for disorder within the realm.

From phoney war to military disaster

At least in the south west the conflict was slower to develop. Philip applied growing pressure on the duke-king through military preparations and agreements with neighbouring lords, actions which may be interpreted as a continuation of royal policy under Charles IV. He was supported in particular by southern lords Jean I, Count of Armagnac (1319–73) and Gaston II, Count of Foix (1315–43), who managed to set aside their disputes for now and accepted to serve as royal lieutenants in the region.

But the king was unable to intervene decisively in the south-west, partly due to the defensive measures of Edward's lieutenants, partly to his own lack of funds. The financial weakness of the French monarchy remained a significant impediment. When the first damaging hostilities occurred, they were launched by Henry of Grosmont, Earl of Derby in a raid that set out from English Gascony into the regions of Périgord and Angoumois. The French were found to be insufficiently prepared (August 1345). After half a century of varying French pressure on the Plantagenet lands, it was the interior of the kingdom, not the maritime flank, which now looked vulnerable.

The following spring it seemed that Edward himself would land in English Gascony. Instead, he attacked through Normandy, bringing with him his local ally Godefroy of Harcourt. The danger of worsening relations with western nobles and their affinities was now becoming apparent. Edward III's campaign was resisted by many Norman nobles. But the nominal head of the duchy's noble networks, Duke John, Philip's eldest son, was engaged in a costly and fruitless siege of Aiguillon in Agenais when the English advance came, and the king's men in the duchy were captured at Caen, including the constable, Raoul II of Brienne, and Jean of Melun, Count of Tancarville, hereditary chamberlain. Although the Norman nobility had prepared an invasion fleet and had contributed to royal levies for the purposes of defence, when war came to them there was little royal help to protect their patrimonies.

The English advance of 1346 culminated in a famous victory for Edward III at Crécy in the county of Ponthieu (August). Ten months later, Calais fell after a hard siege which was long remembered for the heroism of its inhabitants. The town's dogged resistance was an early indication of how important municipal authorities could be in shaping the wider conflict which was now emerging between the two dynasties and their noble supporters. At the same time, the loss of Calais threw the failings of royal government into even sharper relief than defeat at Crécy. Philip was given the opportunity to relieve the siege and failed to do so. In one of the earliest and most striking examples of the many migrations which would result from war, a number of Calaisien families fled to Carcassonne in the far south to make a new life. Others were promised lowly royal offices. Their former hometown would remain an English possession until 1558.

The second half of Philip VI's reign was undoubtedly marked by crises as the central flashpoint of Aquitaine arced outwards to fuel or ignite conflict elsewhere. The emphasis in this story is often rightly placed upon emerging ideas of sovereignty, and how it was increasingly difficult for either side to live with the Plantagenet status of duke-king which was recognised in 1259. Complicating factors had arisen in the form of relations which both sides cultivated in Scotland and Flanders. But from another perspective, the war was also about the French king's relationship with the nobility of western France. The troubles of the monarchy proliferated along the maritime flank of the realm, regions where Plantagenet could compete more effectively with Valois to win over networks of noble support than was possible in the east. The reality of a vast cross-Channel Angevin empire was long dead, and the memory of it no doubt far keener among members of the Plantagenet dynasty than it was among the descendants of noble families in western France. Robert Favreau's story of the bishop of Maillezais who thought the re-creation of a greater Aquitaine under the English in 1346 might be a good thing because his church housed the tomb of one of its eleventh-century dukes, William the Great (990–1030), is surely exceptional. But there can be little doubt that westerners did still find 'a choice of allegiance a very useful weapon in the course of disputes with the [French king]', and that easterners did not have the same option open to them.[4] The manner of Philip's accession should not be accorded greater importance than this long-term issue, particularly as the royal familial community resolved the succession crisis of 1328 to the satisfaction of the vast majority of its members. Edward's actions in defence of English Gascony exacerbated a deeper problem, and it would be many years before the west was won for the Valois kings of France.

From war subsidy to a new age of taxation

Ultimately, that struggle would be won by an ability to raise money in sufficient quantities to buy up noble support and defeat those who refused to back the Valois cause. Unfortunately, not only had Philip VI inherited the problems of his Capetian predecessors, he had also inherited the financial constraints which had limited their ability to act.

The royal *domaine* which had expanded so impressively in the thirteenth century was the main source of what was known as the king's 'ordinary' revenue, in the form of dues, tolls and other levies associated with lordship. The new ruler had further expanded the *domaine* with his substantial inheritances in the west. But it was no easier for the new Valois monarch to 'live of his own' – that is to say, from his ordinary revenues – than it had been for his predecessors. It has been estimated that French royal resources in 1340 may have been no more than two-thirds of those available to Edward III to fight his wars, primarily because of England's 'superior ability to transform itself into a war state' at that stage.[5]

Augmenting royal revenues in a substantial manner would mean unlocking the resources of the kingdom as a whole, generating 'extraordinary' revenues in the form of taxes raised from all the king's subjects. Rulers inevitably encountered a great deal of resistance when they tried to do this. Kings were entitled under certain 'customary' circumstances to seek financial aid from all their subjects, to help them pay for the marriage of their children, for instance, or to go on crusade or meet a ransom. 'Customary aids' were levied by Philip VI on a far greater scale than any of his predecessors. The most notable attempt occurred in 1332, when the king used John's dubbing to knighthood, his daughter's marriage and his own taking of the cross to demand aids, albeit with little success. Another occasion when a king could ask for money from all his subjects was in wartime, to defend the realm. Monarchs had been levying war subsidies for the defence of the realm with increasing regularity since the 1290s, thanks to conflict in Aquitaine and Flanders. Indeed, Philip VI's reign was the apogee of an 'age of war subsidies', as John Bell Henneman has shown in his work on royal taxation – an era that began with Philip IV's wars, and would draw to a close with the emergence of a more regular tax system under Philip VI's successor, John.[6]

Customary aids and war subsidies greatly increased the resources of fourteenth-century Valois kings compared to their thirteenth-century Capetian predecessors (in this respect, as in others, the notion of a late Capetian apogee appears flawed). But aids and subsidies also had their limitations. It was possible for the king to decree a subsidy with a minimum of consultation with his barons, but decrees were only converted into revenue through a great deal of negotiation between a small number of royal officers and many different local authorities – lay lords, ecclesiastical landowners, municipal authorities where they existed. Often some form of revenue-sharing arrangement had to be struck with those authorities to facilitate payment, such as the monies which towns were allowed to keep for municipal wall-building programmes. The authority to raise levies across the kingdom was the king's alone, but a plurality of powers was necessarily involved in the process. Different types of taxes were raised in different places at different times to pay for war subsidies, adding further complexity and delay. Perhaps most importantly of all, there had to be an 'evident necessity' before tax-payers would consent to grant war subsidies, with the result that the king was usually forced to borrow to cover initial costs. And once the cause of taxation ceased, tax-payers expected subsidies to end too – with the result that war subsidies offered little scope for raising revenue during periods of peace, even temporary ones governed by truce.

The development of the estates

The development of an effective fiscal apparatus would be one of the salient features of the political history of later medieval France, and Philip VI's reign did witness important steps in that direction, particularly in the final decade. One of the more important innovations was the *gabelle du sel* or salt tax, for example, introduced in 1341. This tax was to become an important source of revenues for the crown for centuries to come.

Philip's reign also witnessed a more sustained attempt to use representative assemblies to speed up the process of raising taxes. Soon after the start of the conflict with Edward III, in 1339, the *Chambre des comptes* recommended that Philip VI should summon assemblies to explain his reasons for wishing to raise money from them. In 1343 a general assembly (or estates-general) was called, and in 1345–6 it was decided for reasons of convenience to summon northern and southern assemblies separately, in the shape of the estates of Langue-doil and Languedoc. At another level again in Philip VI's reign, local estates began to emerge through consultations with the king's officers, including the estates of Normandy, Auvergne and Burgundy.

The 'plurality of powers' within the kingdom was increasing still further as the authority of the estates took root. The fate of these bodies was closely tied to the development of royal taxation, and forms a major theme in the pages that follow.

In November 1347, a rare meeting of the estates-general at Paris agreed that mounted troops would be maintained in each region by taxes raised in whatever form the local estates preferred. This prescient initiative saw the gradual spread of the office of *élu*, local notables designated by the estates to oversee collection. Large sums were promised for 1348, perhaps ten times as much as those raised by the war subsidy of 1328. The crises confronting the crown under Philip VI were thus encouraging a greater role for estates of varying scale in the political life of the realm. Combined with greater powers accorded to municipalities, these measures reveal how the conflict was effecting an invigorating transfusion of public authority to nascent or existing local bodies. Before collection of the taxes could begin in earnest, the impact of plague brought the scheme to nothing in 1348.

As Elizabeth Brown notes in her work on customary aids, Capetian finances were certainly being radically modified under the first Valois king. But change was not progressing quickly or surely enough to help the second monarch of that line.

John II (1350–64)

The opening years of John's reign (1350–6) were described by Édouard Perroy in his history of the Hundred Years' War as 'among the most incoherent' of the century, dominated by the 'permanent state of panic' of a flawed king.[7] Yet some coherence may emerge if the events of these years are interpreted in the light of relations between the monarchy and noble interests in western and eastern France.

The monarchy and the men of the West (II): Normandy

On the face of it, John came to power with strong credentials as a leader of noble networks in western France, much like his father before him. Duke of Normandy, count of Anjou and count of Maine from 1332, John was the first uncrowned prince to be accorded the titles of the former Angevin dominions since 1204. But closer inspection by Jean Tricard reveals that John was a distant figure in these lordships, and that his father's administration and personnel governed for the most part. John was entrusted with duties elsewhere in the kingdom, mostly in the company of his uncle, Odo IV, Duke of Burgundy. Whatever his titles in the west, therefore, the heir to the throne was closer to the leading representative of the nobility of the east during his formative years. Towards the end of 1347, John was accorded greater powers to govern in Normandy and his role there certainly increased. But the duke's household and council consisted mostly of outsiders placed by families which were influential at his father's court, keen to stake out a place for themselves in the retinue of the heir-apparent. Few leading Normans followed John into power in 1350, with the result that the noble networks of the duchy remained largely disconnected from the royal sphere.

The effects of that missed opportunity were compounded within months of the coronation. In November 1350, Raoul II of Brienne, Count of Eu and constable of France, was executed on the new king's orders for treason. The charge may have arisen from an offer by Brienne to assist Edward III in return for his release from the captivity he had endured since the Normandy campaign of 1346, but the treatment of the constable still 'troubled a great part of the nobility of the realm' (according to the *Chronique des quatre premiers Valois*).[8] Most aggrieved were Brienne's own extensive lineage, particularly when the king did not make the propitiatory gesture of redistributing confiscated property among them. John inherited a difficult relationship with leading western nobles from his father, but his first acts as king did little to improve matters.

Unfortunately the need to address the problem was greater than ever. By 1350, a rather more effective conductor of Norman opposition than Godefroy of Harcourt had emerged in the form of Charles of Navarre, son of Louis X's daughter. Navarre's Norman lands were his principal power base and concern within the kingdom. They included the counties of Évreux and Mortain and the lordship of Mantes, grouped around the left bank of the Seine in a strategically important location between Paris and the sea, to which a further cluster in the west of the duchy, from Avranches to the Cotentin, was later added. The extent and location of these lands meant that with the exception of Edward III, and in the absence of a resolution to the Breton conflict, Charles of Navarre was the most important figure in the west and a natural leader of Norman noble networks. It was a matter of additional concern that Navarre's claims upon a wide variety of lands produced sympathisers elsewhere in the realm, notably in Champagne and Brie where, among more important figures, the poet

Guillaume de Machaut lent his pen to Charles's service. The young prince's appeal was further widened by the fact that his bloodline placed him at the heart of the royal familial community.

John II favoured Charles of Navarre by releasing him early from the terms of his minority, and by granting him the hand in marriage of his own daughter, Jeanne (February 1352). But the king's precautions were undone by two affronts to his son-in-law: first, the non-payment of the substantial dowry which Charles was promised, then the award of the county of Angoulême to a royal favourite, Charles of Spain, without compensation for Navarrese rights there. Because Charles of Spain had also been appointed as royal constable in place of the executed count of Eu, some Normans of the Brienne affinity now made common cause with Navarre. The upshot of this heightened discontent among key Norman noble networks was the murder of King John's favourite in a Navarrese ambush at Laigle in January 1354. The impact of regional political groupings on the regnal stage was brought to the fore in striking fashion.

In the course of the next 2 years, the cracks in the relationship between the king and the Norman nobility widened still further, at times alarmingly. John was not bereft of allies or strategies throughout these troubles. Jean II of Melun, Count of Tancarville, a former supporter of Charles of Spain, had long since returned from English captivity and led an anti-Navarrese party in the duchy which could be relied upon. A royal policy of appeasement reminded Navarre that a settlement with the king could prove more beneficial to his interests in the long term than any binding alliance he might be tempted to contract with Edward III. By making his eldest son Charles duke of Normandy in December 1355, John may also have hoped to channel the ambitions of Norman noble networks in directions that were more profitable for the monarchy. In the short time he was there, Charles established relations with the higher nobility of the duchy which were closer than those of his immediate predecessors, and according to one source he even began to build bridges with Godefroy of Harcourt, who had made his peace with the Valois in 1346. One previously dissenting noble faction could thus be drawn back into the royal orbit.

For all that, John remained unable to control events in the duchy to his satisfaction. In April 1356, possibly under the influence of Charles of Spain's former friends as Françoise Autrand notes, the king adopted a far more aggressive approach to his problems in the west. Navarre was arrested at Rouen while in the company of the king's son, and several leading Normans were summarily executed for treason, including Jean V, Count of Harcourt, Godefroy's nephew. Navarre's claim to Edward III that he enjoyed the support of all the Norman nobility was now put to the test. Around 30 leading westerners joined Philip of Navarre (Charles's brother) and Godefroy of Harcourt in declaring open war upon their king. The number should not be regarded as insignificant given the temerity of the act, and the fact that around 50 Norman lords had believed themselves capable, presumptuously or not, of raising a force large enough – through their vassals, their allies, their kin – to invade England in 1339.

Worse still, Navarrese reaction to Charles's arrest provided an opportunity for English intervention. One thrust of the English advance emerged from Brittany later that year under Henry of Grosmont, now Duke of Lancaster, underlining the continuing weakness of the Valois position in the west. The second thrust of 1356, Anglo-Gascon in composition, was led by the Black Prince from the south: its devastating impact is discussed further below.

The weakness of the king's party

It has recently been pointed out that John could count on the support of a small but determined affinity which did, after all, face up to the Navarrese threat between 1354 and 1356. The 'king's party' – to use Françoise Autrand's term – included figures within the royal familial community, such as the sons of Robert of Artois (Jean and Charles), and great lords like Jean I, Count of Armagnac. Leading noblemen with their own networks of support also stood by the king, notably the Melun family.

And yet it is hard to avoid the conclusion that the princes of the blood and noble affinities closest to John were less weighty allies than those whom his predecessors had relied upon. The sons of Artois were entirely reliant upon the king, and did not bring a substantial network of noble supporters to their master's cause. The count of Armagnac was a major figure, but his ability to recruit widely among south-western noble networks was weakened by the highly effective actions of his regional rival, Gaston III, Count of Foix. None of the princes around John had the resources or influence of the leading figure at Philip VI's court, Odo IV of Burgundy, leader of the men of the east. The Meluns held extensive territories and their lands were geographically scattered, but the support at their disposal could hardly compensate for royal weaknesses elsewhere. Again the contrast is marked with the reign of Philip VI, during which Mile de Noyers brought a remarkable number of Burgundians of his connection to the king's court and administration.

In fact, it is worth emphasising just how 'un-Burgundian' the royal party was under John during the first years of his reign, certainly compared to the entourages of recent kings. Before his accession John was not disinclined, as we have seen, to mix with men of the east. But the Burgundian party at Philip VI's court had been weakened by its association with defeat at Crécy, and the deaths of Queen Jeanne, her brother Duke Odo IV and Mile de Noyers followed over the next few years. The heir to Burgundy, Philip of Rouvres, was a child who remained under royal wardship until shortly before his death in 1361. The only conspicuous Burgundian at the centre of the royal party thereafter was Mile de Noyers's nephew, Geoffroi de Charny, bearer of the royal standard and author of a celebrated treatise on chivalry. Charny was to die honourably in the king's service at Poitiers in 1356.

It may well have been the weakness of traditional networks of royal support in the east which led John to rely on the lesser figures with whom he surrounded himself in his first years as king: not out of suspicion of the great families, as is sometimes suggested, but due to force of circumstance. It is also possible that the same weakness encouraged John to found an order of chivalry in 1352, that 'spectacular but hopeful means of collecting members of an affinity'.[9] The royal order commonly called 'the Star' was intended to bring together up to 500 knights in the king's service: a remarkably large number, possibly as many as one-fifth of all those living in the realm, and certainly far more than the narrow elite of 25 whom Edward III had invited to join the Order of the Garter a few years earlier. By such means, according to the terms of the Star's foundation, John hoped that 'a tranquil peace [would] be reborn in our reign'.[10] Unfortunately a significant proportion of the known membership was killed at Mauron, where the Blois party suffered another reverse in the continuing Breton wars (August 1352). John's ambitious plan to gather a substantial core of the French chivalric community around himself and his successors had failed.

The king now had to confront widespread aristocratic unrest in western regions with limited means, traditional or novel, of raising political support from noble networks elsewhere in the realm. The so-called panics of John's early reign are thus related to deeper fault-lines in the history of royal France.

The battle of Poitiers and the apogee of the estates

Within months of Charles of Navarre's arrest, John himself was a prisoner. The royal army under his command which intercepted the Black Prince at Maupertuis near Poitiers was utterly defeated (September 1356). The resulting crises were undeniably more serious than the aftermath of Crécy.

A reshuffling of fortunes now occurred among members of the royal familial community, although no one element obtained a particularly strong hand. John lost many of his advisers and servants in the battle, but key figures followed him into captivity and remained for varying lengths of time with him in England. The king and his limited entourage in captivity sought to influence events as best they could until John's release in 1360. John's eldest son Charles, the future Charles V, escaped the field, but neither his standing as heir nor his adoption of the titles of royal lieutenant (1356) and regent (1358) was enough to guarantee him a sustained pre-eminence in the affairs of the realm. The circumstances of the king's son-in-law, Charles of Navarre, were little changed at first by the outcome of the battle. But Navarre's eventual escape from prison in November 1357 and his swift return to influence thereafter were certainly a consequence of Poitiers. The main source of pressure for Navarre's release came from a body which was brought to the fore by the military disaster, namely the estates of Languedoil.

The estates acquired considerable importance after Poitiers in both Languedoil and Languedoc. There is little doubt that representative assemblies emerged strongly during this period of crisis because the royal familial community and leading noble affinities of the realm were in disarray. Individual municipalities, even where they were sufficiently competent at this stage in their history, could only fill a vacuum locally. But the estates were also carried forward on a tradition of consultation which had developed in the later years of Philip VI, and which had been briefly resurrected at the start of John's reign (1351). When truces with the English came to an end in June 1355, it was understandable that the second Valois king should have turned to representative assemblies for prolonged consultations (December 1355 to March 1356). Even greater sums than those promised in 1347 were now voted by the estates of Languedoil, all in return for wider powers over the raising and auditing of revenues. The principal outcome on this occasion was revolt at Arras and Rouen, a consequence of the growth of the fiscal state in municipal France for much of the fourteenth century. But the experiences of 1355–6 did at least confirm royal acceptance of a growing role for representative assemblies, and an enhancement of the latter's authority was won. It was therefore a natural reflex for the decapitated and depleted royal council to issue summonses for an assembly of the estates within a week of the defeat at Poitiers.

Several overlapping strands may be discerned in the actions of the nobles, churchmen and deputies of the towns who gathered in the meetings of the estates of Languedoil over the following 18 months. Representative assemblies, like every other political force in the realm, subdivided into a plurality of powers, although the limited survival of evidence does not readily allow us to see them at work. From the beginning, certainly, there was a substantial body of opinion within the estates which sought to remedy the crisis by reform of royal government, and was prepared to use the crown's need for money after Poitiers to achieve its aims. The high watermark of reforming aspirations was reached in the great *ordonnance* of March 1357, which set out – among other things – detailed instructions about how royal officials should conduct their business. Prominent among the reformers were university-trained churchmen such as Robert de Corbie, master of theology, or Philippe de Vitry, bishop of Meaux. The influence of other academics was apparent in the work of the estates, not least Nicolas Oresme, theologian at Paris and later confessor of Charles V, whose celebrated treatise on money influenced the estates' policy on the reform of coinage.

But it was not simply the (ecclesiastical) intellectuals who began to enjoy a greater role in the exercise of royal authority thanks to the estates. The nobility constituted perhaps the most influential group of all. It is striking (as Cazelles found) that the largest single group of noble advisers in the council which was appointed by the estates in March 1357 came from Normandy, where they were joined by others from regions in the north-west which had produced few close advisers to the king in recent decades. For a while at least, it seemed that noble networks might find satisfaction through representative assemblies rather than through the patronage of great men around the king. The estates thus offered new opportunities to groups which were previously excluded from, or relatively uninvolved in, the exercise of royal authority. The reforming measures of the estates also created the possibility that a different kind of monarchy would emerge from the crisis, one that was answerable in everyday matters to a more firmly constituted representative assembly.

But other strands within the estates ultimately precluded that outcome. From the very beginning, calls for the release of Charles of

Navarre emanated from meetings of the assembly. Given the depleted state of the royal familial community after Poitiers, it is understandable that the return of one of its senior members should have been mooted in the estates, particularly among nobles of the north and west where Navarrese support was strongest. The most vociferous Navarrese ally was in fact a churchman, Robert Le Coq, bishop of Laon, whom contemporaries believed to be primarily responsible for engineering Charles of Navarre's release in November 1357. This last development did not make the difficult task of government any easier for the dauphin, who had tried and failed to use the estates to develop his own programme of resistance to the English that same year, and who now had to contend with a rival and increasingly hostile source of authority in the form of his brother-in-law. After recovering his liberty, Charles of Navarre did little to promote the assembly which had served as a platform for champions of his cause. The estates of Languedoil therefore failed to become indispensable to the brothers-in-law who constituted the most important members of the royal familial community at that point. The possibility that a central representative assembly might find a durable place in French political culture receded correspondingly.

A further strand within the estates of Languedoil, Parisian in essence, sealed the fate of this emerging power in French political life. Expertise in governmental affairs among the municipalities of the north was not yet sufficiently advanced to permit every town to send its own *bourgeois* as representatives; several deputed churchmen instead. But Paris had Étienne Marcel, head of one of the capital's leading political clans, ally of key figures within the city's wealthiest trades, and holder of the leading executive post within the city, the *prévôté des marchands*. For one of the few times in our period the capital acquired a preponderant influence in the affairs of the realm, at least in its northern half. Marcel supported the policy of reform advocated by the estates, and he too favoured Navarre's release. But when these policies failed to meet Parisian expectations, the *prévôt* played a leading role in the increasing radicalisation of the estates. The mainly clerical and bourgeois deputies who met at Paris in February 1358 forbad the summoning of lesser assemblies, and demanded that all future meetings of the estates of Languedoil should be held in Paris.

The alienation of the nobility from the estates was aggravated almost immediately when two of the dauphin's constables were murdered in that prince's chambers before his very eyes on Marcel's orders. When the Jacquerie broke out in May 1358 and targeted nobles and noble property around Paris, Marcel lent his assistance to the attacks and encouraged other northern municipalities to do the same. The *prévôt*'s ambitions may eventually have extended to supporting the replacement of the Valois by Charles of Navarre, although his increasing isolation within Paris, and eventually his murder by more conservative opponents within the city (July), brought any such schemes to an end.

What historians have termed the 'Parisian Revolution' in the first half of 1358 under Étienne Marcel can hardly be portrayed as the work of the estates. Nonetheless, that body had served as a vehicle for Marcel to pursue his ambitions, and it was with some degree of plausibility that the last words attributed to the *prévôt* were that he had only ever intended to uphold the estates' *ordonnances*. The dauphin and posterity were well warned that a strong estates-general could generate alarming instability. The chances of the Kingdom of France acquiring a central representative assembly to compare with those which were emerging in other parts of Europe, still weak in 1350, diminished after the experiences of 1356–8 in the north.

In Languedoc, by contrast, the estates took deeper root in this period of crisis, primarily because they satisfied the ambitions of participants more effectively. The southern assembly was more moderate than that of Languedoil, notably in its acceptance of a fiscal policy which did not alienate the nobility. It was also more productive, raising money for the king's ransom and for his lieutenants in the south (first Jean I of Armagnac, then later King John's eponymous third son). Above all, the estates of Languedoc were dominated by the municipalities which derived considerable benefit from joint action through the frequent meetings of the assembly. The southern estates emerged as an effective regional gathering in the second half of the fourteenth century, and it was at this level that representative government would become an enduring feature of French political life in many parts of the realm.

Cutting into the fabric of the events of John's captivity were the interventions of the king himself. The physical absence of the ruler may have strengthened the abstract concept of the monarchy in the minds of his subjects from 1356 to 1360. Recipients of royal grace in this period could find themselves swearing loyalty to the crown rather than to the king, for instance, as they had customarily done in the past. But in many ways John remained directly present at the highest level in the affairs of the realm throughout his captivity. In March 1357, his announcement of a separately negotiated truce with the English undermined the reforming work of the estates of Languedoil. His envoys travelled back and forth between London and Paris, transmitting news to the king and conveying his views to the council. His separate negotiations for peace with Edward III in January 1358 and March 1359 (the so-called first and second treaties of London) were conducted with little reference to the concerns of the dauphin or other political forces in France, as indeed was the final settlement which was agreed, after further English campaigns in 1359–60, at Brétigny (May 1360; finally ratified at Calais in October).

The Treaty of Brétigny

The terms of the treaty of Brétigny resembled one proposed 6 years earlier at Guines, when John, already facing the Navarrese threat but still undefeated, was not prepared to come to an agreement. Then, Edward had sought full sovereignty over Aquitaine, Ponthieu and Calais, and the same tenure of territories which were to be ceded to him by the proposed settlement, notably Maine, Anjou, Touraine, Poitou and Limoges. All of these concessions figured in the Brétigny peace, with the exception of the formerly Angevin lands of Maine, Anjou and Touraine. In addition, Edward was to receive territories in the north (the county of Guines, Montreuil-sur-Mer) and a great deal more in the south (the Angoumois, Périgord, Agenais, Quercy, Rouergue and Bigorre), all in full sovereignty. The *Parlement*, already profoundly disturbed in its functions by the crisis, would no longer be the court of appeal for up to one third of the realm. In addition to the extensive territorial and jurisdictional concessions, John's ransom was finally set at 3,000,000 *écus* – a sum which was perhaps fifteen times the ordinary annual revenue of the crown.

The French monarchy's drive to push unqualified obedience to the shores of the Atlantic had ended, it seemed, in expensive failure; indeed, much of the west was to be lifted from its grasp. Municipal authorities and noble landowners in the countryside began to swear allegiance to Plantagenet commissioners (August 1361 to Spring 1362). Edward did appoint some Englishmen to existing royal offices (such as William Felton, seneschal of Poitou, who made his career and contracted a marriage in France), but on the whole existing administrative posts and even indigenous office-holders were retained, particularly in municipal government. There was little redistribution of land in favour of the English victors, unlike the fifteenth-century conquests. In 1362, the Black Prince was rewarded by the creation for him of a principality of Aquitaine under the sovereignty of the English crown.

French contemporaries were keenly aware of the disastrous consequences of Poitiers, and a literature which emphasised the failings of nobility and the sins of their compatriots in general began to emerge even before Brétigny confirmed the full extent of what had been lost, notably in François de Monte-Belluna's harangue, *Tragicum argumentum de miserabili statu regni Francie* (1357). But perhaps we may be permitted to see chinks of light where contemporaries did not.

First, ratification of two crucial clauses of the treaty, separated out into a document known by its opening words, *C'est assavoir*, was delayed and eventually never performed. These were the clauses by which Edward renounced his claim to the throne, and the French crown gave up its sovereignty over Edward's lands. The reasons for non-ratification appear to have been practical, and do not put in doubt either side's acceptance of the agreement. But the potential consequences were far-reaching. Edward (or indeed his successors) could revive the claim to the throne at a future date. French royal sovereignty over Plantagenet territories was in principle not abolished. We will see later that such loopholes could be converted into recovered territory under different circumstances.

And then there is the matter of the cost of Brétigny. The ransom settlement was certainly enormous, but the release of the king was undeniably an 'evident necessity' – one of the essential circumstances under which a king could demand aid from his subjects. The ransom subsidy, an old means for the crown to raise money, contributed to something essentially new in French history, the emergence of regular peacetime taxes. After payment of a substantial first instalment to obtain the king's release, much of it raised from forced loans from wealthy individuals and corporations who could expect repayment from the proceeds of taxation, an important royal *ordonnance* (December 1360) established new indirect taxes to meet the ransom cost. The office of *élu*, formerly associated with the estates, was appropriated by the crown and became a mainstay in the raising of extraordinary revenue thereafter. The process of inuring the French to regular taxation progressed considerably, although the ransom payment formed only part of it as we shall see.

Finally, the great territorial losses of Brétigny encouraged careful consideration of what remained in the king's hands. Within a year of John's return it had been decreed that all alienations of the royal *domaine* since Philip IV would be abolished, and once again that future kings were to swear upon their coronation to uphold the inalienability of the lands joined to the crown. Just as the monarchy sought to reabsorb or preserve its most basic resource, the royal *domaine*, attention was paid to the best use of the crown's lands. One important result was an extensive programme of apanage grants within the royal familial community in John's last years. The king's second son, Louis, held a large apanage incorporating the newly erected duchy of Anjou, to the west of the duchy of Orléans which John's brother, Philip, had held since 1344. The king's eponymous third son was given the duchy of Berry, along with Auvergne to the south. These central lands straddled the major fief of a royal son-in-law, Louis II, Duke of Bourbon (1356–1410). John's fourth son, Philip, was the beneficiary of the grant of the duchy of Burgundy in September 1363, which had been incorporated into the *domaine* nearly 2 years earlier following Philip of Rouvres's death. Territorial power was thus concentrated, not directly in the hands of the king (although his jurisdiction and rights were preserved, as always happened in apanage grants), but within a wider royal familial community. The young princes were clearly placed at the head of regional noble networks, and it was possible that these might now be more firmly connected to the monarchy than had previously been the case in John's reign.

The granting of apanages was not a novel policy as we have seen, and there was no way of knowing how or when its effects would be felt, particularly as Louis of Anjou and and Jean of Berry left for an English prison to serve as hostages until their father's ransom was fully paid. But the grants of 1360–3 did represent a further transfusion of public authority into the regions and localities of the kingdom, and this at a time when local authorities – specifically, municipalities and estates – were also acquiring greater powers with royal consent as a way of tackling local pressures. The greatest of those pressures after Brétigny, and for the remainder of the 1360s, was the mercenary band.

The companies

Theatres of conflict had grown steadily in number since the early 1340s, and increased still further under John, notably in Normandy where Navarrese action was conducted by Charles's brother Philip during the later 1350s, and in the south-west where Gaston III 'Phoebus', Count of Foix resumed his attacks on his rival, Jean I, Count of Armagnac (1319–73), culminating in Foix's victory at Launac (1362). Private war remained a perpetual threat to the public weal, and was fuelled by the needs of a soldiery which was recruited from abroad, from the nobility of the realm, and from those elements of French society which had been dislodged by economic crises and war.

Mercenaries in their thousands made their careers in France under captains who contracted for service in such wars, many of them from the south-west: men such as Menaud de Villiers, alias Espiote, who served the count of Foix and Charles of Navarre, as well as his own interests at the head of a substantial body of men. The truces which followed John's capture and the peace of Brétigny were bad news for the companies of freebooters, and many resolved to continue their activities regardless. The result for much of France was a peace which brought no security, particularly in Normandy, Auvergne, Champagne, Burgundy, Languedoc and the Rhône valley, where captains like Seguin de Badefol made a good living from ransoms, protection money and theft.

Once released, John attempted to restore security to these lands. But even when royal forces could be paid for and mustered, they were not always successful against the skilled companies. The count of Tancarville and others discovered this to their cost in March 1362, when they were heavily defeated at Brignais south of Lyon. Brigands might be deterred by effective urban defences and could be bought off with money raised locally, practices which continued to encourage the growth of municipal government and local estates in the period. But where such measures worked, they simply redirected the problem elsewhere: a concern, if not for all, then at least for the supra-regional monarchy and its representatives to whom the victims of any given moment might turn for redress. The ransom payment of 1360 had marked an important stage in the development of the fiscal state, and now the ravages of the freebooters increased the pressure for further change. In December 1363, a second important royal *ordonnance* on taxation was promulgated to raise funds to fight the companies, extending the levying of the hearth tax.

The problem of mercenaries and the regional noble networks which employed or joined them had been addressed once before by the French crown and Holy Church when the Albigensian crusade was directed against disturbers of the Christian peace in the south-west. The Avignon papacy and the king were troubled as never before by the soldiery, and since 1361 plenary indulgences had been given to those who took the cross against the freebooters. John himself took the cross in March 1363, and was accorded a tenth of all ecclesiastical revenues in the kingdom for a period of 6 years to help pay for the undertaking. During the last months of his reign he made strenuous efforts to raise the money and men to restore peace to his kingdom.

In an effort to secure English non-intervention in this plan (and not in misguided fulfilment of the chivalric obligations of his ransom, as was once thought), the king crossed the Channel in January 1364 to treat with Edward III. While in London, John fell ill and died. It was left to Charles V – a prince more tested than any before he came to the throne, save perhaps his grandson – to further his father's plans.

Charles V (1364–80)

The first 6 months of Charles V's reign witnessed resolutions to the longstanding problems of Navarrese dissent and Breton divisions which had dogged relations between the crown and the nobility of the north-west for a generation. The outcomes in both cases were not wholly to the king's immediate advantage, but they helped lay the foundations for the gradual re-establishment of royal power which was the salient characteristic of Charles V's reign. Once again the fortunes of the kingdom turned on the relationship between the ruler and regional nobilities.

The demise of the Navarrese threat

Charles of Navarre's renewed rebellion against the Valois monarchy, this time over his exclusion from the succession to the duchy of Burgundy after Philip of Rouvres's death, provoked a determined reaction in the last months of John II's life. The campaigns of the summer of 1364 against Navarrese forces – including Constable Du Guesclin's victory at Cocherel in Normandy (May) – greatly reduced Navarre's room for manoeuvre. Charles of Navarre was reduced thereafter to contracting alliances with mercenary captains who acted elsewhere in the kingdom in his name, not least in and around Burgundy, but most of their actions were in fact geared to their own interests rather than those of their supposed sponsor. Navarre had already been discredited in the eyes of some nobles by his association with the radical estates of Languedoil, and it is likely that subsequent events made noble networks in Normandy and elsewhere in the north more receptive to the benefits of loyalty to the crown. When he eventually came to terms with the king in 1365, Navarre agreed to swap his strategically important lands in the Seine basin for the valuable but distant city of Montpellier, where his chances of recruiting large numbers of noble supporters to his cause were extremely small.

In the south, meanwhile, there was little scope for a Navarrese revival based on Charles the Bad's Pyrenean kingdom. The dominant power in that region now was clearly Gaston III of Foix. Having prevailed over Armagnac in 1362 at Launac, Foix followed up his success by repudiating Navarre's sister, Agnès, whom he had married when Charles the Bad's star was in the ascendant. Phoebus was not a core member of the royal familial community and was more interested in establishing regional hegemony for himself than gaining any wider influence over the kingdom. To this end he extended his protection over Bigorre and parts of the Languedoc, and countered the efforts of Jean I and Jean II (1373–84) of Armagnac to restore their authority. His influence over local noble networks was unproblematic so long as it was not used against the king. The declining influence of Navarre in both north and south meant that the power of transregional noble factions to disrupt the exercise of royal authority faded for a generation.

Montfortist victory in Brittany

In Brittany, meanwhile, the long-standing succession conflict finally came to a head. Since Jean of Montfort's death in 1345, the war had been perpetuated by English and mercenary garrisons acting in the name of Jean's eponymous son. Neither side achieved a decisive breakthrough, and the duchy itself was plundered by the soldiery. But in 1364, Charles of Blois met his death at the Anglo-Montfortist victory of Auray, an outcome the new French king accepted by terms agreed at Guérande the following year with Duke Jean IV (1364–99).

On the face of it, the crown had suffered a serious reverse in Brittany, but Montfortist success had quite the opposite result. The advent of firmer ducal rule and continued Montfortist reliance on English allies alienated important sectors within the Breton nobility in the years following Auray. The emergence of regional princely powers was clearly not always to the liking of nobilities who found themselves within their orbit. As Michael Jones has shown, Montfort's popularity among lesser nobles in particular reached its lowest point in the 1370s. Some of the alienated Breton barons entered into the service of the French crown, most famously Olivier V of Clisson, husband of the duke's first cousin and a leading military commander in the realm in his own right.

Ultimately it was internal opposition of this calibre which forced Jean into exile in England (1373–8), like several great western lords before him. Added to the fate of Charles of Navarre, the rallying of leading Bretons to the royal cause under Charles V represented a further shift of the nobility of the north-west away from the anti-Valois stance adopted by some of its number in the recent past. The French crown gained a greater say in Breton affairs in the 1370s than it had enjoyed since the time of Jean IV's great-grandfather. Only when French royal confiscation of the duchy was pronounced in 1378 and annexation seemed imminent was Jean IV accepted back by key sectors of a Breton polity which resisted firm control, whatever its provenance. Stronger institutional and ideological bases of ducal power would begin to evolve from that point on, but their evolution was not marked during the royal reign that concerns us here.

The heyday of the companies

Increasingly favourable relations with the nobility of north-western France, combined with the signing of treaties (to 1369) or truces (after 1375) with the English, created conditions which were conducive to peace for much of Charles V's reign. Unfortunately the organised depredations of the mercenary companies prolonged insecurity throughout the 1360s. Disconnected from their princely and noble paymasters, the companies set about making a living for themselves.

Damage was widespread, but the worst-affected regions lay in central and eastern France. The companies controlled over 60 fortresses in the regions of the Maconnais, Forez and Velay alone. Papal crusade proposals to draw the soldiery away from the kingdom were launched once more in 1365, first to fight the Turk in Hungary under the mercenary captain Arnaud de Cervole (a former cleric known as 'the Archpriest'), then under Du Guesclin in support of Enrique de Trastámara, the French crown's preferred candidate in a war of succession in Castile. Even the second of these ventures, which was better-supported and more successful than the first, can hardly be described as a turning point in the struggle against the soldiery, as Kenneth Fowler has shown. The problem would persist until the renewal of Anglo-French war in 1369, when the king was able to recruit a greater proportion of captains than his enemies due to circumstances discussed below. Many of the remainder were defeated in English service, as we shall see.

The 'decisive decade': Taxation and the estates

Efforts to deal with the companies accelerated significant changes in the exercise of public authority under Charles V. In both Languedoc and Languedoil there was growing acceptance of peacetime taxes to try to keep the brigands in check, an important precedent for the future and a boost for the crown's resources when the Anglo-French conflict resumed in 1369. Under the weight of these pressures, the 1360s became the decisive decade in the history of medieval French taxation, just as the 1190s had witnessed a great leap forward in Capetian finances as a result of the crusade preparations of Philip II. Although much of the benefit was felt in Charles V's reign and that king made his own contribution by instituting a durable apparatus for the levying and control of taxes in the form of the *généraux conseillers* (1369), the impetus had in fact come from the ransom payment and first *fouage* of John's reign. John Palmer estimates that the extraordinary revenues of the French crown now outstripped those of the English monarchy several times over.

Charles V would eventually discover that increasing the fiscal burden to fight wars – even successful wars – carried considerable risks. The taxes which Louis of Anjou continued to raise in Languedoc in the king's name during the later 1370s provoked urban revolts which persisted into the early 1380s, not least at Montpellier, the city granted to Charles of Navarre, where royal levies raised on each hearth were 21 times greater in 1368 than they had been 40 years earlier. On his deathbed in 1380, the king himself was led to cancel taxes he had ordered to be levied. But from the crown's perspective, the contrast with the position of 1340 was stark. The greatly expanded revenues now available permitted the recruitment of the forces of the first Caroline reconquest, among them many of the mercenaries and nobles who had previously been so troublesome.

Growing resources at the centre were accompanied by strengthened powers in the locality. The concession of widening powers to municipal governments to protect the towns, first apparent under Philip VI and John, continued apace under Charles V. Local and regional estates were the only types of assembly to play a part in these important developments. Charles did not eschew consultation with the estates, but perhaps wise from his experiences in the later 1350s, he did avoid regular summonses of large representative assemblies. In the Languedoil, the estates voted Charles V money in 1369 to maintain an army that was several thousand strong in the field. The estates did not meet again until the end of the reign, effectively rendering taxation permanent for that period. The estates of Languedoc met separately and voted large sums of money for the use of the king's brother and lieutenant, Louis of Anjou. The kingdom thus continued to move away from its brief but intense experience of powerful central representative assemblies in the 1350s. As the royal centre and the municipal periphery grew stronger, the potential intermediary of the estates remained weak and unformed.

The renewal of the war

French intervention in Castile failed to rid the kingdom of the soldiery in 1365, but it did contribute to the recovery of Valois fortunes in the wider conflict over the French crown. In 1367 the Black Prince, ruler of the principality of Aquitaine as we have seen, countered French success in Castile by campaigning in support of his own preferred candidate for the throne, Pedro I. But victory at Najera (1367) was costly for the Prince, and he was forced to place heavy financial demands on his lands in south-western France. The fiscal charge was particularly unwelcome to southern lords such as Arnaud-Amanieu lord of Albret (1358–1401) and his uncle Jean Iof Armagnac whose lands had passed under English overlordship in 1360, and whose finances were already severely depleted by the effects of warfare in the region, notably their defeat by Foix. Since the clauses of the Treaty of Brétigny relating to the suppression of royal sovereignty over Aquitaine were never ratified, appeals against the Prince's levies might still be addressed to the French crown. From 1368 on, the appeals emanated from Aquitaine in their hundreds, illustrating the permeability of princely authority in later medieval France to royal sovereignty. When, according to the chronicler Jean Froissart, the Black Prince was summoned to Paris to answer for his actions, he could only vent his frustration by promising to attend with 60,000 companions in his company and a helmet on his head.

In the war that followed in 1369, events in Castile worked again to the advantage of Charles V. Enrique of Trastamara prevailed over Pedro I at Montiel that year, creating an enduring alliance which introduced Castilian sea power into the conflict on the French side. The war at sea remained a secondary zone of conflict, but attacks on the English coast now became a feature of hostilities, sustained over the following 20 years by renewed ship-building at the *Clos des Galées* (royal shipyards) in Rouen. The Franco-Castilian naval victory near La Rochelle (1372) weakened the English position in Aquitaine, although by that stage great advances had already been made on land. The most intensive phase of the Hundred Years' War to date was now emerging in the form of many small but cumulatively important military successes for the French crown between 1369 and 1375.

French gains under Charles V were undoubtedly attributable in large part to the revenues at the crown's disposal in these years – proof, if any were needed, of the striking development of royal taxation in the third quarter of the fourteenth century, and of the effective redistribution of its product among the military classes whose support could now be paid for. English errors of judgment played a role too, notably in the extensive deployment of manpower in *chevauchées* (large mounted raids) which were countered by constant surveillance and harrying, rather than in garrisons which might have slowed territorial losses. But the reconquest was also greatly advanced by the involvement of the western noblemen whose increasing adhesion to the Valois cause since the traumas of the 1350s we have noted above.

In the northern theatre the 'largest and most coherent group' of war leaders consisted of Bretons linked to the Constable Du Guesclin and his successor Olivier V de Clisson; around them there formed a majority among the captains in royal service which came from the western seaboard of the realm, from Saintonge in the south to borders of Calais in the north.[11] Of the 2,657 men-at-arms serving Louis I of Anjou in Languedoc in 1374 whose geographical origins may be identified, more than half were either Bretons (1,007) or Normans (345). These mobile north-western specialists in war were usually accompanied by locals, by definition men of the west or south-west to whom the king now turned to drive out the English or Navarrese. In the campaigns in the south-west, Charles also tried to rely on hungry locals for leadership, although here he arguably backed the wrong horse. The king's lieutenant-general in Languedoc, his brother Louis I of Anjou, encouraged Charles V to ally with Gaston III of Foix, whose control over local noble networks had become extensive. But the king over-ruled Louis of Anjou, first by supplying Jean I of Armagnac with funds to aid the recovery of his lands from the English, then by appointing Jean II of Armagnac for a brief period as royal lieutenant in Languedoc. Gaston III's influence in the south was too great for any lasting Armagnac recovery, and recruiting his support might have speeded up the advance in the south-west. But Charles V's support for the Armagnacs, combined with the fact that the counts were commonly chosen as the king's lieutenants in the south, did at least draw this important southern clan further into the mainstream of regnal politics. By 1374, a gradual reversal of virtually all the gains made by Edward III had been achieved: first the Agenais, the Armagnac lands, Quercy and Rouergue (1369), then the Limousin and Périgord (1370), Poitou (1372–3) and finally Saintonge (1374–5).

The activities of the king's brother Louis I of Anjou in Languedoc are illustrative of the governmental role accorded to close members of the royal familial community under Charles V, a further factor which is commonly identified in the restoration of royal authority. The royal familial community was an effective body of men, capable of mobilising the support of noble networks in the lands they had been granted. In marked contrast to his Valois predecessors, Charles had three able brothers, all close in age and well-established long before either of the king's sons were born (the future Charles VI in 1368, the future Louis of Orléans in 1372). Scope for sibling rivalry was certainly considerable under the circumstances, but was reduced by generous grants of title and office. Louis I of Anjou was made lieutenant-general of Languedoc in 1364, and of Brittany in 1373 during Jean IV's exile. He was partly maintained by the extensive apanage which his father had granted him in the west, as we have seen. In 1369 Jean, Duke of Berry was made lieutenant-general of a vast swathe of France from Normandy in the north-west to the Lyonnais in the south-east, and continued to hold his apanage in the form of Berry, the duchy of Auvergne and the county of Poitou. The youngest of Charles's brothers, Philip, was made lieutenant-general and duke of Burgundy in 1363, and the following year the new king extended his lieutenancy from the Lyonnais to Autun. Finally, Louis II of Bourbon, brother of Charles's wife Jeanne, held the duchy of Bourbon in central France as a fief and served Charles V in numerous campaigns. Royal powers delegated to the king's brothers across much of the realm were extensive, including the authority to treat with enemies, raise troops and taxes, appoint officers and prosecute crime: rights normally exercised by the king in his council.

Raymond Cazelles has suggested that as a result of these measures, Charles V became ruler of a small royal *domaine* which amounted to little more than the territory governed by Hugues Capet four centuries earlier. Although the remark points to the possible dangers of over-reliance on the royal familial community, we should not underestimate Charles V's ability to lead his brothers, or indeed their own proven willingness to serve the interests of the anointed king in return for a substantial slice of the expanding revenues which were raised in his name. The granting of apanages and lieutenancies to princes of the blood extended rather than limited royal authority under Charles V. The same was true at the local level of the revenue-sharing arrangements between the king and the municipal authorities.

But French recovery under Charles V cannot simply be portrayed as the achievement of an enlarged and united royal familial community. Philip of Burgundy and Louis of Anjou certainly contributed to the reconquest of Poitou (1370–2), but Bertrand du Guesclin was the key military figure in this campaign as in several others. His fellow Breton Olivier V de Clisson is credited with the adoption of the defensive tactics which nullified the English threat. Men of the west were therefore a key component of Charles V's successes. The princes were regular attenders of the king's court and council, but they co-existed (and sometimes had to contend) with influential non-princely servants when they were there. Prominent among the latter were easterners upon whom the crown had so often relied for counsel since the beginning of our period. The eclipse of the Burgundian party at the close of Philip VI's reign and its continuing weakness under John were reversed under Charles, partly through the activities of his brother, Philip, whose tenure of the duchy served to channel local noble ambitions, partly because Brétigny forced the monarchy to look east anyway. The return of the western regions ceded in 1360 was far from certain. Of around 60 key figures around Charles V who can be identified, the 'immense majority' came from the 'oriental flank' of the realm.[12] Valued servants from eastern France included Bureau, lord of la Rivière in the Nivernais, a chamberlain of Charles V from his time as dauphin and first chamberlain of that monarch and his successor, Charles VI. De La Rivière and Bertrand du Guesclin were buried beside Charles V's tomb at the king's express request – a particular mark of favour which surely warns against overestimating the role of the princes of the blood in the royal recovery under Charles V, and which demonstrates, at the same time, the fact that the nobilities of eastern and western France had both found a place close to this particular king.

Later, as we shall see, several of the non-princely servants who enjoyed influence with Charles V would come to dominate royal policy under his son. These men were known as the Marmousets, little monkeys which frolicked at court, clearly a dismissive term implying they were cheeky upstarts compared to some of the princes within the royal familial community whose actions they opposed. The Marmousets were not an isolated or powerless group, however. As John Bell Henneman has shown, they drew the bulk of their support from the military aristocracy, particularly the men of north-western

regions of the realm where no member of the royal familial community had an apanage, but where Charles V, in contrast to his two immediate predecessors, had successfully recruited and rewarded noble
supporters thanks to the resolution of the Breton and Navarrese
problems.

The participation of the princes in Charles's plans was therefore
just one reason for that king's success. We should also note that their
involvement came at a cost. The king's closest relatives had rights and
expectations that legitimately surpassed those of his other traditional
advisers and servants. In return for their efforts to maintain 'the honour, well-being, conservation and exaltation of us, of our lineage,
kingdom and subjects' (as one royal *ordonnance* put it), the princes
of the blood had come to expect a share in the crown's growing revenues. Under Charles V, concessions to the king's closest relatives
were still proportionately limited. Figures calculated by Maurice Rey
enable us to say that the king's finances amounted to at least ten
times the combined annual expenditure of Jean of Berry and Philip
of Burgundy in the years 1372–4. A wise king could control predatory
princes; an immature or impaired one might not as we shall see.

The crown augmented

Charles V was remembered as the archetypal wise king. It is true that
some of this reputation was partly created by the work of Christine
de Pizan writing after his death, and that like most eulogies of a dead
monarch her work was partly a commentary on the reign of his successor. But Christine's was not a solitary voice: those who concurred
included the royal *bailli* and celebrated poet Eustace Deschamps, or
the royal counsellor Philippe de Mézières, a tutor of the king's eldest
son who emphasised the devout nature of this king's wisdom. During
Charles's lifetime the Carmelite friar Jean Golein accorded the epithet 'the Wise' to the monarch who had entrusted him with the task
of writing a treatise on the coronation ritual (*Traité du sacre*).

Reflection on the crown and on the rights of the monarchy had
figured prominently in the dispute with the papacy under Philip IV,
but it attained a new intensity under Charles V. The king himself
passed important edicts on matters such as the age of majority for
rulers, arrangements for regencies and the tutelage of royal minors
(all 1374). Political thinkers around Charles presented a variety of
views on the role of the king as we saw in Chapter 1, notably Nicolas Oresme and the author of the *Songe du Vergier*, identified as Évrart

de Trémaugon. Cazelles suggested that exaltation of the crown by intellectuals in its service in the 1370s was a sign of the monarch's insecurity, but surely the reverse was true. In the reign of Charles V, the royal familial community pulled with the king, the fiscal state attained unprecedented powers, and a balance was struck within political society between the men of the east (most active in council) and the men of the west (most active in the field). The proliferation of such writings reflected the increasing role of intellectuals in the political sphere, a trend already apparent under John as we have seen, and which would continue to evolve in our period. The next two reigns would give them much to comment on.

*   *   *

The ability of the king of France to deal with the threat of his most powerful vassal and rival to the throne depended on the support of the royal familial community, the mobilisation of noble networks behind his cause, and access to money to reward loyalty and defeat his enemies. Philip VI's accession was made easier by the support of his close relatives and his good standing with eastern and western noble networks. But as his reign progressed, relations with leading north-western nobles deteriorated, particularly after Sluis. His adversary began to have more success recruiting in those same milieux. In the east, meanwhile, Burgundian noble support grew weaker after Crécy. Although great changes were occurring in the sphere of royal finance, they did not yet give the French king any kind of advantage.

Under John, relations with leading nobles along the maritime flank worsened considerably, partly due to the king's actions, partly because of the emergence of Charles of Navarre. The king's inability to muster eastern support and the weakness of the royal familial community left him further exposed. These underlying problems meant that when a third military defeat came at Poitiers, the political crisis was particularly deep, permitting the estates of the realm to attain their apogee, and the mercenary companies to do their worst.

The elements of recovery were already beginning to emerge late in John's reign. Crucial developments included the development of regular taxation from the husk of the random subsidy, and the granting of apanages to young princes of the royal familial community which created the possibility of reconnecting the monarchy with networks of noble support. Early in Charles's reign, the resolution of the Breton succession and Navarre's effective demise brought more nobles on the maritime flank into the royal orbit. Eastern and western noble interests found satisfaction under this king; the royal familial community pulled together; and the benefits of the fiscal initiatives launched in the 1360s were fully felt. But despite the military success of the period 1369–75, the progress of the monarchy was far from linear from that point on, as we shall now see.

Chapter 4: Royal France, c. 1380–c. 1461

Charles VI (1380–1422)

Charles VI came to the throne aged 11 and remained under the control of his uncles until late in 1388, during which time the senior members of the royal familial community grew more accustomed to the powers (and dependent upon the resources) acquired under Charles V. The end of the king's tutelage was followed by three and a half years of personal rule under the influence of the Marmousets, led by Olivier V of Clisson, Bureau of La Rivière and Jean Le Mercier, and supported by members of that north-western military aristocracy which had played such a key role under Charles V. Under the new king, the Marmousets pursued policies which had been effective in the 1370s, notably the avoidance of open battle with the English and the preservation of the king's *domaine* and financial reserves.

Then, in August 1392, Charles VI experienced a public attack of mental illness. Contemporaries observed periodic returns to sanity throughout the king's life, at which points he resumed his powers to rule. These apparent recoveries help explain, in part at least, why no deposition took place, even if it was clearly contemplated. Unfortunately, as Richard Famiglietti has convincingly argued, it is highly likely Charles remained impaired at these times too by a condition which may have been schizophrenia. For fully 30 years France was governed by a king whose affliction, it seemed, might only be remedied by the prayers of his subjects.

The king's madness

The consequences of the king's illness were soon felt. Shortly after the onset of the crisis, the most prominent Marmousets, notably Clisson and Le Mercier, were dismissed. The royal familial community now closed in around the king and apportioned itself a more substantial role in his affairs.

The critical difference compared to earlier reigns was the utter incapacity of the monarch for long periods, an absence at the centre far more marked even than that experienced during John's captivity. The king's absences diminished the most effective natural check on princely rivalry. Tensions among the princes of the blood grew but did not cause irrevocable damage until 1404, when Philip the Bold, Duke of Burgundy, whose pre-eminence was broadly recognised, died. Thereafter, the contest between the king's only brother, Louis of Orléans, and John the Fearless (1404–19), Philip the Bold's successor, escalated dramatically. The result was assassinations of a kind not seen since the murder of Charles of Spain in 1352.

The first killing was that of Louis of Orléans in Paris (November 1407) on John's instructions, an act which eventually gave the duke of Burgundy control of the king and capital. John remained in the ascendancy in the capital until 1413, when his rivals returned to power. In September 1419, 1 year after he had recovered his hold over the hapless king, John was himself hacked to death at Montereau (September 1419) on the nod of the Dauphin Charles, Louis of Orléans's nephew. These unnatural events demonstrated that the crisis arising from the king's madness was unmanageable for the royal familial community.

Around the main protagonists there formed shifting coalitions made up of patrons within royal organs of government, brokers between these men and the wider polity, and their political clients across the realm. The problems which arose were more acute than in earlier periods of division, notably the Navarrese threat in John's reign, partly because the stakes were so much higher now thanks to the tremendous increase in the extraordinary revenues since the 1350s and 1360s. Moreover, the struggle between Navarre and the Valois kings had affected a narrower polity, mainly consisting of nobles, prelates and towns connected by commerce to Paris. But growing municipal autonomy since 1350, combined with the experience of paying taxes over two generations, ensured that party conflict at the royal centre had a greater impact in the municipalities in the early fifteenth century. Pre-existing local rivalries tended to fuse with factional interests at the regnal level. The Burgundian party was particularly adept at mobilising popular support in the municipalities, for reasons which are discussed below. The conflicts of the 1410s developed into something resembling a civil war.

Against the Burgundians stood a party which can be described in its first guise as 'Orleanist' on account of its support of the king's brother, although that term was not used by contemporaries. John Bell Henneman has demonstrated that Louis of Orléans was close to the leading Marmouset, Olivier V of Clisson, with the result that at the core of the Orleanist party were key members of the military classes of the north-west. After Louis of Orléans's murder in 1407, leadership of his party passed to Count Bernard VII of Armagnac (1391–1418), Louis's former ally and father-in-law of his heir, Charles of Orléans (1407–65). The Orleanists were now identified by contemporaries as 'Armagnacs', whose emergence as a party may be dated to the creation of the anti-Burgundian military league of Gien (April 1410) under Charles of Orléans, Bernard VII of Armagnac and Jean, Duke of Berry. When the count of Armagnac was himself murdered by Burgundian supporters after they recovered Paris in 1418, the Armagnacs gathered around the king's last remaining son, the Dauphin Charles.

Following years of limited hostilities in the Anglo-French conflict, divisions within the kingdom contributed to spectacular English successes under Henry V. The first and most famous of Henry's victories was won at Agincourt (1415) against a French army swollen by both Armagnac and Burgundian elements. Just as Crécy was followed by the more important capture of Calais, Agincourt was followed by the conquest of Normandy (1417–19). Many Norman nobles were expelled or exiled from their patrimonies. With an apparent air of finality, Henry's achievement attained its apogee in the form of the treaty he signed at Troyes (May 1420) with Charles VI and John the Fearless's young heir, Philip the Good (1419–67). Henry became regent of the kingdom and heir to the throne of France. He and his own successors would rule in perpetuity after Charles VI's death. In the meantime, to avenge his father's murder, the young duke of Burgundy entered into an alliance with England which would remain in force until 1435.

Such, in brief, were the principal events which may be traced back to Charles VI's madness. It is clear from our synopsis that the king's youth and subsequent illness were critical to the fortunes of the realm. This remained an age of personal rule. Such was the nature of the small world of royal government – based on informal mechanisms of brokerage and clientage, rather than numerous 'civil servants' running a well-oiled machine – that government did not simply run itself. A vacuum at the centre was always likely to draw in a plurality of powers to fill the void. Constitutional arrangements were drawn up to cope with the king's 'absences' and the related possibility of his demise while his sons were minors, principally in 1393, 1403 and 1406. Unfortunately these measures failed to command consensus among the various interest groups within the royal familial community. Matters were further complicated by the short lives of two of Charles's three sons who grew beyond childhood, namely Louis (d. 1415) and John (d. 1417). Reconciliations or peace treaties were negotiated between the main protagonists at Paris in 1405 and 1407, Chartres in 1409, Bicêtre in 1410, Auxerre in 1412, Pontoise in 1413 and Arras in 1415, but the results were insubstantial and temporary. Throughout this period of division, it seemed to the author of the so-called anonymous Parisian journal that France suffered more than it had 'since the time of Clovis, who was the first Christian king'.[1]

Fundamental though the king's madness clearly was, it is clear that the problem was also aggravated by structural factors which we have traced in previous reigns. Foremost among these was the view that France was governed by a royal familial community under the king. This natural conception of power had proved its worth on the accession of Philip VI and during the recovery under Charles V, but always carried with it the threat of discord and division. A second (and often overlapping) structural element to emphasise is the continuing role of noble networks in the political life of the realm. The conflict of 'Burgundian' and 'Armagnac' touched a wide variety of groups, but at its core lay a longer-term contest between eastern and western noble interests which we have traced in earlier reigns. Last but not least, the events of Charles VI's reign must be understood in the light of the attraction of the revenues from taxation which had grown remarkably through the second half of the fourteenth century. Royal income was sufficient to 'excite cupidity without managing to satisfy it'.[2] Since the revenues of the crown were at the heart of the struggles for power, a fuller discussion of events might usefully start there.

The king's riches

The revolts which had threatened to cut the stream of fiscal revenue to the crown at the end of the 1370s erupted more widely in the early years of Charles VI's reign, notably in the towns of Picardy and Languedoc (1380), at Rouen and Paris (1382), and in certain rural areas such as Auvergne. Royal suppression of the revolts was decisive, with the result that by 1384 the king's ability to tax was more firmly established than ever. The continued buoyancy of royal resources is of added importance because theatres of conflict – and therefore the 'evident necessity' which justified taxation in the eyes of the king's subjects – were significantly reduced after the early years of the reign.

In Brittany, the second Treaty of Guérande (1381) inaugurated a period of Franco-Breton peace which was seriously threatened on only one occasion (as a result of an attempt on the life of the leading Marmouset, Olivier V of Clisson, enemy of Duke Jean IV, in 1392: it was during a campaign into Brittany to punish this misdemeanour that Charles suffered his first attack of mental illness). In the south, meanwhile, Gaston III of Foix's desire for regional hegemony and his raids on Armagnac lands were curtailed by a peace agreement with Count Jean III (1384–91), one of the main achievements of a rare but lengthy tour Charles VI made of Languedoc in 1389–90. Gaston's successors – first his nephew, Mathieu de Castelbon (1391–8), then Mathieu's brother-in-law, Archambaud de Grailly, *captal* de Buch (1398–1412) – were obliged to accommodate the king's wishes to a greater extent than their illustrious predecessor had ever done. The threat of a dominant southern principality now waned, and in this region, as in Brittany, the crown did not have to expend heavily.

Demands on royal resources further decreased as the war with England entered its slackest phase. The possibility of peace was genuinely contemplated and explored in conjunction with efforts to resolve the Schism in the church. The principal French concern of the 1380s was to preserve Charles V's reconquests and even, in a series of costly but ultimately fruitless projects, to take the war to England (1385–7). With exceptions such as the French military initiatives against Calais and in the region of Guyenne in 1404–5 and 1406–7, hostilities were infrequent between the negotiation of truces at Leulinghem in 1389 and Henry V's invasion of 1415.

Of course, it would be misleading to say the crown ceased to incur expenses for the defence of the realm and the preservation of peace in these years. Diplomacy, garrisons in frontier regions and measures to counter troublesome strongholds were among the more obvious costs which had to be met. Nonetheless, thanks to decisive action early in the reign to preserve fiscal resources, the crown enjoyed a better balance between income from taxes and expenditure on war during the 1380s than in any earlier decade in French history. In the reported words of the royal constable Olivier V of Clisson in 1389, 'the king ha[d] riches in abundance beyond all bounds.'[3]

The continued eclipse of the estates

Before exploring the consequences of royal wealth in the first dec
of Charles VI's reign, it is worth emphasising that the king's
ity to tax had been sustained without any corresponding grow
the powers of representative assemblies. On the contrary, Ch   s
VI's reign witnessed a further decline in the role of the e   s,
both in Languedoil and Languedoc and to a lesser extent with   1e
localities.

Admittedly it did appear that the estates of Languedoil migh   on
the point of a resurgence at the start of the reign. At least three   rth-
ern assemblies between November 1380 and January 1381 so   it to
widen the abolition of taxes initiated by Charles V on his d   bed.
When it became clear that taxes would still have to be ra   , the
estates sought a return to the role their predecessors of   5 had
acquired in the apportioning, raising and auditing of levies.   empts
to recover the former influence of the estates were short-l   1, however. Repression of the revolts of the early 1380s weakene   he case
for representative assemblies, and the new king was surr   1ded by
a government of dispendious uncles who had little inte   in sub-
mitting revenue flows to the scrutiny, let alone control   outside
agencies. The next assembly of the estates of Languedoil   curred in
1413, to raise funds to fight the English. Due to the con   t between
Burgundy and Armagnac, the meeting was poorly atte   d and did
not succeed in its calls for the reform of royal governm   .

In Languedoc, assemblies which had been frequen   m 1369 to
1382 met less regularly under the lieutenancy of the   ke of Berry
to 1389, then under the royal governors who succee   him in the
region to 1393. Despite protests from southern to   s which had
obtained tangible benefit from the estates, there wer   more southern assemblies from this last date until the closing   rs of Charles
VI's reign. The pattern of declining summonses was   ilar in the case
of local estates in many other parts of the realm. Ob   ving the fate of
assemblies at this time, James Russell Major notes   'not until well
into the seventeenth century was the crown agai   o exercise such
unilateral tax powers'.[4]

The king's uncles: Angevin decline and Burgundian ascendancy

It remained the strongly held conviction of members of the royal
familial community that they should share in royal resources which

now came to a very large extent from taxation, rather than from the royal *domaine*. The incomes of princely apanagists and the king himself were diverted on several occasions during Charles VI's early reign into projects led by princes of the realm – projects that were pursued outside the boundaries of the kingdom or on its periphery, but which had a significant long-term bearing on events within it.

The king's oldest uncle and therefore the next most senior member of the royal family, Louis I of Anjou, was adopted as the heir of Queen Joanna of Naples in her southern Italian kingdom and its associated county of Provence in 1380. The Angevin succession in Naples formed the basis of later royal interventions in the Italian peninsula under Charles VIII (1483–98). In the short term, however, the extra-regnal interests of the house of Anjou were a drain on its limited resources, encouraging a degree of dependency upon the monarch among Louis I's successors which contrasts with the growing financial independence of the dukes of Burgundy. More immediately, Louis I's death in Bari in 1384 left his 7-year-old son, Louis II (1384–1417), as the leading representative of the house, thereby clarifying the hierarchy of the royal familial community in Burgundy's favour.

Louis I of Anjou had been the most acceptable of the king's uncles in the eyes of the Marmousets and the north-western military aristocracy of the realm. His lands lay in the west, and he had had a military career among the western nobles who had contributed to the recovery under Charles V. Close relations with Olivier V of Clisson also contributed to the bond. Anjou's demise therefore weakened the western party in French political life, and it would be some time before this important group was able to gather around another member of the royal familial community. When that happened, it would be Louis of Orléans, the king's brother, who attracted their support. But until then, and for fully 20 years after Louis I of Anjou's death, the senior Valois prince was unquestionably Philip the Bold, Duke of Burgundy. The balance between eastern and western nobilities around the king in Charles V's reign had tipped markedly in favour of the former.

Philip the Bold's territorial interests outside the kingdom lay in the Low Countries, and arose from his marriage in 1369 to Margaret, daughter of Louis of Male. At the time it was contracted, the union prevented an English marriage for Margaret of Male, which would have resulted in the lands her father had gradually acquired since 1356 passing into enemy hands. In addition to Louis of Male's counties of Flanders and Rethel, Margaret was heiress to her grandmother's counties of Artois and Burgundy, and the county of Nevers where her father and grandfather ruled jointly. Philip the Bold did not wait until the death of his father-in-law in 1384 to make his influence felt in the regions he would later rule. The distribution of princely largesse among local noble networks, the contracting of alliances and several personal visits built up support. In 1382, Philip led a French royal army into Flanders to defeat the second major Ghentish rebellion of the century under the leadership of Philip van Artevelde, son of Jacob, at the Battle of Roosebeke.

On his accession in Flanders, Philip the Bold became ruler of the largest and most populous complex of territories ever ruled by a Valois prince. Within a decade, Richard Vaughan has estimated, the duke's revenues amounted to around one-third of those at the king's disposal, more than half of them from the lands he now ruled over. The contrast with the position in 1372–4 mentioned above is striking. It was resources such as these which enabled the duke to meet the enormous costs of his son's crusade preparations and ransom after Nicopolis in 1396 – a great Christian defeat in itself, but one which augmented the reputation of the future John the Fearless within his own lands. Through the distribution of favours among the nobility, a judicious marriage policy and other diplomatic initiatives, Philip the Bold consolidated his position in the Low Countries and created opportunities for integrating further blocks of imperial territory. Most important in this category of potential future acquisitions were the duchies of Brabant and Limburg, where Philip's father-in-law had already succeeded in having himself appointed heir in 1356; and the counties of Hainaut, Holland and Zeeland, where the ruling house of Bavaria contracted marriage alliances with its powerful Burgundian neighbour. The men of the east in Philip's service now formed part of a wider dynastic empire which looked northwards towards Artois, Flanders and beyond, not simply up the Seine towards Paris. A fundamental shift in the outlook of a key group in French political society was occurring in the last decade of the fourteenth century.

An expensive and unsuccessful royal campaign in 1388 against one of Philip's new regional rivals in his northern lands, William of Juliers, Duke of Guelders, was a step too far in the pursuit of Burgundian interests for some royal advisers, even if the duke of Guelders could be portrayed as an ally of the English. Within weeks of his return from the Low Countries, Charles VI liberated himself from the tutelage of his uncles. The decision was made public by the young king at Reims, symbolically important as the place where the ruler's pre-eminence within the royal familial community was affirmed at every coronation.

The loss of pre-eminence in France late in 1388 was a setback for Philip the Bold, albeit one which only lasted until the king's first attack of mental illness in 1392. Despite his growing importance in the Low Countries, the kingdom remained at the centre of the duke of Burgundy's concerns, not least for the favours and revenues it still procured him. But as a result of Philip's acquisitions, his successors were the only Valois princes to enjoy substantial resources outside the kingdom. Burgundian expansion into the Low Countries also gradually encouraged a more accommodating attitude towards the kings of England, for Anglo-Flemish economic links remained strong. For the first time in our period, the political leader of the men of the east had an option which was usually more readily available to the aristocracy of the western seaboard, namely an alliance with the ruler of England. It was an option which Philip and his son did not take up, but which Philip's grandson felt compelled to pursue in 1420.

The king's brother: Louis of Orléans

As the only brother of a ruling king, Louis of Orléans was well placed to enjoy a key role within the royal familial community – especially once Charles VI's condition became apparent in 1392. By that stage, however, the royal uncles, Philip the Bold foremost among them, were pre-eminent, and the 20-year-old prince took a secondary role. Brothers and uncles of ruling kings were usually natural allies because they came second to their regal brothers in the division of the dynastic patrimony, as Michel Nassiet has pointed out, but in this instance circumstances dictated otherwise.

There were few compensations to make up for the role Louis of Orléans was forced to play in the 1390s. His union to the daughter of the duke of Milan, Valentina Visconti, made him a natural candidate for French projects in the Italian peninsula, and gave rise to the claims which his grandson, Louis XII (1498–1515), would pursue there a century later. In the Empire, Louis contracted numerous alliances from 1398 which were explicitly intended to strengthen the French crown against English threat. But these were costly ventures, and unlike the acquisition of Flanders by Philip the Bold, which was also intended to thwart the English, they brought little by way of territorial gain for Louis of Orléans.

It may be, as Françoise Autrand has suggested, that the Marmousets regarded Louis of Orléans as a new type of prince who would not expect the benefits traditionally received by senior members of the royal family. Louis certainly began to associate more with the Marmouset party from the early 1390s, recruiting to his household men like Jean Le Mercier and an increasing number of prominent military commanders from the west. In 1396, in Henneman's view, the king's brother and this once-influential group drew more firmly together in opposition against Philip the Bold. Closer association was motivated, on Louis's side, by Orleanist failure in Italy that year, and on the Marmouset side, by the loss of many former western military figures at the battle of Nicopolis (a defeat which, by contrast, had more positive consequences for the Burgundians). A struggle for influence within the royal familial community was beginning to overlap once again with a long-established contest between eastern and western noble groupings.

But whatever the Marmousets might have wanted for him, Louis of Orléans chose not to follow an innovative path of princely self-denial. Louis began to acquire territories and alliances which befitted his rank and were comparable in extent to his uncles' possessions. Although it would be misleading to portray the three main groups of lands which he now began to assemble purely as an attempt to block his most powerful uncle, the duke of Burgundy, Louis's purchase of the rights to the duchy of Luxembourg in 1402 most certainly was, potentially splitting the two main blocks of Burgundian dominions by Orleanist territory. By that stage the power struggle between senior uncle and nephew had become quite open. Louis's greater proximity to the king enabled him to recruit support in the organs of royal government and retain an ever greater proportion of royal taxes. For his part, Philip used his superior resources to put on a show of force in Paris, and to publicly attack the fiscal policy of a government increasingly influenced by his nephew (1401–2).

Perhaps it was Philip the Bold's conscience which led him to advocate the reduction of taxes in the Kingdom of France, like his father in 1380. But it seems pertinent to note two related points. Thanks to his territorial acquisitions since 1384, the duke of Burgundy was much less reliant on the product of royal taxation than his nephew and rival. Moreover, in calling for the restriction of taxes, Philip identified the Burgundian party as one of fiscal reform. This was a potentially popular policy given the growth of royal demands over the previous generation, especially among the populace of the towns whom taxes hit hardest. A contest between two members of the royal familial community, each supported by different noble interest groups in the realm, was now expanding outwards to touch a wider population of tax payers. This key difference helps explain why the conflict of Burgundy and Orléans had even wider ramifications than the actions of Charles of Navarre half a century earlier.

Philip the Bold's death in 1404 clarified the hierarchy of the royal familial community in Louis of Orléans's favour, and for 3 years he finally achieved pre-eminence within the royal familial community. Philip's successor, John the Fearless, was the grandson and cousin of a king, not the son and brother as Philip had been, and as Louis of Orléans still was. These differences mattered. Louis's rightful control over the king and the royal family enabled him to divert substantial amounts of the proceeds of royal taxation to his own ends, and place his men within the king's administration, not least among the *généraux des finances* who took charge of the king's enormous extraordinary revenues. Meanwhile, John the Fearless saw the Burgundian share of royal revenues dwindle to virtually nothing, and this as early as 1405. For a Burgundian used to a long tradition of dominance in France, the situation was increasingly intolerable. After a failed coup in 1405 and an unconvincing reconciliation which saw both princes participate in the military action against the English in the north and south-west, John the Fearless resorted to assassination to achieve mastery in France.

Burgundian against Armagnac

Some contemporaries were prepared to believe that the duke of Burgundy's real goal was to supplant the ruling monarch. The example of a royal cousin (Henry of Lancaster) usurping the throne of a less obviously incompetent king (Richard II) was there for all to see across the Channel. But as Barthélemy-Amédée Pocquet du Haut-Jussé argued, John the Fearless's actions suggest that he, like his father before him, sought primarily to control royal authority to his own ends. In this respect the duke was acting, not simply like many members of the royal familial community before him (albeit a particularly ruthless and successful one), but as a conventional political leader from eastern France. His mastery of the kingdom from 1408–13 and 1418–19 represented the apogee of a deeper structural trait in French noble geopolitics.

Against John stood shifting coalitions which, despite their changing composition and leadership, had at their core a strong presence of westerners. Orléans's murder in 1407 decapitated but did not destroy that duke's party. Military leadership of the opposition to Burgundy eventually passed to Armagnac and the Gascons in his service. But Armagnac was part of a wider coalition as we have seen, the princely members of which sought to mobilise the aristocracy of their western lands behind them – not least Louis II of Anjou (1403–34), Jean I of Alençon (1404–15) and Louis of Orléans's successor and oldest son, Charles.

John's success against this opposition depended on the popularity of the Burgundian party in Paris and other leading towns, and his ability to control the king and the immediate royal family. The demise of Louis of Orléans was not unpopular because of that prince's association with heavy taxation, and the other members of the royal familial community were slow to take action against the prince responsible for his murder. Instead, it was John who took the initiative in 1408, first by returning to the capital where a public justification of the assassination of Orléans was made on his behalf by Jean Petit, master of theology at the University of Paris, then by effecting a reconciliation of sorts the following year with Charles of Orléans. John also acquired greater control over the king's government by engineering the downfall of Jean de Montaigu, grand master of Charles VI's household (1409). According to the chronicler Enguerran de Monstrelet, 'At that time, the duke of Burgundy had more power than all the other princes, and affairs were carried on by him and his supporters'.[5] The military action of the league of Gien in 1411–12 failed to prevent John from tightening his grip, and the duke's self-conscious support of reform increased his popularity in many of the cities of the realm.

When John did begin to lose control in 1413, it was his support of reform which was partly his undoing. Moderates around the king had at first been persuaded of the need for reform of royal government, and saw John the Fearless as a possible champion. But the violent actions of a popular party led by the Parisian butcher Simon Caboche (April–May) encouraged the moderates to enter into discussions with the Armagnacs. One of those particularly affronted by the riots in the capital was Charles VI's eldest son and heir, Louis of Guyenne. Despite Guyenne's young age, John was unable to counter the growing independence of the heir to the throne, and it was Louis who played the key role in the events which saw the duke of Burgundy finally flee Paris in August 1413. For now, the ascendancy of the men of the East was brought to an end.

Armagnac control over the king and the capital during the next 5 years was never particularly secure. As Richard Famiglietti has shown in his study of Louis of Guyenne, the eldest son continued to seek a third way between the warring factions, and his status as prospective heir meant that he was difficult to resist. The Armagnacs were no more successful than John the Fearless in controlling this key figure. When Louis died unexpectedly in December 1415, aged just 18, the

Armagnac party was certainly strengthened in Paris. Unfortunately for them, the next heir to the throne, Charles VI's second surviving son, Jean, Duke of Touraine, was married to John the Fearless's niece. The young duke was even resident at the Burgundian court. Once again, control of a key member of the royal family lay with the men of the east.

A further weakening of the Armagnac party resulted from war with the English. Both Burgundians and Armagnacs negotiated with the English in the second decade of the fifteenth century, but it was the occidental Armagnac party, conforming to earlier precedents, which travelled first and furthest in this direction. In 1412, the anti-Burgundian coalition approached Henry IV, offering to restore the duchy of Aquitaine and the lands in their own possession which were ceded at Brétigny. In 1414–5, Henry V approached the Armagnacs in control of Charles VI and was made a similar offer. In both instances the opposing sides in France reached a peace settlement before an English alliance could have any great effect, and on the second occasion Henry V responded with his devastating invasion of 1415.

Although the French army at Agincourt contained both Burgundian and Armagnac elements, it was the latter which suffered most. John the Fearless lost both his brothers in the battle, but these deaths simplified succession arrangements within his family. Crucially, neither the duke of Burgundy nor his heir was present. By contrast, the eldest representatives of the houses of Bourbon and Orléans were captured at Agincourt (respectively Jean I [1410–34], never released, and Charles, released 1440), while another signatory of the league of Gien, Jean I, Duke of Alençon, was killed in the engagement, leaving a 6-year-old son and successor, Jean II (1415–76). On top of these losses, the opposition to John the Fearless was weakened by the death of Jean, Duke of Berry in 1416 (who left no heir). Louis II of Anjou also died the following year, and the eldest of his three sons had only just attained the age of majority at that time. The impact of these developments within the royal familial community revealed once again just how important that body of men was to the fate of the kingdom in our period.

In the course of 1417, then, John the Fearless's position grew stronger. Despite many negotiations and his own interests in Flanders and Artois, John never publicly sided with the English as his rivals were prepared to do. But it was surely no coincidence that the duke's renewed military offensive in the summer of 1417 coincided with the beginning of the English conquest of Normandy. As many of the major French towns went over to John in his campaigns in northern France (August–September), the English forces which landed in August set about the task of capturing the duchy. In the process, the power base of the north-western military aristocracy was reduced still further, and new areas found themselves under threat, notably Anjou.

The unexpected death of the Dauphin, John, in April 1417 was a setback for the Burgundian party, and the next-in-line to the throne, the future Charles VII, was subsequently active in resisting John the Fearless's partisans, notably at Rouen. But towards the end of that same year the duke of Burgundy recovered his influence over the royal family when the Queen, Isabeau of Bavaria, was prised from the grasp of the Armagnac party. John and Isabeau established a rival government at Troyes early in 1418, and existing organs of royal government in Paris – the *Parlement*, the *Chambre des comptes* and the *Trésor* – were declared abolished. Gradually the situation of the Armagnacs in the capital was becoming untenable, and a small contingent of Burgundians eventually took the city by surprise in May 1418. Although the Dauphin was smuggled out by Armagnac supporters, Bernard VII was not so lucky. The count of Armagnac was one of many among his party who were slaughtered in prison in July, shortly before John the Fearless and the queen made their return to the capital.

After the killings in Paris, the remaining men of the west had little option but to rally round the Dauphin, Charles, who had been in their midst for several years already. The struggle now seemed very uneven: a Burgundian duke who controlled the king, queen and capital faced a much weakened opposition around Charles VI's only surviving male heir. As Philippe Contamine has noticed in his great study of the French royal armies, the military establishment which the Dauphin now created around himself at Bourges – his war treasurers, marshals, admirals, masters of the artillery and crossbows – was composed primarily of men with Orleanist and Armagnac traditions of service, usually of western origin. The struggle between eastern and western interests was therefore perpetuated, despite another change in leadership. In his study of the ramifications of the murder of Louis of Orléans, Bernard Guenée notes that Charles's closest advisers during his peace negotiations with John the Fearless throughout the summer of 1419 were predominantly Angevins, Normans or Bretons. And it was from this western milieu that the idea of killing the leader of the men of the east, John the Fearless, finally emerged. This was the act which led to Charles VI disinheriting his only remaining son, the appointment of Henry V as his heir, and to the new duke of Burgundy, Philip the Good, allying with the English.

By the early 1420s, a striking reversal of roles had thus occurred. The men of the east retained their influence over the monarchy, but the Treaty of Troyes envisaged that the monarchy in question would be Lancastrian rather than Valois. Henry V's early death (August 1422) cast the future of the Treaty of Troyes into doubt, but the men of the east remained central to English plans. On his deathbed, according to the chronicler and provost of Arras, Pierre de Fenin, Henry V told his brother John, Duke of Bedford, regent for the infant Henry VI, that the Burgundian alliance was critical to the survival of the Lancastrian regime in France, and that he should maintain it at all costs.

Meanwhile, the remnants of the leadership of the north-western military aristocracy which had for long opposed Burgundian power was to be found around the disinherited dauphin. With noble support of this calibre, added to the resources of lands in his power where growing municipal autonomy had produced seasoned taxpayers, Charles was certainly not weak. But to prevail, the young prince would have to overcome the strength of his ancestors' ancient enemies, combined with that of his ancestors' most trusted allies. Should Charles be anointed king, the Burgundians would find it difficult to accept his authority, just as he would find it hard to trust their service. A profound shift had occurred in French politics. Charles was destined to be the 'least Burgundian of kings', as Gareth Prosser has perceptively observed – by inclination in this case, and not by force of circumstance, as Charles's great-grandfather John had been.

The events of the last three decades of Charles VI's reign tested the French and ultimately divided the kingdom into three parts, albeit with significant gaps, overlaps and differences within or between them. One part was Lancastrian, located across the north and in the south-west of the realm. Another was Burgundian in the east and north-east. The third was delphinal, situated in the centre, the south and the west as far as Anjou and Touraine. The legacy of the division would last at least a generation as we shall see.

Strengths and weaknesses of the monarchy in 1422

For all its travails, the institution of monarchy did draw strength from these years. From 1392 to 1422, France was governed by an absent king – a king more profoundly absent than even John had been, despite his imprisonment in England. The monarchy was, more than ever, an abstract idea around which the French could rally in hope. In his study of the chronicle of Michel Pintoin, Bernard Guenée finds that 'the illness of Charles VI taught the kingdom to live (or rather to survive) as best it could, without the king, but by exalting royalty.'[6] This was a different form of exaltation from that which surrounded the crown under Charles V or Philip VI, but perhaps it was not any less important in the long term.

Calls for the reform of the administrative bodies which derived their authority from the monarchy were revived under Charles VI for the first time in any significant way since the 1350s. But compared to the events of that decade in John's reign, the reformers did not greatly interfere in the workings of the royal state. The Marmouset regime is attributed with significant reforms which increased the competence and authority of the relatively small number of office holders at the centre of royal administration. Several efforts were made to restrict the spiralling costs of royal government, the most famous of which was the reforming ordinance of 1413, halted in its tracks by the Armagnac reaction to the excesses of Caboche's party in the capital. Outside the period 1388–92, any attempt at reform was heavily dependent upon the political support of members of the royal familial community, and as we have seen the support of this group, with the possible exception of the duke of Burgundy, was difficult to count upon.

If the royal administration which emerged from Charles VI's reign had much the same strengths and weaknesses as its predecessors, the means at the king's disposal to raise revenue were, by contrast, in tatters. All sides in the civil conflict had used royal resources as best they could to further their own ends, but the reforming stance of the Burgundian party had had the dangerous effect of exciting popular opposition to taxation. Both sides abolished the *aides* in 1418 to garner support, and collection of the *gabelle* was disrupted. The means of raising taxes could be rebuilt, but restoring popular willingness to accept taxation would be more difficult. In one respect at least, the future Charles VII was better off than his father. The young prince found himself surrounded by fewer, less mighty princely subjects than his father had been. The concept of rule by royal familial community was not destroyed by the events of Charles VI's reign, but it would be fair to say it was cherished more by princes than it was by later kings.

Charles VII (1422–61)

To the Burgundian chronicler George Chastelain writing after the king's death, it was clear that Charles VII's reign had been double in character, one part adverse, the other prosperous.[7] Having declared himself regent (1418) and cleared overt Burgundian support from Languedoc (1420), Charles became *de facto* ruler of his father's realm south of a line from Lyon to Poitou via the region of the Loire, extending into parts of Maine, with pockets further north such as Mont-Saint-Michel and Tournai. This territory was sometimes referred to as 'the kingdom of Bourges' on account of his frequent sojourns in the capital of Berry.

By 1452, the anointed king's circumstances were very different. Charles had recovered all the lands won by Henry V and Bedford in the northern half of the realm, and his armies had all but driven the English out of the south west. Only Calais remained in their hands. That same year a royal officer could claim without fear of contradiction that 'since Charlemagne, no king of France had been more powerful' than his master.[8] The central achievement of the reign seems clear, although when and why the king's fortunes changed are matters of differing opinion.

Turning points?

Broadly speaking, three points in the reign are commonly identified: the intervention of Joan of Arc in 1429–31; the Treaty of Arras signed with Philip the Good duke of Burgundy in 1435; and the creation of a French standing army by an *ordonnance* promulgated in 1445. By discussing each in turn, it will become apparent that there was a more fundamental problem for the king to address before he could prosper, namely how to establish a stronger measure of control over the western military classes. Only by absorbing and rewarding noble networks could the process of state formation under the crown be advanced.

Posterity has sometimes dated the turning point of Charles's fortunes to 1429, when Joan of Arc reportedly restored the king's confidence before helping to raise the siege of Orléans, recover Champagne and bring the Valois ruler to his coronation at Reims. John, Duke of Bedford himself told Henry VI in his council, in June 1434, that 'all things [in France] prospered for you 'till the time of the siege of Orléans, taken in hand by God knows what advice'.[9]

The war against the Anglo-Burgundians had been fought in or around the territories of Charles's enemies to that point, but substantial military victories eluded his forces after Baugé (1421), and resounding defeats had to be endured at Cravant (1423) and Verneuil (1424). Joan's 15-month-long career (1429–30) certainly weakened the Lancastrians, leading Christine de Pizan, in the *Ditié de Jehanne d'Arc* she wrote before the Maid's capture, to hope that the French might 'reach peace/ from out of the great storm'.[10] The loss of Champagne drove a wedge into the Anglo-Burgundian territories in the east, and even tenure of Normandy, the hub of the English regime in France, became less secure.

And yet territories lost to the Valois in and after 1429 were partially recovered by the Lancastrians, notably Maine in 1433–4. Lands that were held on behalf of Charles VII continued to suffer English attack, even as far inland as the Limousin in 1432. The king's attempt to take Paris was repulsed in 1429, and Henry VI was crowned there 2 years later. Whatever its shortcomings, the Anglo-Burgundian alliance remained in force for more than 5 years after Joan's capture.

Indeed, the Maid herself became a problematic figure following her conviction and execution. The king and his supporters were understandably wary of being associated with a 'sorceress and heretic and invoker of devils', at least until after the trial of 1456 which annulled the sentence passed on Joan. It was the English who showed most interest in linking her with Charles VII's subsequent successes. Soon after her capture, indeed, chancellor Regnault de Chartres, the very archbishop responsible for anointing Charles VII in Joan's presence, wrote to his flock in Reims to say that the Maid had become headstrong, proud and vain, and that this was why God had permitted her to be taken.

Even before Joan's career began, two seasoned commentators – the royalist secretary and poet Alain Chartier, and the Bourbonnais writer Pierre de Nesson – expressed the view that peace could only be achieved by detaching the duke of Burgundy from his English alliance. Once the two branches of the Valois reached agreement at Arras (1435), Burgundian authors inevitably referred back to this particular event as a turning point in the king's reign. The end of hostilities between Charles VII and Philip was a primary goal of Valois diplomacy, and an option seriously entertained by the duke for many years before it was secured.

The restoration of relations with the most powerful member of the royal familial community raised the possibility of a return to more effective corporate government. During much of Charles VII's early reign, the princes who had been captured at Agincourt (Orléans, Bourbon) or otherwise detained in England (Angoulême) remained in confinement. There was not a single royal brother or uncle alive. The young king had been able to strengthen ties with the house of Anjou, but Angevin resources in western France, inherently weak and also under threat from English conquest, hardly matched those which Burgundy could bring to the Valois cause. In any case, the ruling duke, Louis III (1417–34), spent much of the 1420s attempting to enforce his claim to the kingdom of Naples. The renewal of relations with Burgundy at Arras made the reintegration of the men of the east, the source of so many influential royal advisors and noble supporters in previous Valois reigns, a realistic prospect.

The cost of the Burgundian alliance in 1435 seemed high to many contemporaries, and the benefits were not apparent to all. In return for renouncing his alliance with the English, Philip the Good gained the strategically important Somme towns (subject to a buy-back clause set at a high cost), and was personally exempted from performing homage to the king. The westerner Raoul le Bouvier, who represented the duke of Alençon at the negotiations in Arras, later recounted how he and others of the royal household thought it was scandalous that 'the king had been ransomed by his vassal and subject.' Alençon's chronicler, another westerner, Perceval de Cagny, thought Charles had preferred to surrender his lands rather than put up a fight.[11]

Such sentiments among the western noblemen could not have been assuaged by the negligible military gains of the Franco-Burgundian alliance after 1435. In April the following year, Burgundian troops helped recover Paris, but it must have been far from clear to contemporaries that this success made Valois victory in the wider conflict inevitable. Paris was now disconnected from the economic region to which it traditionally belonged, and remained so until the recovery of Normandy. The new masters of the capital were in many ways just as reliant as the old on Burgundian support, at least in the early years. Control of the city remained insecure thanks to the continuing English presence nearby at Meaux, Creil, Pontoise and Mantes. Given these circumstances, it is unsurprising that the king and his court were infrequent visitors to the capital, and that the Loire region remained the political centre of France.

The Treaty of Arras released troops who might otherwise have been tied up in military action against the Burgundians, as some had been in 1433–4, but this increased military potential brought few lasting gains. Dieppe and Harfleur were recaptured in the winter of 1435–6, but the second port was recovered by the English in 1440; the first was repeatedly besieged in campaigns which returned much of upper Normandy to their control. In 1436 Philip the Good did attack Calais, but the campaign ended in chaos when the Flemish militia abandoned their prince. As Christopher Allmand has shown, even Burgundian brokerage of Anglo-French peace negotiations in 1439 produced little immediate result.

In light of these developments, Burgundian claims for the importance of the Treaty of Arras appear overstated. A more dispassionate assessment was offered, with the benefit of hindsight, by Guillaume Hugonet, chancellor of Duke Charles the Bold (1467–77): 'after the treaty of Arras the English remained in great power in Normandy and Guyenne, and for fear of them the French kept the peace.'[12] Without allies in France, the gains the English made at Brétigny were quickly lost to a king who enjoyed the support of leading members of the royal familial community and networks of noble support in eastern and western France. It remains to be seen why the same did not occur after the Treaty of Arras.

As late as 1440, Jean II Juvenal des Ursins, bishop of Beauvais, was advising Charles VII to seek peace with the English: they remained strong and the king's own armies lacked discipline. But within just 5 years, as Philippe Contamine has noticed, des Ursins had changed his tune: it was time to strike against the English. The change can be explained by the third of the turning points usually cited in the historiography, the impact of the military reforms promulgated in May 1445. The principal creation of the royal *ordonnance* that month was an army of 1,500 lances, each lance comprising four combatants and two auxiliaries, apportioned to companies under the command of leading captains. Pay was regular, provisioning and review were subject to regulation, and the companies were stationed across the realm in designated locations. These forces were joined from 1448 by contingents of *francs-archers* (volunteer archers and crossbowmen raised at parish level in return for exemption from direct taxes), and enjoyed the support of the king's artillery under the Bureau brothers. The action of the army of the *ordonnance* in the regions of Normandy and Guyenne in 1449–51 was highly effective. As Paul Solon's study of popular attitudes towards the standing army demonstrates, many contemporaries were aware that a landmark change had occurred. The *ordonnance* of May 1445 therefore has more obvious credentials than Joan's career or the Treaty of Arras as a turning point in royal fortunes under Charles VII.

If that is true, then it is important to emphasise that the companies were not created, in the first instance at least, to achieve the brilliant victories for which they are most remembered. The king's reforms occurred during a period of Anglo-French truce agreed at Tours, around the very time that Henry VI was formally celebrating his marriage to Charles VII's niece, Margaret of Anjou. Truce and dynastic union were considered the prelude to the negotiation of a more enduring peace between France and England.

Charles VII's reforms in 1445, in fact, addressed a more pressing problem than that of the English presence in France, namely how to control the military classes ostensibly in the king's service, the noble networks of western France and the wider soldiery. This was a problem with a long history. The *ordonnance* of 1445 was one in a series of similar initiatives under Charles VII himself, notably in 1424, 1425, 1434 and 1440. In turn, Charles's initiatives represented a return to measures taken to raise the army of the first Caroline reconquest of 1369–75. It was proposed in 1445 that designated captains and the men they selected would be constantly retained exclusively in the king's service, just as Charles V had done. The reforms of 1445 differed from their immediate or distant predecessors in important ways: compared to those of Charles VII's early reign, they succeeded; compared to those of Charles V's time, they became permanent. The king had gradually acquired sufficient money to maintain the military classes effectively and direct their energies. It is this gradual and unpredictable change, rather than any single event or personal intervention, which we need to focus on.

Money and manpower

The king's ability to raise money and men was limited indeed at the start of the reign. While it is true, as Gaston Dodu argued long ago, that the territories which acknowledged Charles as their ruler in 1422 were far from exiguous or bereft of resources, important losses had occurred. The re-establishment of the fiscal strength of the monarchy as it had been in Charles VI's early years would be a long and difficult process.

The western military aristocracy which the king was left to rely upon was also greatly diminished, most recently due to the fall of Normandy. Some among the military classes of the duchy abandoned their patrimonies and sought refuge elsewhere, such as Jacques d'Harcourt who fought against the English in the *Pays de Caux* before finally withdrawing to Anjou. Those Norman noblemen who remained in the duchy were lost for now to the Valois cause, for they had submitted to their new English rulers and were expected to provide them with military service throughout the 1420s, as Anne Curry has shown. Charles VII's efforts to detach Jean V, Duke of Brittany (1399–1442) from the Anglo-Burgundian orbit met with only partial success, and were damaged by reports that members of his entourage had colluded in the kidnap and 5-month detention of the duke in 1420 by the heirs of the Penthièvre claim to the duchy.

In the absence of traditional sources of money and men, Charles VII resorted to expedients which, by their nature, could only be temporary. Compared to John II's attempt to create a military order, at least these measures met with some success. To raise a credible military force Charles VII relied heavily at first on foreign soldiery, principally Scots. The first of three waves of these soldiers of fortune arrived in 1419 at La Rochelle, and in 1424 the Scots numbered 2,500 men-at-arms and 4,000 archers. Victory at Baugé over Henry V's brother, Clarence, was important in establishing the reputation of the Scots' army in France, and John, Earl of Buchan was made royal constable soon after. Archibald, Earl of Douglas was given the duchy of Touraine for him and his male heirs, a possession previously only granted to royal siblings. But Cravant and especially Verneuil (where Douglas was killed) were heavy defeats for the Scottish army in France, and the demands they placed on the French were high. In the Loire region, their requisitioning and robbery led locals to dub them 'mutton guzzlers and wine bags'.[13] By this stage, the crown's ability to recruit and pay the soldiery that fought in its name had become badly degraded.

Irregularity and absence of pay were among the explanations for the behaviour of the soldiery in Valois service. To alleviate the financial pressure, Charles and his advisers resorted to another temporary expedient, the debasement of coinage. The policy was made possible by royal control over mints since the fourteenth century, and by the preparedness of royal subjects across the 'kingdom of Bourges' to put up with the inflationary pressures which inevitably resulted. At their height, the sums raised were substantial, 'as large as the *grandes tailles* of the 1380s and 1390s', and several times greater than the ordinary revenues raised from the royal *domaine*.[14] But by 1422, the profits from the mints were in marked decline as buyers and sellers discovered ways of circumventing the consequences of debasement.

The limitations of extraordinary measures such as debasement and importing foreign soldiers led the king to return to more conventional royal policies. For money, he turned to the estates; for men, the military classes of western France.

The resurgence of the estates

Bearing in mind the decline of the estates after the first decade of Charles VI's reign, the increased instance of summonses issued in the name of his son in the 1420s and 1430s is striking. The first meeting of the estates-general since 1413 was held at Chinon in 1428, and more numerous assemblies of the estates of Languedoc and Languedoil can be identified, the latter further divided into eastern and western regions. Emergent local assemblies were summoned more frequently to meet with crown representatives, such as the estates of Poitou which assembled 14 times in these decades. Others which had not been called for some time resurfaced, such as the estates of Touraine. These developments go some way towards justifying the claim that Charles VII's early reign witnessed 'the most persistent experiment in the use of national and regional representative institutions in France before the Revolution'.[15]

Increasing recourse to representative assemblies under Charles VII certainly helped the gradual restoration of the fiscal state. Important contributions to the king's circumstances were made by the estates-general, notably those meetings (Chinon in 1428, Poitiers in 1435 and 1436) which voted for the restoration of the *aides* (sales taxes). But we should not overestimate the importance of the assemblies of this period. Meetings of the estates-general remained infrequent under Charles VII for a number of reasons, including difficulties of attendance for delegates appointed in far-flung corners of the realm. When they did meet, the estates-general made few demands of the ruler, at least compared to those which assembled under Parisian leadership during the reigns of John II or even Charles VI. And although the estates-general consented to taxes, the crown's representatives still had to conduct many local negotiations with provincial estates and public authorities in the localities to obtain the money they required. More frequent consultation in the 1420s and 1430s therefore failed to create a role for a French estates-general to compare with that of representative assemblies in some other parts of Europe. Charles VII's suspicion of the estates appears to have been as great as – if not greater than – that of any previous king. Once he felt able to take taxes without summoning the estates, as his father's government had done from the early 1380s, or as his grandfather's had done from 1369, he did so. The estates-general fell into desuetude once more after the abortive assembly of Bourges in 1440, and were not summoned again until the following reign, at Tours in 1468.

At the levels of region and locality, many assemblies shared the same fate as the estates-general: revived by dialogue with the monarchy in its time of need, they faded away when no longer called upon. But there is marked evidence of continuity at this level too, and the fate of local estates was often quite different from that of their regnal counterparts.

In Auvergne, for instance, Antoine Thomas finds that the estates played an active role in the defence of their region in the 1420s and 1430s, to the extent of attempting to establish five companies of men-at-arms and archers paid 1 month in advance to stand in readiness against military threats. In 1452, Charles VII stopped asking the estates in Auvergne to consent to taxation and handed tax-raising duties over to the *élus*. But the estates did continue to be summoned in whole or in part throughout the fifteenth century, as James Russell Major has shown, usually at least once a year. Although their role in fiscal matters declined, the estates of Auvergne were nonetheless charged to discuss weighty problems such as the revision of custom law or royal treaties.

In Languedoc, where the estates had carved out an even more influential role for themselves in the 1420s, royal irritation came to a head in 1443. The king responded to a refusal to meet his tax demands by declaring he no longer wished such assemblies to meet. Through negotiation and well-targeted gifts to royal advisers, as Henri Gilles has shown, a solution was nonetheless found which maintained the estates in their privileges and fiscal role, and helped guarantee their continued existence into the early modern period.

Provincial assemblies also continued to flourish in princely territories which were reintegrated in the later stages of Charles VII's reign. In the Dauphiné, as Auguste Dussert's work demonstrated, Charles's eldest son Louis boosted the provincial estates by regular consultations and requests for subsidies when he took up residence there from 1447 to 1456. In Normandy and Guyenne, consultations with the estates were a regular feature of English government. These lands returned to direct royal rule before Charles VII's death, and were later joined by others with equally strong (or even stronger) traditions of representation during the reign of his son, notably the duchy of Burgundy in 1477 and the county of Provence soon after. By the close of the fifteenth century the *pays d'états* extended across large swathes of the kingdom.

Did regional and local survivals of representative assemblies change the nature of the monarchy? If we reduce the problem to the narrow question of taxes, it is clear we should not overestimate the ability (or even the ambition) of the estates to impede royal tax-raising. The estates of Normandy studied by Henri Prentout continued to meet and voted large sums for the king in their annual meetings at the close of the reign. The estates of the Landes in Guyenne discussed by Robin Harris consented to taxes to pay for garrisons and refortification after the recovery of the region in 1453. Where provincial estates were obstructive and conflict arose, an accommodation was generally reached which suited the king's interests, as we have seen in Languedoc.

But if we take a broader view of royal government, the survival of representative assemblies clearly contributed to the devolution of public authority to local bodies which stretched back to the middle of the fourteenth century, and which was noticeably accelerated by the adverse conditions of Charles VII's early reign. Indeed, regional or local estates sometimes added to that process by their own demands. Four years after Charles created a sovereign *Parlement* for his territories at Poitiers in 1418, it was pressure from the estates of Languedoc which led to the establishment of a second *Parlement* to provide justice for the king's subjects in the south. The preoccupations and requests of local and regional estates did not mark assemblies out as dangerous forces to be reckoned with, and this is probably a major reason for their continued survival.

The problematic leadership of the men of the West

Raising money posed Charles VII one set of problems, raising men another – particularly after the destruction of the Scots army at Verneuil. Douglas's successor as constable of France was Arthur, Earl of Richmond (Richemont), brother of Jean V, Duke of Brittany. The appointment marked a return to royal reliance on the leadership of the military aristocracy of the western flank of the realm which had served Charles V so well, and which Charles VII had no real option but to follow. This time, however, the results were mixed, and the degradation of the crown's ability to recruit and pay for its soldiery worsened to a point where decisive action became essential for the common weal.

Prominent in the political manoeuvrings which made Richemont's appointment possible were the interests of the house of Anjou, pursued by Charles VII's mother-in-law, Yolande of Aragon. Earlier dukes of Anjou were among the most dependent of the princes of the blood on royal resources as we have seen, and English success at Verneuil left the house's patrimony vulnerable to attack. A Breton alliance was a useful means of shoring up the Angevin position. Moreover, by helping secure Richemont's nomination, the Angevin party also raised the possibility of improving relations between Charles VII and Philip the Good, Richemont's brother-in-law since 1423.

The hope that the constable's appointment might effect a grand alliance of eastern and western noble networks turned out to be misplaced, but for a few years at least Richemont's mainly Breton forces, combined with the local nobility of Anjou, Maine and Le Perche, impeded further English advances. Among these local noble groups were dynasties like the Lavals, studied by Malcolm Walsby, which were forced to decide whether to go over to Bedford and recover lost patrimonies, or stick with the Valois for the long haul. Charles VII was planning to recover the military initiative by renewed recruitment of Scots in 1428, preparing the ground by arranging the marriage of his eldest son Louis to Margaret, daughter of James II. In the end, however, it was Joan of Arc's intervention which provided fresh impetus for the Valois military effort. The leading figures who achieved success with Joan were also from the military classes of the western flank of the realm – not Richemont (for reasons outlined below), but certainly Jean, Count of Dunois (1439–68), bastard brother of the captive duke of Orléans; Jean II, Duke of Alençon; René of Anjou, Duke of Bar; and Gilles de Laval, lord of Rays, marshal of France.

It has even been suggested that Joan's intervention may itself be linked to western noble interests. The Maid's journey from her village of Domrémy in eastern France to an audience with the king at Chinon was facilitated by Charles II, Duke of Lorraine (1390–1431), father-in-law of René of Anjou. Joan's village was an enclave in René's duchy of Bar situated a little to the north, and it was René's vassals who first brought Joan to Charles II's notice. Whether the Angevin party was then responsible for introducing the Maid to Charles VII is impossible to prove, although 'it is easy to discern the involvement of this faction at every subsequent stage of Joan's career up to the coronation at Reims'.[16]

In the end, growing royal dependence on the leadership of the military aristocracy of western France proved just as hazardous for Charles VII as it had for Philip VI after 1340. Neither the king nor his western allies had much choice but to rely on one another, but unfortunately the king still had limited resources with which to reward his military leaders or channel their ambitions. If the war went well, recovered lands and the grant of others still in enemy possession might be offered as incentives. In August 1429 the Edict of Compiègne stipulated that territory recaptured from the enemy should be returned to its former owners in its original state, and that any inheritances they had been denied in the interim would be made over. With the possible exception of the successful years of 1429–30, the lasting recovery of patrimonies and inheritances must have seemed an increasingly unlikely prospect in the early part of the reign.

Satisfaction would have to be found instead within the boundaries of the kingdom of Bourges. To meet the needs of his noble supporters among western noble networks, Charles VII gave out parcels of the royal *domaine*. As Robert Favreau has shown, virtually all of the *domaine* in Poitou was alienated in this way, save Poitiers and Lusignan. The other expedient was to let the soldiery under western leadership take its living from the land. As Philippe Contamine notes, the stabilisation of the Angevin frontier in the mid-1420s was financed by allowing royal troops (in a revealing conflation of terms) 'to raise an *aide* [tax] known as *appatiz* [protection money]'.[17] Clearly neither expedient could last for long.

To add to these problems, the distribution of the limited resources of the kingdom of Bourges eventually became a source of tension among the western noble networks. One of the beneficiaries of alienations in Poitou was Georges de La Trémoïlle, whose lands, alliances and power at court brought him into conflict with Arthur of Richemont, another major beneficiary of royal largesse. The veritable war fought between the two and their allies in western France between 1427 and 1433 paralysed Charles VII's government, and brought about Richemont's temporary fall from grace. Others who believed their service and loyalty had not been adequately rewarded began to cause further trouble. The impoverished duke of Alençon sought to better his lot by demanding money he believed was owed to him by his uncle, Jean V, Duke of Brittany. Alençon's declaration of war on Brittany reduced still further Jean V's willingness to give up the English alliance which he maintained, for a variety of reasons, for much of the 1420s and 1430s. In the south-west, it proved impossible to satisfy the ambitions and mobilise the support of both Jean IV, Count of Armagnac (1418–50) and Jean I, Count of Foix (1412–36). The two rivals had been won round to Charles VII's camp after an early period of alliance to Henry V, but problems grew as Foix's ascendancy became increasingly clear, notably with the acquisition of the county of Bigorre (1425) and the grant of the royal lieutenancy of Languedoc. Good relations with the French monarchy gave Foix the possibility of pursuing his interests south of the Pyrenees. The count of Armagnac responded to the growing danger of Foix's dominance by encouraging the depredations of the mercenary captain André de Ribes in royal territories across the south-west.

The relationship between Jean IV of Armagnac and André de Ribes highlights a further problem which compounded the problematic nature of the leadership provided by the military classes of western France. The crown's ability to recruit and retain the soldiery had degraded to such a point that mercenary captains were often in the pay, not of the king himself, but of leading figures such as Jean IV of Armagnac, Arthur of Richemont or Georges de La Trémoïlle. Although the constable directed these forces towards legitimate goals for the king (such as the recovery of Meaux in 1439), other leaders placed their interests above those of the crown.

The point may be illustrated by a brief discussion of the career of the most infamous of the captains, Rodrigo de Villandrando, which was studied in detail by Jules Quicherat. The Castilian nobleman's formidable company of *Rodigois* cropped up in 1432 in the service of La Trémoïlle, favourite of the king, in his war against Charles of Anjou, brother-in-law of the king. The following year Villandrando was hired to resist the military expedition of the king's lieutenant in Languedoc, Jean I, Count of Foix, to secure for his brother Pierre, cardinal of Foix, the governorship of Avignon and the surrounding Comtat-Venaissin (both of which lay outside the kingdom, of course). The Castilian was also courted by the Bourbon ducal family for its own purposes. Charles I (1434–56) borrowed substantial sums of money from the great mercenary captain, and Villandrando took a female bastard of the ducal line as his wife. The duke's illegitimate brothers, Alexandre and Guy, became leading mercenary captains themselves.

It was probably pressures such as these which led Charles VII to make substantial concessions to Burgundy at Arras in 1435. Even then, his difficulties were far from over. Some mercenary captains were persuaded to uphold the peace, such as the Anglo-Burgundian warlord Perrinet Gressart whose career was studied by André Bossuat. Many others remained in arms, just as they had after Brétigny, causing such destruction and hardship in Languedoc, the Limousin and Burgundy that they became known by the wider populace as *écorcheurs* (flayers). It would be another decade before a strong measure of royal control was established.

The close relationship between the leading members of the military aristocracy and the mercenaries was a further encouragement for urban communities in Poitou, Languedoc and elsewhere in the 'kingdom of Bourges' to protect themselves as best they could, thereby consolidating or accelerating the development of urban institutions. But the king, who is our main concern for the moment, was left with a growing problem of public order. Here we touch on the principal reasons why Charles VII and his closest allies had great difficulty in maintaining the military initiative, and why the creation of the army of the *ordonnance* was a vital development. The incentives for noble networks to put themselves wholeheartedly behind the king's cause were not yet greater than the attractions of putting their own local objectives first.

Angevin bases of recovery

It helped that for much of the period after Arras, key members of the royal familial community were firmly attached to Charles VII's cause, above all the Angevin party led by his brother-in-law, Charles, Count of Maine (1440–72). The fate of the Angevin patrimony was closely bound up with the crown's ability to resist further English advances. Maine replaced La Trémoïlle in 1433 in the Angevin coup supported by Richemont which helped make peace with Burgundy possible. Maine was joined by his brother Duke René of Anjou after the demise of that prince's hopes of becoming king of Sicily in 1442.

Partly as a reaction against Angevin influence over the king, several other princes drifted away from the royal camp, drawing strength as they did so from the support of leading mercenary captains for whom war was good business. In 1436–7, a coalition consisting of Jean IV of Armagnac, Jean II of Alençon, Jean V of Brittany and Charles I of Bourbon planned to oust advisers close to the king and replace them with their ally from the south-west, Charles II, Lord of Albret (1415–71). The venture, which enjoyed the backing of Villandrando, was uncovered and thwarted, but it underlined the king's inability to draw the western military classes unreservedly behind his cause.

Soon after, Charles VII began to address some of the fundamental problems which shaped his relationship with the troublesome noble networks of his dominions. In December 1438 the king ordered the revocation of all alienations of the royal *domaine* over the previous 20 years, thereby removing an important cause of rivalries among western military leaders. In October 1439 a royal *ordonnance* sought to bring the leadership to heel by forbidding seigneurial levies of *tailles*, ostensibly intended for the king's wars, but all too often used for the princes' own goals. He also reserved the right of recruitment of the companies to the king alone. These were key steps in regaining control of the money and men the crown needed.

A strong minority of western military leaders felt threatened by the measures the king and his Angevin supporters had taken. In

February 1440, a new coalition formed around the Dauphin Louis, Jean II, Duke of Alençon, Jean, Count of Dunois (who later withdrew), Georges de La Trémoïlle and Charles, Duke of Bourbon. The conspiracy was dubbed the 'Praguerie' by those who saw distasteful parallels with the actions of rebellious nobles in the Kingdom of Bohemia. The goal attributed to the confederates, admittedly by Charles VII, was more ambitious than that of 1437: not simply the replacement of royal advisers, Charles of Anjou foremost among them, but of the king himself, by his son, Louis.

Reform was part of the princes' public agenda in 1440 as it had been in the conflict of Armagnac and Burgundian. Despite their populist call to abolish the recently restored *aides* (a measure which would now harm the king's finances, rather than their own), no wider support was forthcoming. Municipal authorities in the west were steadfastly loyal to Charles VII, notably those of Saint-Maixent and Poitiers who resisted the rebels and informed the king of their actions at the earliest opportunity. Under Alençon's leadership in Poitou, and Bourbon's in central France, the latter supported by his half-brothers and their mercenaries, the rebels made little progress. The king, by contrast, acted decisively, and in doing so enjoyed the support of Anjou, Richemont and others among the western military classes. The rebels came to terms in July after a series of failed attempts to restore the momentum of their campaign.

The Praguerie was certainly not the last noble revolt in later medieval French history, but it had been an important showdown, and crucially the king had won. After 1440, restive elements among the leadership of westerners constituted a much reduced threat to Charles VII's authority. Indeed, the king's ability to harness and direct the energies of these men was a vital prerequisite of the second Caroline reconquest, just as it had been of the first. The 'extreme moderation' of Charles's treatment of the rebels certainly helped restore a degree of unity.[18] An amnesty was extended to the principal participants, and Louis was given possession of the Dauphiné to which he would eventually withdraw in 1446. The western rebels were mostly brought back into the fold. The Praguerie did have an epilogue of sorts in the form of the princely assembly which gathered at Nevers in 1442, where a number of familiar requests were made (notably the restoration of the corporate government by princes of the blood which had prevailed under Charles VI). But these calls were made with the support, rather than under the aegis, of the leaders of the Praguerie, and there is little evidence that they were taken up by the king.

The most recalcitrant westerners could now be isolated and punished. Jean IV, Count of Armagnac was arrested for a range of misdemeanours in 1443, and was required to swear upon his release 3 years later that he would renounce all alliances with the English and never again claim to be count 'by the grace of God'. To the resurgent monarchy such claims seemed treasonous at this precise point in time, and the formal process of treason trials became a feature of the king's dealings with the princes at the close of the reign. Jean II of Alençon's continued willingness to contemplate an English alliance, like many dissatisfied western military leaders before him, would eventually lead to his arrest in 1456 and treason trial 2 years later.

But the treatment meted out to Alençon and Armagnac was not typical of the king's relations with the western noble leaders. He needed them too much. The 1440s witnessed improving relations among the western military classes, built around a steady base of Angevin bonds to the crown. The conditions necessary to persuade the men of the west to break their ties with mercenary captains in their employ had begun to emerge in the peace negotiations which settled the Praguerie at Montferrand, and were boosted by the signing of the truces with the English at Tours in 1444. At first it was hoped, yet again, that the mercenaries might be led from the kingdom and eradicated in a conflict that served royal purposes. A campaign against Metz in support of René of Anjou as duke of Lorraine (1444–5) may be interpreted in this light. Such campaigns could never provide more than a temporary alleviation of a structural problem, as we have seen on numerous earlier occasions. At Nancy in February 1445, it was agreed in council by the western leaders of the military classes, foremost among them Maine, Anjou, Richemont and Pierre de Brézé, seneschal of Anjou, the king's principal adviser in these years, that they would discretely secure the agreement of leading captains to disband and return home, leaving a select few to form the core of the army of the *ordonnance* which was promulgated soon after.

The growing revenues of the restored fiscal state were boosted by significant reforms of royal finances (1443–7) which Jean-François Lassalmonie has studied, and would last well into the sixteenth century. But the forwarding of enormous sums from the royal *argentier*, Jacques Coeur, the realm's leading entrepreneur, was still necessary to field the armies of the reconquest, and the debts incurred were never repaid after Coeur's convenient downfall in 1453. Gradually, the crown was succeeding in rebuilding its capacity to raise money and men.

The unity of purpose which made possible the tricky business of disbanding the mercenaries and creating the royal companies was evident in the king's relations with leading political figures in the west. After an awkward start, Gaston IV of Foix (1436–72) grew better acquainted with the royal court than any of his predecessors. He acquired the post of seneschal of Guyenne and Gascony, and established strong alliances with leading figures such as Pierre de Brézé. Stable relations with the French monarchy helped Gaston pursue objectives beyond the Pyrenees and were maintained until Charles VII's death. In Brittany, meanwhile, François I (1442–50) was also better connected than any of his recent predecessors to royal circles, not least through his marriage to René of Anjou's sister, Yolande. It helped that a strong Breton group had formed around Charles VII, just as it had under Charles V, particularly in the king's military establishment. The pro-English stance of the duke's brother and rival, Gilles, further encouraged François I in his inclinations, as did the increasingly hostile attitude of an English government which watched the withering of its traditional Breton alliance with dismay. It was a series of attacks by the English (or by captains in their pay) to destabilise the duke of Brittany which led to the rupture, in 1449, of the truces signed at Tours.

The renewal of war

As in 1369, the war was renewed by a French king acting in support of westerners. In the final phases of the Anglo-French conflict which followed, Gaston IV of Foix attacked the southern frontiers of English Guyenne in 1449, while François I accompanied his uncle, Richemont, in the reconquest of western Normandy (at least until the onset of a fatal illness). Gaston IV participated fully in the conquest of English Guyenne in 1450–1, as did the new count of Armagnac, Jean V (1450–73), whose service of the royal cause while viscount of Lomagne had generally been more reliable than his father's to that point. François I's successor, Pierre II (1450–7), provided Breton troops for the reconquest of Guyenne which was necessary in 1453 after a brief return of the English.

The recovery of English territory gave the king the opportunity to reward his supporters, further strengthening the crown's relationship with the military classes of the west and south-west. Dunois, Brézé and Richemont were amply provided for in Normandy, as Gareth Prosser's work on the duchy after its recovery demonstrates. In Valois Guyenne, which Robin Harris has studied, lands and office were given to loyal leading noble families, such as the Beynacs and the Bourdeilles, and to those whose defection played an important role in establishing and maintaining Valois rule, such as the Abzacs in Périgord.

Paradoxically, it was the growing permanence of their occupation after 1420 which had diminished the ability of the English to recruit allies among the western military classes. Just as the threat of the estates had persuaded westerners of the value of the alliance with the monarchy in the 1350s and 1360s, so the threat of Lancastrian domination now encouraged their descendants to make the king's cause their own. The men of the west looked to the Valois king, not across the Channel as their ancestors were sometimes wont to do, to further their interests. The Norman nobility played an important role in expelling the English they had formerly accepted as their masters. And the rebellion which briefly returned Guyenne to English rule in 1452 was the result, not of widespread indigenous noble rejection of the new Valois régime, but of a limited conspiracy combined with a late show of force by English arms.

Of course, it would have been a mistake to underestimate what the English could still achieve in France. The continuing need to defend the realm helped make the army of reconquest and the taxation to pay for it permanent features of the French political landscape. But the English had little to offer to the western military classes after 1420, still less after 1453. By contrast, Charles VII drew heavily on the support of westerners, not just in the field as his predecessors had done, but also in his council. As Pierre-Roger Gaussin has shown in his prosopographical work on this last body, the majority of royal advisers whose geographical origins may be identified in Charles VII's reign came from the Loire region, Poitou, Saintonge, Normandy, Brittany or the south-west. The monarchy and the men of the west were finally firm allies, more so even than under Charles V.

The continued exclusion of the men of the east

According to the official historian of Philip the Good, Duke of Burgundy, George Chastelain, the Burgundian court followed the reconquest of Normandy and Guyenne with joy. But Philip the Good did not take part in the second Caroline reconquest, as his grandfather, Philip the Bold, had done in the first. The men of the east were not readmitted to the king's trust and favour after the Treaty of

Arras – and this despite the betrothal in 1438 of Philip the Good's only surviving child, Charles, Count of Charolais, to Catherine, daughter of Charles VII, or the duke's efforts 2 years later to mediate during the Praguerie.

Continued exclusion of the Burgundians was most noticeable in the non-implementation of key clauses of the Treaty of Arras, a matter to which the duke's representatives returned in conferences at Nevers (discussed above), Châlons-en-Champagne (1445) and Paris (1448). Nor did the Burgundians begin to re-occupy the royal council after 1435, a body their predecessors had dominated under earlier Valois kings as we have seen. Gaussin has shown that just 2 per cent of the royal councillors who can be identified in this reign came from what might be termed Burgundian circles, although in reality these men were either leading lords who were relatively independent of the duke of Burgundy, or high clerics who appeared only briefly at the king's court. The significant shift of 1420, whereby the predominance of the men of the east in Valois government was broken, was thus maintained after 1435. That the responsibility for the continuing exclusion of the men of the east lay with the king, rather than with the duke of Burgundy as is sometimes maintained, is revealed by a discussion of the actions of Philip the Good from the Treaty of Troyes to the end of Charles VII's reign.

The growth of Burgundian dominion in the Empire, much of it the consequence of dynastic alliances contracted by Philip the Good's grandfather discussed above, was spectacular in these years. Between 1428 and 1433, Philip became ruler of the duchy of Brabant and the counties of Holland, Hainaut and Zeeland, to which he later added the duchy of Luxembourg (1443). Expansion in the Low Countries is often taken as an indication that after the traumas of 1419, the duke of Burgundy had turned his back on the ambition of his father and grandfather to play a leading role in France. In the long-term, Burgundian power in the Low Countries certainly altered the geopolitical balance of the realm, creating challenges to royal authority from the north-east and east which were more typical of other periods in French history. But throughout Philip's lifetime, Burgundy remained very much part of the French body politic, and it this perspective which is relevant here.

The Burgundian alliance was important to the English after 1420, not so much in Normandy where the Lancastrian government relied on land grants and the cultivation of Norman particularism to bolster its rule, but certainly in Paris and points north-east, where Philip's

regional influence and his status as a peer of the realm lent credibility
to Lancastrian dominion. Bedford followed his late brother's advice
to maintain good relations with Burgundy by marrying one of Philip's
sisters in 1423. Later, in 1429, he appointed Philip as the king's
lieutenant. But a fundamental weakness of the Anglo-Burgundian
relationship lay in the fact that it was based more on shared animosity towards Charles VII than on any particular common goals. Philip
the Good sought to extend Burgundian influence through his proximity to the crown: in very different circumstances from the way his
forefathers had pursued this tactic, granted, but essentially the goals
were the same. Bedford, on the other hand, wished to use Philip's
influence to his own ends.

An example of ill-fitting objectives may be found in 1424, when
Bedford granted Burgundy the recalcitrant city of Tournai, an
enclave in Philip's territories with a majority of the population which
was openly loyal to Charles VII. The grant of so large a city might
appear a substantial concession to Philip and something of great
value to an ally whose loyalty one prized. In reality, the grant was of
very limited appeal. For it to have any effect, the duke would have to
take the city first. Once he had done so (no mean feat, and something
Edward III had failed to achieve in 1341), the duke would not be
allowed to keep the profits of the important royal mint in Tournai –
these were to be reserved for the Lancastrian king of France. Philip's
successor would have to return the city to the king on his death. Given
all these conditions, it is little wonder that Philip the Good struck
an arrangement with the Tournaisiens whereby they remained loyal
to Charles VII in return for an annual tribute paid to the duke of
Burgundy. Philip the Good understandably became a lukewarm ally
of the English as a result of these and other developments, and the
terms of a reconciliation with Charles VII were secretly formulated as
early as 1423.

The Anglo-Burgundian alliance persisted for as long as it did
because of a number of factors. So long as peace was not concluded,
Philip needed effective support against Charles VII. The alliance also
gave the duke a free hand to make territorial acquisitions in the Low
Countries. He may even have feared the English themselves, as Mark
Warner's study of the dual monarchy points out. It was possible that
the proven strength of Philip's allies could be turned against him if
he abandoned the English. Among the English leadership were men
who were avowedly his enemy, notably (but not only) a rival claimant
to the counties of Hainaut, Holland and Zeeland, Henry V's youngest
brother, Humphrey, Duke of Gloucester.

With hindsight it may seem that the duke had plenty to occupy himself with in the Low Countries thanks to the acquisitions discussed above. In reality, the duke's tenuous grip over his burgeoning empire made the 1430s, in Richard Vaughan's phrase, a 'critical decade' in Burgundian history, marked as it was by war with Liège in 1430, defections of certain leading nobles to the Valois cause in 1433–4, rebellion in Ghent (1432) and Bruges (1436–8), and the consequences of conflict between the Dutch and the Hanseatic towns of the Baltic (1439–41). The threat of war with Emperor Sigismund in 1434–5 came to nothing due to the very imperial weakness which had facilitated Burgundian expansion in the first place, but it demonstrated once more the diverse range of problems which the Valois prince faced as he stretched his reach eastwards and to the north.

It is therefore no wonder that Philip, like his grandfather before him, sought to strengthen his ties within the Kingdom of France after Arras. Burgundy's role in the release of Charles of Orléans from England in 1440 provided him with one ally, albeit a weak one, and his offer of membership of his chivalric Order of the Golden Fleece to Alençon, Orléans and Jean V of Brittany was accepted that same year. The quest for allies met with less success in the case of Jean V's successor, François I, who refused the offer of membership of the Order in 1445. Philip's efforts that same year to restore relations with René of Anjou by cancelling debts outstanding since René's defeat and ransom by Burgundian allies at Bulgnéville in 1431 had disappointingly little effect too. A German observer noted in 1447 that Philip the Good was profoundly unpopular at the royal court, where the Angevin party still held sway.

It is difficult to say whether limited Burgundian participation in the reconquest of Normandy improved the situation much, but peaceful relations with Charles VII certainly enabled Philip to suppress the rebellion of Ghent in 1453 – a bloody war over the duke's right to levy the *gabelle*, and a clash which provided further proof that ducal dominion in the Low Countries could still face serious challenges. Once Philip had prevailed over the Flemish city and Charles over the English in Guyenne, the duke of Burgundy proposed, like John the Fearless before him, to lead a French crusading army under the royal banner to avenge the fall of Constantinople. But once again crusade failed to provide unity around the Most Christian King. Still Charles would not readmit the Burgundians to his grace. Whether this was due to the hard lessons of his early years, or the understandable desire to avoid the risk of domination by eastern interests that were stronger than ever, is hard to say. Perhaps both motivations played a part.

In fact, relations between the king and the duke worsened in the closing years of the reign. The principal cause was the seemingly unplanned but nonetheless prolonged welcome which Philip extended to the king's oldest son Louis, who had already dabbled in princely conspiracies in 1440, and who abandoned the Dauphiné in 1456 under paternal pressure to take refuge with the duke in his imperial territory of Brabant. Just as the future Charles V seemed to be making inroads into Norman noble networks to his father's irritation in 1355, so a century later Louis seemed to be striking up a potentially worrying relationship with the powerful men of the east. Louis refused to return to the royal court, despite the king's threats and the duke of Burgundy's mediation. As Charles VII's reign drew to a close, and in order to bring a recalcitrant member of the royal familial community and his powerful allies to heel, it seemed that the monarchy was about to turn its renewed might against the men of the east – its erstwhile servants under the first Valois kings, its masters under Charles VI, but its enemies since 1420.

On 17 June 1461 Charles summoned the Norman nobility and archers to arms. In early July, news of his illness reached Burgundy. Before that month was out, the king was dead.

*   *   *

What had really changed by 1461? The English king/duke had been driven out of his lands, certainly, and contemporaries regarded this event as epoch-making, much like the fall of Constantinople to the Turks in the same year. No wonder the epithet 'Most Victorious' was soon linked with Charles VII's name. The king ordered that the 12th day of August would be a holiday, as a perpetual commemoration of French victory in the war against England: another exaltation of the monarchy, one of the many ways in which it became a focus for loyalty and identity in the late Middle Ages.

But the problem of a mighty French prince buoyed by great resources outside the kingdom still persisted in 1461: not the duke of Gascony, certainly, but the rich duke of Burgundy, ruler of Flanders, Brabant, Holland, Zeeland, Hainaut and Luxembourg. Philip the Good clearly still wished to be a dominant influence in the kingdom, much like his ancestors. The old problem of eastern and western noble groupings in French history still persisted, albeit in a different guise from the period 1328–1420. The dauphin's flight to the Burgundian dominions also demonstrated how readily that problem could become entangled with the interests of key members of the royal familial community.

Although the Kingdom of England itself had descended into civil conflict between the houses of York and Lancaster, it was far from clear that peace for France would be the long-term outcome of that struggle. The last time the English had changed kings, the new dynasty had sought to strengthen its position back home by leading a conquest of France. No renunciation of the English claim to the French throne had occurred since 1453, nor would there be one for centuries to come.

Finally, it is true that the French king had greater revenues at his disposal in 1461 than at any time in the previous half century, thanks to the restoration of the fiscal state and the recovery of lands formerly held by the English. These developments had occurred with the help of representative assemblies in Charles VII's reign, but without the estates becoming a political power of note in the kingdom. As the events of the first half of the fifteenth century demonstrated, however, fiscal progress was easier to unmake than to make. Lands which had been recovered could be lost to able adversaries. We should not take it for granted that 1461, any more than 1380, marked an apogee in the history of Royal France.

In at least one key respect the position of Charles VII was stronger than that of Charles V. The establishment of a permanent standing army thousands strong created an important new way of encouraging – if not guaranteeing – a degree of dependency upon the crown among the kingdom's noble networks. Philippe Contamine has shown that perhaps 10 per cent of the kingdom's noble families could find a place in the king's service by this route. Added to the pensions, offices and other forms of patronage the king was able to distribute, more so now after the reconquests, it becomes clear that 'the budget of the state was to some extent a budget of noble assistance.'[19] Given what we have learned about seigneurial incomes, perhaps that budget was simply a welcome addition to noble wealth, rather than a necessity. In any event, it created the possibility of influencing the behaviour of noble networks across the realm in a way that had not existed before. Henry Heller has argued that the ability of the crown to absorb and channel the energies of the military classes was more important to the process of state formation than any growth in bureaucracy. Given points made earlier about royal government in this book, we are bound to agree.

Indeed, perhaps the point should be taken further. State formation was determined by the crown's ability to accommodate other elements in that 'plurality of powers' which made up French political society, not just noble networks referred to by Heller: churchmen, for instance, whose teachings, technical skills, and resources contributed significantly to the exercise of authority by late medieval kings. As we shall now see in our closing chapter, the same point can be extended to townsmen.

Chapter 5:   Municipal France, c. 1300–c. 1500

At several points in earlier chapters, we have had cause to signal the importance of towns and townsmen in late medieval France. Urban communities were the destination of many rural emigrants, and urban wealth was invested in land, sometimes for profit, often for social status. The walls which many towns began to construct after the battle of Crécy were the most obvious (but not the only) manifestation of growing distinctions between life in rural and urban France. We have also seen that urban defences contributed to the developing role of towns in the political life of the realm. Municipal authorities entered into contact more frequently with elements of the royal administration, sometimes employing specialists to help them (legal advisers, for instance, or bilingual clerks in the south). Townsmen were sent as representatives to the estates, locally, within the region, more rarely at the level of the kingdom. Others raised taxes as *élus*. The widespread acceptance of the term *bonne ville* was an acknowledgment of the importance of municipalities to the monarchy, even if revolts against taxes were a peculiarly urban phenomenon, and urban communities could become embroiled in factional struggles.

The present chapter will build upon these points. We will see that municipal authorities, like leading churchmen and noble networks in the countryside, figured prominently in that plurality of powers through whom the king ruled. Once we have considered the impact of late medieval demographic change in French towns (**'Population'**), we will consider the functions they served in the surrounding area. This was the age of the regional capital, and the importance of the main towns within their regions assured a certain economic buoyancy (**'Functions'**). One of the roles the town acquired within the life of a region was that of spiritual capital, a point which naturally leads to a discussion of religious life (**'The Church and Religion'**). Here too, growing distinctions between town and country were becoming apparent, not least in the range and frequency of interventions by municipal authorities in areas which were previously the preserve of churchmen. If municipal authorities were more ambitious in this area of public life, the explanation lies in the increasing scope and competence of urban government (**'Government'**). The powers of the ruling group lay almost everywhere in the hands of an oligarchy which had few internal rivals (**'Governors and Governed'**), and was only really threatened by the frequent urban revolts of the period (**'Urban Revolt'**). The crown generally came to the aid of municipal authorities who were, after all, one of its most important collaborators. This last point emerges at the end of the present chapter, where the role of towns in the wider kingdom is discussed in more detail (**'Extra Muros: Towns in the Kingdom'**).

Population

The problem of numbers

The Kingdom of France had few very large cities compared with northern Italy or Flanders, but many substantial regional centres by comparison with England. Even such simple statements are difficult to quantify. Historians have made estimates of urban population levels based on documentary snapshots, such as lists of tax payers, people eligible for the watch, sometimes even the number of mouths to feed in the city. But such records are rare, and their use is problematic: what of those exempted from taxes? How many people actually lived in the single households mentioned on tax lists? Bernard Chevalier eschews population estimates altogether in his general study of French towns in the period. It might be more helpful here to follow Robert Favreau, who thinks it is possible to identify the main cities, and to say something about their size in relation to one another. In the north, then, Tournai was probably larger in the fourteenth century than Lille, Arras or Amiens, but declined thereafter. Heading south-east, Pierre Desportes finds that Reims was the most significant of the towns of Champagne, at least until the fifteenth century when it is said to have been surpassed by Troyes; below both lay Châlons, Laon and Soissons. Dijon remained the main town in Burgundy throughout our period, and was the largest community in the east of the realm until the absorption of Lyon. Provence did not become part of the kingdom until 1481, with its main cities of Marseille, Arles and Aix.

Up to that point, the group of largest cities in France was to be found in the south east, led by Montpellier, Toulouse and Narbonne.

As we noted above, it is striking how few urban centres of comparable stature figured along the western seaboard and its immediate hinterland. Poitiers and La Rochelle were the most significant cities which remained under royal control for most of our period, while Bordeaux, under English rule until 1453, was by far the largest community in the west. Nantes and Rennes were the only urban centres of note in ducal Brittany. Along the Loire lay a corridor of cities, the most significant of which were Angers and, much further inland, Tours and Orléans, with Bourges a little to the south, all thought to have been of a similar size. Heading up through Maine, Laval and La Ferté were very small communities by comparison, and Caen in Western Normandy experienced markedly declining fortunes in our period. Rouen was probably the second largest city anywhere near the seaboard from Bordeaux to Boulogne, although it was at some remove from the Channel. When we speak of 'municipal France' and the contribution it made to the political life of the kingdom, it is worth emphasising at an early stage that we are referring mainly to continental rather than coastal parts of the realm.

Further inland from Rouen lay Paris. Estimates of the capital's population vary enormously, but even the most modest figures proposed would make Paris three or four times larger than any other city in France. For scores of miles around the capital its economic influence could be felt, and the pull of Paris drew immigrants in numbers sufficient to restrict the growth of other towns in the immediate environs. Guillebert de Mets from Flanders wrote a remarkable description of the city in 1434, with its 310 streets and 4,000 taverns.[1] One could 'plunge into Paris' to hide away, as the Great seneschal of Normandy Pierre de Brézé did in 1461 during Louis XI's purge.[2] But as we shall see, the capital's pre-eminence within the realm was pronounced only in the first half of our period, and its political importance was eclipsed from the later stages of Charles VI's reign onwards. This was the age of the regional capital rather than the regnal capital in French history. Here, too, 'plurality of powers' is a helpful concept for understanding the features of our period.

Evidence of demographic decline

Crude estimates might help us grasp the contours of urban France, but of course populations varied greatly in size throughout due to the impact of plague, war and famine.

Of the three flails, war affected French towns to a greater extent, and for longer, than their counterparts elsewhere in Europe. Towns which were regularly exposed to military action (or simply the threat of it) could suffer long-term consequences. Henry V's capture of Normandy in 1417 created a wave of panic and emigration to Brittany from the city of Caen, an experience repeated to a lesser extent during the War of the Public Weal in 1465, both contributing to that city's decline (as analyzed by Denise Angers). At Toulouse, Philippe Wolff finds that the renewed outbreak of hostilities between the counts of Foix and Armagnac in 1372 led some city dwellers to take refuge in Aragon. The wholesale destruction of towns, such as the sack of Limoges by the Black Prince in 1370, was uncommon, not least because towns were hard to capture as we shall see. But even the raising of local taxes to pay for war could provoke an exodus, as Philippe Lardin finds in Normandy in the course of the 1370s.

Gleaning a sense of the impact of plague, famine and war, although not necessarily the respective weight of each, is sometimes possible through hearth tax records of municipal authorities which recorded the number of heads of household. These documents reveal, in Albi, a fall from 2,669 heads of household in 1343 to just 1,200 9 years after the plague pandemic struck. Falls of this magnitude – around 54 per cent – are not unusual: in Millau it was a little less (−46 per cent, 1346–63), but it was much the same at Carcassonne (−53 per cent, 1370–87), Castres (−57 per cent, 1348–73), Toulouse (−58 per cent, 1335–1405) and Paris (−53 per cent, 1328–1423); at Chalon-sur-Saône the decline was worse (−64 per cent, 1360–1400), though not as bad as the smaller towns in Dauphiné (−69 per cent, 1339–83). The number of people living under the same roof as heads of household may have increased or decreased in size under differing circumstances, and fluctuations in periods not covered by records are very likely. But clearly the trend was downward to around the middle of the fifteenth century, just as it was in the countryside.

Town and country

What is striking, however, is that urban population decline seems directly comparable in scale to that of the countryside, with drops of around 50 per cent commonly recorded. Towns have been described as 'veritable tombs' and 'great devourers of men' due to the higher death rates which prevailed there, so one might legitimately expect greater decreases in the urban population than those which have been proposed.[3] Jean Tricard's study of *Livres de raison* (family record books) kept by a number of urban families in the Limousin reveals that urban infant mortality rates could be very high indeed: of 59 children whose births are mentioned in the sources from 1357 to 1502, just 16 lived to adulthood, and this despite the fact that the milieux in question were relatively well-off.

If urban populations were not replenishing themselves, it follows they were bolstered by immigration. At Toulouse between 1350 and 1450, contracts for employment and apprenticeships in notarial records allow Philippe Wolff to demonstrate immigration at work. Of 1,100 surviving contracts, 73 per cent concerned immigrants, many of them young enough to embark on a trade, or at least of working (and reproductive) age. Where it is possible to judge, immigrants came primarily from rural milieux, affecting the balance of population between town and countryside. In French Flanders, admittedly the most densely urbanised region of the kingdom, Alain Derville finds that the wars of the later fifteenth century led to a decline in rural hearths of nearly 29 per cent, compared to just 12 per cent in towns. In the more rural region of Burgundy, Hannelore Pepke-Durix finds that the proportion of urban households among those counted in tax records for the *bailliage* rose from 25 per cent to just over 30 per cent between 1375 and 1430. The security provided by city walls offered increased attraction in our period for the rural immigrants who had traditionally replenished thinning urban populations.

The impact of immigration into towns was marked in many urban centres throughout the kingdom. At Rennes from 1421 on, Jean-Pierre Leguay finds that the city walls were expanded in a series of building programmes, partly due to the influx of Norman immigrants abandoning the duchy under English rule, partly due to local immigration. Le Puy, studied by Étienne Delcambre, experienced little enemy action and acted as a magnet for rural dwellers weary of the greater insecurity they had to face. The number of recorded heads of household increased by nearly a third between 1367 and 1408 (from 912 to 1264). It is even possible for Robert Latouche, the historian of Quercy, to consider the later medieval period as the *belle époque* of towns like Saint-Antonin, Caylus or Montpezat. The turmoil of the later Middle Ages accentuated the regional importance of urban centres in this part of France, as in many others. There has never been much of a debate among French historians, unlike their English counterparts, over whether the late Middle Ages was a period of urban decay.

Geographical mobility

Relative to the countryside, indeed relative to other parts of Europe where warfare was less present, the population of French communities thus appears to have held up well or indeed even expanded. Underpinning such observations is an equally important demographic trend: the very great mobility of the population of French urban communities. At Chalon-sur-Saône, Henri Dubois finds that 93 per cent of the family names in hearth tax records for 1361 had disappeared within 20 years, far more than one would expect to be lost due to plague. At Avignon on the edge of the kingdom, Jacques Chiffoleau notes that around 62 per cent of surviving wills from the city were made by people born somewhere else, and only 24 per cent by testators who came from the city. Individual cases of people on the move emerge with great clarity from the sole surviving criminal register of the Châtelet in Paris from the last decade of the fourteenth century, studied by Bronislaw Geremek. There we find the blacksmith born in Le Mans in the west, who worked at Bapaume and Arras in the north and in small towns like Saint-Denis and Montereau in the region of Paris before eventually settling in the capital; or the tanner who learned his trade in Orléans, who moved to Coulommiers east of Paris where he married, and thence to the capital where he also found work as a mason's mate. Mobility and masculinity may be linked in the tendency for unattached younger men to move to cities for employment or education. In Reims between 1351 and June 1360, Desportes finds that recorded newcomers to the town included 1,572 men of working age, but just 242 women. Male students may have accounted for around 15 per cent of the population of Poitiers and Orléans. As Jacques Rossiaud's work on Dijon has shown, young women did come to cities alone, sent by their families to become servants or arriving as widows. He often encounters them in criminal records, as victims of attack.

A proportion of the immigrant population inevitably joined the ranks of the marginals who failed to insert themselves into urban society. In 111 of the 126 cases mentioned in the Châtelet register, the accused came from outside the Paris region – almost half of them from communities which lay over 80 miles from the capital. As the work of Claude Gauvard and Nicole Gonthier on violence in cities has shown, neighbours tended to look out for one another, and the new immigrant was potentially exposed by a lack of friends, family or patrons. He or she was also an important figure in social and religious change in late medieval French towns, as we shall see at a later stage.

No less important was the relatively small core of families whose presence is attested generation after generation in towns and cities across France. So frequent are references to them in the documentation that we know their names. At Bourges, Alain Collas finds that the 'people who mattered' were the Pelourdes, the Bouers and the Chambellans, families mentioned in the records of the town over a period of more than two centuries, usually holding public office of varying distinction. At Dijon, Thierry Dutour notes the Pèlerin, Le Vertueux and Chauchart families in records from the thirteenth through to the fifteenth centuries. It was often from the ranks of these durable clans that the oligarchs emerged – a group whose political significance we will examine below.

Functions

The view that urban history is shaped by the region surrounding the city walls seems particularly relevant in the case of later medieval France. The size of the kingdom combined with the destabilising forces of the period encouraged the emergence and development of the regional capital, which may be defined in economic, commercial, administrative and spiritual terms. Diversity of function marked these larger towns out from the *ville champestre* or the fortified *bourg* which remained close to the agricultural pursuits of the countryside. Examples of such smaller communities would include Pau, where a tax survey (1385) reveals a population predominantly made up of rural workers, or St Émilion in Guyenne, where the town's statutes (1485) prescribed the number of the beasts which locals could put to pasture in the town and its suburb.

In more densely urbanised regions of Europe, the supply of manpower, capital and technical knowledge made specialised production for wide markets possible. Such circumstances applied in few parts of later medieval France. The multiple roles of *bonnes villes* at the heart of large rural regions encouraged a more diverse manufacturing base, which in turn protected urban economies from some of the worst effects of contraction associated with the period.

Industry

Cloth production was the industry which lent itself most readily to large-scale specialisation, particularly in the north and Languedoc. Changing economic conditions caused contraction in specialised urban economies, but in France the experience was less severe than elsewhere. While around 56 per cent of the working population of Ypres was involved in the production of woollen cloth for export by the fourteenth century, Geremek estimates that fewer than 12 per cent of Parisian workers were similarly employed, with more than half of that estimated total engaged in diverse artisanal production just for the large local market. No French town witnessed an economic reorientation as marked as that of Ghent, where David Nicholas has shown that the grain trade supplanted cloth-making over the fourteenth century as the leading activity. In small towns like Bressuire in Poitou, studied by Favreau, townsfolk involved in cloth production often had secondary activities to ensure their income.

There was one industry in which many French towns did develop a potentially lucrative specialisation, namely arms production. In Poitiers, arms manufacturing was, after drapery, one of the few industries actively promoted by the municipal authorities in the fifteenth century. Some towns developed a widespread reputation for the weapons and armour they made, such as Tournai (where Berry herald noted 'they make a lot of mercery and military equipment'), or Tours, where Chevalier finds that local manufacturers were able to supply 95 per cent of the suits of armour required by the king's companies of the *ordonnance* in the 1470s.[4] But because the manufacture of more mundane weaponry and armour was simply an extension of other urban trades, arms production occurred in most big towns to meet local demand. Candlestick makers, bell-founders and brass-workers turned their skills, when required, to the casting of culverins and bombards, while demand for less advanced military equipment drew upon the general expertise of those who worked with wood, leather and metal. Jacques-Jean and Jacques Berret, manufacturers of mortars for grinding and of other metal vessels, were also sellers of firearms at Dax and Montauban during the 1420s and 1430s. War, even just the threat of it, was good for many existing businesses in the towns of late medieval France, just as some rural areas benefited from economic dislocation arising from warfare in neighbouring regions as we have seen in Chapter 2.

The general lack of large-scale specialisation in urban manufacturing made for a diverse economic base. Many towns must have resembled Montbrison, described by Étienne Fournial. Here the visitor could find the cobblers in their own street, the tanners in the rue Saint-Jean, the smiths and the weavers in the rue de Moingt: tradesman supplying first and foremost the town's population and the inhabitants of the surrounding countryside. The larger the town, the greater the range of manufacturing, most of it aimed squarely at the local market. Industry of this kind was workshop-based and centred on the family unit, supplemented – as resources allowed – by apprentices. The organisation of family units into autonomous interest groups is an issue which we shall examine below.

Trade

Long-distance trade also played a limited role in urban economies in France, for it was the local or regional market which counted more in commerce. This feature further strengthened the regional capital.

Some towns were simply not suited to international commerce. Bernard Chevalier notes that port facilities at Tours were poor, and the flow of the Loire varied greatly from summer to winter. The city's hinterland had little to offer to specialised markets. On the western seaboard, Yves Renouard observes that Bordeaux was a city of truly international importance due to its commerce in wine. At the start of the fourteenth century, the port may even have witnessed the largest volume of trade in Christendom, most of it in the hands of Gascon merchants. With this exception and that of La Rochelle, no city in France had a dominant presence in international markets, not even the capital itself. Paris was well placed to supply goods to central France and Burgundy, so long as political circumstances were favourable. Specialisation in luxury goods developed as a result. But Paris could never be described as a hub of international trade in its own right, dependent as it was upon relations with communities further up the Seine (especially Rouen) and an international market centred on Bruges. Indeed, as Jean Favier's study of the commercial life of Paris makes plain, the international importance of the Flemish city still eclipsed that of the French capital in the economy of north-western Europe in the fourteenth century.

In any case, some long-distance trade in France was conducted, not in urban markets, but in the more occasional fairs which were widely advertised by proclamation and held within striking distance of major trade routes, such as the Lille fair, or that of Chalon-sur-Saône in Burgundy. The west had only modest regional fairs, a fact which underlines the differences between coastal and continental France. The fifteenth century witnessed the rise of the fair of Lyon, closest in the kingdom to the great fair of Geneva which had long since attracted French merchants. Fairs certainly benefited

towns, but only indirectly. Henri Dubois notes that around one-fifth
of heads of household in Chalon-sur-Saône participated as vendors
or administrators in the fairs which were held in the great wooden
halls twice yearly on the edge of town – a large proportion, but not
enough to account on its own for the town's mercantile wealth, a
good part of which derived from the local wine trade. Travelling merchants were the main figures in such gatherings: men like Barthélemy
Bonis of Montauban in Languedoc, whose surviving ledgerbooks
record the sales of silks he acquired from Lyon, and the fine cloths
from Flanders which he had bought during his annual journey to
the northern fairs. In their home town, the activities of such men
were bound to leaven the economy. The fifteenth-century Chartres
merchant Jean des Freux bought products from afar, like Flemish herring and Orléanais wine. The vast majority of his business –
which Claudine Billot has followed through an exceptionally rich
series of 170 notarial acts – was conducted within a 25-mile radius of
Chartres.

But we should not forget that such entrepreneurs were in a
minority among traders. Much commerce was local, the countryside
supplying the town with food, the town supplying the countryside
and surrounding communities with manufactured goods, services
and – as we saw in an earlier chapter – a degree of investment.
The relatively diverse and regionalised economies of French towns
thus offered protection against the contraction which weighed heavily upon many larger European centres of commerce and industry
during our period.

And in any case, none of the *bonnes villes* of France relied primarily
on trade or commerce.

Administrative and spiritual capitals

In the towns of the Loire, indeed, 'administration was by far the
largest industry'.[5] Administration did not simply mean the work of
the municipality, but also the organs of royal and princely government which came to be located in relative security behind the walls
of the regional capital. The arrival of wealthy jurists and other public
servants brought new opportunities, most famously to the Bourges
merchant Jacques Coeur who shifted his business from his hometown to Tours to be closer to his principal market, the household
of Charles VII. The governors of Lyon asked the king for a *parlement*

in 1462 because they believed it would help 'people and maintain the town'.[6] André Bossuat was even led to wonder whether urban prosperity depended more on a town's role as a seat of justice than it did on its markets or the proximity of fairs.[7]

The regional primacy of many major towns was also grounded in prayer. The flow of pilgrims to celebrate saints' cults, particularly in episcopal cities with their rich stock of relics, was substantial. The Black Virgin of Le Puy greatly boosted that city's fortunes from the mid-thirteenth century on. Towns on major pilgrimage routes were also stopping-off points for large numbers of penitents, including Paris itself, where Pierre-André Sigal finds that the hospital of the confraternity of St James gave shelter, in the space of just 12 months (1368–9), to 16,000 pilgrims travelling to and from Mont-Saint-Michel. Religious processions brought penitents onto the town streets on a regular basis. Annual events like the procession of the Holy Sacrament at Aire-sur-La-Lys, studied by Paul Bertin, had a primarily local resonance, reinforcing existing hierarchies in urban society through the roles ascribed to various groups in ritual performances. But they also drew in large numbers from further afield. The annual procession at Tournai brought participants from northern France and Flanders throughout the late Middle Ages, with the cities of Ghent and Bruges sending deputations to process every year with local confraternities and parish groups. From the later fourteenth century on, towns were also venues for large-scale religious theatre (particularly but not exclusively in the north and north-east). At Lille, Graham Runnalls finds that two to three mystery plays were staged every year in the period 1382–1544. More routinely, episcopal courts attracted a steady trickle into the chief diocesan centres. Even in a small city like Carcassonne, Monique Bourin is able to show that the bishop's jurisdiction was a strong pull-factor: between May 1338 and July 1341, more than 1,200 named individuals paid their dues for the bishop's justice in the city, nearly two-thirds of them from outside its walls. Sacred objects found their way in from the countryside too. The reliquaries of the small Breton parish of Orvault were deposited in Nantes, presumably diminishing the spiritual life of peasants who bequeathed money and possessions in their wills for the upkeep and glory of such important objects.

Clearly the town was a spiritual capital for the surrounding countryside. But in important ways we should now explore, religious life in urban France was also quite different from rural experiences discussed earlier in this book.

The Church and Religion

The clergy

The most striking difference between town and country was in the number and range of clerics resident in the former. In Reims, the seat of a large northern bishopric, Desportes thinks the clergy amounted to around 12 per cent of the population, while elsewhere – Toulouse, Poitiers, Besançon – a still-impressive estimate of 5 per cent is more common. Parish priests could be numerous in cities (20–30 in Poitiers, Orléans or Metz, nearly 40 in Paris), but their numbers were as nothing compared to the clerical supernumeraries who congregated in towns, many of them immigrants from peasant backgrounds who found employment as reserve priests servicing the needs of the dead. At Aurillac, the members of this clerical proletariat grew from around 30 in 1344 to over 100 in 1508 (and this in a population of a few thousand at most).

Clerics in the town were part of a denser vocational network than their counterparts in the country, enjoying more opportunities for association within their group. They were also less likely to be living near (or even among) their lay relatives than their counterparts in the country. Universities are probably the most extreme example of a clerical community within towns. Perhaps it was complete immersion in that milieu which caused the Occitan-speaking Cahorsin pope John XXII (1316–34) to retain only the most superficial command of French from the early years he spent studying in Paris and Orléans. But urban parish priests were also further from their flock than their rural counterparts, often from reasonably well-off urban families with the benefit of a higher level of education. Thomas Du Marest was one such. This priest at Coutances in Normandy came from a wealthy Carentan background, and his unique *Livre de comptes* includes mention of the 6 years he spent studying at Paris, at a cost of 40 lbs a year for his food and lodgings.

Religious practices

Differences between town and country are emphasised in the work of Jacques Chiffoleau, whose research on Avignon wills identified a number of changes in specifically urban religious mentalities in the late Middle Ages. Mass mortality and greatly increased immigration combined to turn late medieval men and women in towns into 'orphans', disconnected from their rural or small-town kin groups, fearful of a solitary and unremembered demise, eager to express their individuality and status in death through 'flamboyant' religious practices like multiple masses and funeral processions. Growing numbers of reserve priests both caused and resulted from such developments, for it was from among their ranks that townsfolk hired the priests to participate in their funerary processions and to perform masses for the dead.

A key further element in the changes identified at Avignon was the growing popularity of the confraternity, serving as a form of surrogate family and offering mutual assistance, for burials in particular. Fifty-five per cent of the population who left a surviving will at Avignon were members of two or three confraternities, in contrast to the countryside where, as we have seen, there was usually no more than one confraternity to which the vast majority of parishioners belonged. Membership lists for three Avignon confraternities reveal their recruitment of immigrants from across the south-east of France, from Burgundy, the Île-de-France and the Low Countries. At Rouen, one of the many spots enlightened by Catherine Vincent's work on confraternities, these associations tended to be concentrated in artisanal districts of the town, where the immigrant population usually settled.

One should perhaps be wary of exaggerating contrasts between religious life in town and country on the basis of the Avignon evidence. As Chiffoleau himself acknowledged, that city experienced a particularly remarkable expansion in the fourteenth century as a result of the prolonged presence there of the papacy. Elsewhere, historians find differences between town and country to be less marked, or at least the rate of change to be slower. At Toulouse (studied by Marie-Claude Marandet) there were indeed developments in funerary practices comparable to those discernible in Avignon, but only in the fifteenth century, fully two generations later; and when change did emerge, burials were less ostentatious, the increased demand for masses more modest. Urban society in Toulouse took the greatly increased mortality of the period in its stride, continuing for longer to follow traditional religious practices in keeping with those of the surrounding countryside. Here urban religious practices were still changing, but at a slower rate than in some other cities.

The municipality and the church

Where urban religious life certainly did differ from that of the
countryside was in the increasing involvement of civic authorities.
Churchmen were numerous in urban society, and the church was a
substantial owner of property there, but the number of regions where
the clergy played a formal role in municipal government (such as
Dauphiné) was small, and in some (such as Gascony or Provence)
they were excluded altogether. By contrast, municipal authorities
were taking an active interest in a number of roles previously dominated by the church.

Schooling was still usually carried out by clerics, but towards the
close of our period municipalities were beginning to take responsibility for founding new schools and lodging existing ones, in 1476 at
Châtellerault, in 1488 at Albi. Higher authorities were instrumental
in the creation of universities by the pope, but at Cahors (1332) and
Bordeaux (1441) the municipality figured prominently among petitioners for the creation of a university, and at Poitiers (from 1431)
Favreau finds that the town authorities helped meet the costs of the
construction of the buildings used by the masters, their salaries, and
even the purchase and care of books for the library. Poor relief also
witnessed a gradual degree of municipalisation towards the close of
our period, when civic authorities in Lyon (1478) took on responsibility for the *Hôtel-Dieu* at a time of growing indigence. Preaching
and the performance of mystery plays mobilised the clergy in considerable numbers, but municipal authorities took a close interest in
both, not least because public order might be at stake. At Amiens
in 1485, a preacher was imprisoned for stirring up trouble between
the municipality and the church authorities. Many such preachers
were mendicants, of course, men who were not complete strangers
to the countryside by any means, but who belonged to a primarily urban organisation which was increasingly popular with well-off
townsfolk.

None of these trends amounted to the emergence in later medieval
France of what historians have termed 'civic religion', if by that one
means the control of the sacred by civic authorities to their own
ends. The municipality was 'a support and an ally' of the church
in such instances, 'nothing more'.[8] But as a consequence of the
growing involvement of municipal authorities in the affairs of the
church, the conditions for the heterodoxy of the sixteenth century
were gradually emerging, more strongly in the town than in the countryside – a development accelerated by the greater distance between

urban clergy and their flock compared to the countryside, and in differences between religious practices in both.

Government

Municipal authorities were able to take on a greater role in matters previously dominated by the church for the simple reason that the reach and sophistication of urban government developed considerably in our period. Compared to the attention paid to the growth of royal administrative structures in the late Middle Ages, the topic is a relatively neglected one – unjustifiably so, for the administration of the 'good towns' was increasingly perceived as a service to the king.

Struck by the spread of consulates in the south and of communes in the north, scholars of French towns used to identify the twelfth and thirteenth centuries as the great age of emancipation and institutional development. Extricated from seigneurial or episcopal power by the energies and abilities of their leading inhabitants, endowed with many of the characteristics of lordship themselves, French communes and consulates represented a new form of public authority in the kingdom whose origins and organs of government found parallels in many other parts of Europe. The later Middle Ages, by contrast, attracted less attention. For those who did write on the subject, notably Henri Sée in his study of the towns under Louis XI, the fourteenth and fifteenth centuries witnessed the decadence of municipalities and the increasing tutelage over them of the royal state.

Closer inspection has revealed fundamental flaws in this interpretation of the later medieval period. Most communities in the kingdom were in fact left untouched by the high medieval spread of communal and consular government in France, particularly (but not exclusively) the towns in the geographical centre of the realm. Bernard Chevalier has estimated that only one-quarter of the urban communities of the realm existed as legal authorities in their own right by 1300, governed by a mayor and *échevins* (mainly in the north) or by consuls or *jurats* (mainly in the south and south-west). The exercise of public authority in the great majority of French towns was therefore very limited indeed at the start of our period. In these cases, it was the later Middle Ages which constituted the great age of emancipation and institutional growth. Second, whatever the origins of the municipality and the nature of its early development, existing forms of urban government were transformed by late medieval pressures of war and taxation. Consultation within a wider polity consisting of taxpayers and other interest groups became more regular. At the centre of the developing urban polity, the oligarchy which commonly provided members of the governing executive strengthened its hold on power. The political history of later medieval France, unlike that of Italy, is not predominantly the history of its towns. But such was the growth in municipal government that the development of public authority in the realm cannot be properly understood without reference to the *bonnes villes*.

Walls and taxes

The main forces driving forward the transformation of municipal government were defence and finance. Although urban fortifications existed in some regions in the twelfth and thirteenth centuries (in the Languedoc, for instance, as a result of the Albigensian crusades), the spread of wall-building programmes from the middle of the fourteenth century onwards was remarkable. In the wake of Crécy (1346), new walls were built and existing defences were strengthened in many towns across the realm. Following Poitiers 10 years later, the practice became widespread.

The expense of defence measures was very great. In addition to raw materials, there was usually some cost attaching to acquisitions and demolitions so construction could go ahead. Urban authorities occasionally succeeded in cajoling inhabitants and even nearby villagers into contributing labour free of charge, but the hire of workers remained a major item of expenditure, one which was rising in precisely this period due to changing conditions. In his study of urban fortifications, Philippe Contamine finds that no less than 71 per cent of the expenditure of the authorities of Troyes was devoted to reinforcing the walls from March to November 1359.

It would be fair to say that the greatest efforts to build walls were located in the period 1340–80. But given the insecurity which prevailed in much of later medieval France, no town could afford to neglect its ramparts for long. The existence of walls also generated ancillary costs: the acquisition of artillery to dissuade or repel aggression, or of chains to control access to streets, gates and waterways; the arming and organisation of the watch, of key-keepers, and of crossbowmen and archers to man the towers. Even allowing for Louis IX's crusades or Philip IV's tax demands for his wars in Flanders and Aquitaine, the urban walls of later medieval France mobilised money and manpower on an unprecedented scale in that kingdom's history. The story is harder to tell than the massive expenditure of the crown on warfare, but it is scarcely any less important.

Where was the money to be found? Municipal revenues, much like those of the crown, were still classified as 'ordinary' and 'extraordinary' by contemporaries. Ordinary income consisted of profits from municipal property and rights, often farmed out to private individuals who guaranteed the town a regular revenue for a fixed period, such as fishing rights in the town moat noted by Édouard de Barthélemy in his study of Châlons in Champagne, or rights to the dung which dropped on the roads, mentioned by Henri Delsol in his work on Brive. Virtually every local monograph of a late medieval French town emphasises the hopeless insufficiency of ordinary income in these testing years, certainly compared to the greater profits available from the same source in Flanders. At Aire-sur-la-Lys, studied by Paul Bertin, ordinary income amounted to one-sixth of total receipts in 1484. Hence the financial weakness bordering on insolvency of many northern municipalities at the start of our period – the achilles heel of communes which, even if had they acquired much-vaunted liberties in an earlier age, rarely had the means to become an enduring and influential form of public authority.

Extraordinary revenue was the answer to the problem, most commonly indirect taxation on the sale of goods and produce (such as the *maltote* on wine or beer) or direct taxes levied on property and/or income (commonly known as the *taille*). Municipalities did not wait for the development of royal fiscality to begin taxing those who lived within the city walls, particularly in southern France. Urban taxes preceded and in many ways prefigured royal taxation, as Albert Rigaudière and others have shown. But if municipalities had the means and experience to tax, successive royal administrations took care to remind them that they needed the king's permission to do so. It became increasingly common, from the reign of Philip VI onwards, for tax-raising powers to be granted to civic governors, upon request and on a temporary basis, to carry out royal instructions to restore or build walls. In this respect the crown endorsed revenue-sharing arrangements with municipal authorities which bear comparison with the rights accorded to the more important territorial lords of the realm. The king was effectively 'introducing the principle of royal sovereignty into municipal fiscality'.[9] Later, some towns (especially in the north) began to supplement extraordinary revenue by selling life-rents – that is to say, an annual income for life drawn on the future income of the municipality in return for a loan of money. Again, higher permission was sought for such local initiatives.

The municipality was born of the duty to build walls in many towns across France in the later Middle Ages. At Clermont, discussed by Gabriel Fournier in his study of fortifications in Auvergne, Philip VI's instructions to build a single wall round the city was followed, in 1379, by the grant of the right of assembly to the inhabitants, and with it permission to elect three representatives. Early in the fifteenth century the town acquired royal permission to appoint nine *conseillers* to advise the executive. Right of assembly, the election of an executive, the appointment of an advisory body, the employment of municipal subordinates and the emergence of a bureaucracy: these were the main elements of municipal government as it developed under the pressure of royal fiscal needs in later medieval France.

Municipal assemblies

The right of town dwellers to gather and discuss their affairs free from suspicion of illicit assembly was a prerogative of some communities by the thirteenth century, and was justified by the legal principle that what concerned all should be agreed by all (*Quod omnes tangit*). But many communities did not acquire the right of assembly until our period, and assemblies became more frequent from the reign of Charles V on, when grants of tax-raising powers were made on the condition that levies be raised by general consent. At Sens from 1343, the inhabitants were permitted to assemble once a year to elect representatives. As the need for more regular meetings grew, the king granted the Sénonais the right to assemble 'as often as they like under the authority of one of the magistrates' (1430).[10] Large assemblies numbering several hundred participants were summoned by the town bell at Troyes, to hear news of monetary devaluation in February 1430, for instance. Such assemblies brought together elements in urban society which might otherwise seek to maintain a distance between themselves: clerics of different hues, royal officers, members of the urban nobility, heads of households and the *menu peuple*. The presence of the latter was something many municipal executives usually sought to avoid. At Langres, studied by Ferdinand Claudon, notables acquired permission from Charles VII in 1445 to elect *échevins* who could act without reference to a general assembly, because in their view the presence of townsfolk of low estate was a source of division and disorder in municipal affairs. We might hesitate to describe all of those present as active participants in assemblies, given the strong evidence from assembly minutes that there was an eloquent, influential minority and 'the majority that says yes'.[11]

Those provisos made, the role of assemblies in urban politics was significant. Even where the constitutional role of assemblies was relatively limited, their existence is proof enough of an emerging urban polity which was clearly linked to a wider community of the realm: hearing and sharing news, forming opinions, deliberating, anticipating and planning. And as Bernard Guenée notes in his study of the chronicler Michel Pintoin, the so-called Religious of Saint-Denis, the opinions of urban notables were beginning to preoccupy those who recorded the history of our period. 'It was in the towns that the destiny of the kingdom was being played out.'[12] Urban assemblies – in ways that were both similar to and different from the experience of processions and meetings of the estates – created an occasion for the king's subjects to reflect on the fact that they were part of a wider polity.

Executive, council and servants

The eloquent minority which tended to dominate proceedings in general assemblies commonly emerged from two sub-groups in municipal political life, the one overlapping the other. The first of these subgroups was the elected executive (*échevins, consuls, syndics* or *jurats*), the second the *conseil*.

Increasingly, the executive was subordinated to the overall authority of a single officeholder, whether mayor or first consul, with the result that whether towns were communes, consulates or seigneurial communities in an earlier age, constitutionally they began to resemble one another in the late Middle Ages. The numerous tasks which befell the magistrates may be grouped around three basic responsibilities: to judge, lead and represent. Municipal jurisdiction was not, as is sometimes claimed, systematically eroded by the encroachment of higher courts in the later Middle Ages in France. Many towns still exercised high, middle and low justice in the fifteenth century, an important point given the widely held view among contemporaries that the exercise of justice was the most convincing proof of authority. These responsibilities made for a heavy workload, leading Agnès Vagnon to describe the duties of the consuls of Lyon as Herculean. Historians are used to seeing the later medieval period as one of accelerated governmental growth under the pressure of war, but it is vital to recognise that growth was particularly marked in the municipalities.

Eligibility for office and election practices varied from one town to the next, but both tended to restrict office-bearing to a select group within urban society. At Bordeaux, according to the *Livre des Bouillons* (c. 1375), one could only be considered for election as a *jurat* if one was born in the city or its immediate region and resided there; if one was at least 25 years old, of legitimate birth and of non-servile condition; and, most restrictive of all, if one possessed property and capital to the value of 1000 *l.b.*, or an annual income amounting to 200 *l.b.* As the conditions of office-holding remained narrow, so the dignity and privileges of office-bearing increased through the later medieval period. At Le Puy, Delcambre has shown that the consuls, their families, and even their servants enjoyed the king's safeguard in the fifteenth century. At Saint-Jean-d'Angély, those guilty of slighting the mayor were fined and required to seek his pardon, cap in hand and on bended knee. Here, as in Dijon, the funeral expenses of a mayor who died in office were met by the municipality.

An executive which sought to make itself exclusive and exalted was generally assisted in its work by an advisory body known as the *conseil*, recruits to which very often came from the same milieux as *échevins* or consuls. At Eu in the north, Suzanne Deck has shown that it was normal practice for one intake of *échevins* simply to become the town's *conseillers* the following year. But as the volume and complexity of business increased, so expert and experienced advisers became increasingly desirable. The rise of the legist in municipal government was as marked as his progress in the service of the king or prince. Legists were often appointed quite separately from the *conseil* to advise the municipal executive, but were also becoming more common within this body too. At Amiens, studied by Édouard Maugis, one such legist was Master Trystram de Fontaines, active until 1446, whose opinion was usually the first to be sought on matters of importance, and who was sometimes called upon to replace the mayor to explain sensitive matters to general assemblies. The rise of the legists did not strike all contemporaries as a welcome development. At Dijon in 1450, Phelippot Martin, then an inspector of taxes on wine, declared that 'the people don't want advocates and procurators as mayors, ... it would be better to have a merchant who knows the condition of ordinary people, and how to deal with a legal case in just 2 days.'[13] But the *homme de loi* was fast becoming an essential feature of municipal government, and dealings with external agencies was a major reason for the change.

Appointed by and answerable to the municipal executive was a group of servants who were small in number, but far more numerous in proportion to the rest of the population than royal officers were within the kingdom. A list from Tournai in 1421 includes over 60 such men, from the key administrative staff (procurators, clerks or receivers) to keepers of the peace (among them 24 sergeants) and other specialised personnel (messengers, clock keeper, executioner, town surgeon). The most important figure among these subordinates was undoubtedly the town clerk, commonly nominated from among the ranks of the notables himself, often a notary in origin. Unlike magistrates, town clerks usually served until they resigned, were dismissed, or died. At Lyon, studied by René Fédou, Guillaume de Cuysel served as *procureur-secrétaire* for 26 years until 1407; later, Rolin de Mâcon managed 21 years in the post. Town clerks were responsible for keeping the first town council minutes. Between 1307 and 1488, at least 64 *bonnes villes* began to keep these practical documents, three-quarters of which predate the first known examples from England. The relative precocity of French municipal government is further evinced in the emergence of town accounts, widespread from the second half of the fourteenth century on, when wall-building programmes began in earnest. The growing volume of documentation (to which we might add registers of tax assessments, legal judgments of magistrates sitting as a court, collections of municipal correspondence and so forth) necessitated the keeping of archives, a task which also often fell to the town clerk or his growing number of auxiliaries.

The upsurge of governmental activity in French towns did not touch all parts of the realm equally. In the region of Forez to the west of Lyon, consulates were only gradually beginning to appear in the second half of the fourteenth century. In the small Auvergnat town of Ussel studied by Jean-Loup Lemaître, there is no sign of a *conseil* or town clerk to assist the consuls in their work until the eighteenth century. But elsewhere the role of the municipality gained considerably in substance and definition. It is important to try to identify in whose hands that authority typically lay, and how secure their possession of it really was.

Governors and Governed

The oligarchy

According to a plea made before *Parlement* in 1447, the men who ran the consulate at Montferrand had generally made their money on the cattle market. In Arras, as Jean Lestocquoy has shown, the leading group consisted of families which had made their fortune in commerce, money-lending, inn-keeping, tapestry-making and the law. In Rennes, notes Jean-Pierre Leguay, it was the merchants who held sway.

The extent of the monopoly over public office which such families held can be startling. Pierre Desportes notes that it was theoretically possible for 492 different men to have held the office of *échevin* at Reims between 1290 and 1330 (based on annual elections for 12 posts per year). But just 81 names occur in the complete election lists for the period, and these men themselves came from 53 families. It would perhaps be a mistake to overemphasise the homogeneity of the oligarchy, because they were quite capable of falling out with each other. But whatever the differences that might arise between them, the ruling group also knew how to stick together. Guy de Valous has shown how the genealogies of around 30 leading lineages in Lyon intertwine with one another in our period, even for second and third marriages. The oligarchy's stamping ground is recognisable from patterns of property ownership in Dijon, where Françoise Humbert finds that the notables tended to settle in the parish of Saint-Médard (where the town hall was also located).

Historians of a few earlier and many later periods in French history will be familiar with the phenomenon of the urban oligarchy; the same is true of England or the Low Countries. Already in the Kingdom of France in the late thirteenth century, Philippe de Beaumanoir was well aware that urban government lay in the hands of a wealthy few whom the rest of the population feared. In the capital, that oligarchy began to emerge when the merchants who made their fortune by control of river traffic came to form the core of the magistrature. But the key point is that rarely in French history have conditions been so favourable to the exercise of oligarchical power as they were between c. 1350 and c.1450.

Kleptocracy, plutocracy and technocracy

Historians have not been slow to single out the crimes of the oligarchy, above all their tendency to deflect the weight of the fiscal burden away from the wealthy and onto the population at large. This goal could be pursued through indirect taxation which affected consumers generally, as opposed to direct taxation which expected (in theory at least) that 'the strong carry the weak'. At its most extreme, the redistribution of the tax burden made civic government resemble, in the view of the historian of Lille, Alan Derville, 'a vast business organised to profit the great families'.[14]

Recourse to the direct taxation was certainly rare in some towns, particularly northern ones, and here the oligarchy might have derived benefit from its influence over fiscal mechanisms. But elsewhere, the *taille* remained a central plank of civic finances. At Saint-Flour, as Albert Rigaudière notes, direct taxes accounted for nearly 40 per cent of municipal revenues between 1378 and 1466, while at Albi in 1359–60, Jürgen Neyer finds that over 70 per cent of revenues were raised that way. There is no reason to suppose the wealthy were any more enthusiastic about paying their dues than other groups, but it is clear that they were most likely to have the liquid cash to do so. At Reims, at the height of Philip IV's tax demands, Desportes finds that citizens whose fortunes exceeded 1,000 *l.t.* paid five-sixths of the town's total contribution. The raising of indirect taxes relied on the willingness of rich bidders to take on the farm of the tax and guarantee a fixed income to the town. Payment of direct taxes could also require the intervention of the rich, mainly because raising the *taille* was always a slow process and usually an incomplete one. No wonder the consuls of Saint-Flour consistently came from the top 30 per cent of the city's taxpayers. While we might suspect that French towns were run by kleptocracies in the later Middle Ages, we can say for sure that government by plutocracy was difficult to avoid.

The dominant position of a small group in urban society should also be understood, in part at least, as the result of the growing demands of running a municipal administration. Criticisms of the inability of municipal executive office holders to speak well, to read and write, and even to know Latin suggest that these skills were becoming requisites of office in some towns. Once possession of the necessary attributes had been proven, able men could find it very hard to retire. In January 1415, Marc Vilain was re-elected as procurator of Tournai, despite having announced his unwillingness to serve on the grounds he was '62 years of age or more, feeble, corpulent, one-eyed and diminished to such an extent he could no longer go out in the dark, work hard, or ride a horse like a young man as the office required'.[15] Legal training was increasingly central to the work of municipal government, and such expertise was most likely to be found among the ruling families. It would be inaccurate to conclude that late medieval French towns were ruled by a meritocracy, but rule by technocracy was becoming a necessity. One can readily understand that to hold public office might seem an honour, or that service could seem an end in itself, although we should remember that public office was also the best way to advance one's interests, and those of friends and family. The work itself was lightly remunerated or not at all: the consuls of Le Puy received an annual salary of 10 *l.*, but not the magistrates of Amiens or Chartres.

Rivals or allies?

There were at least three groups with the potential to rival, or ally with, the urban oligarchy in municipal affairs: religious institutions, the nobility and the guilds.

Struggles between bishops, chapters or local abbots and the emerging lay authority were still a feature in many parts of France in our period, and some municipal executives only gradually emerged from the shadow of their church, such as that of Angers studied by Jean-Michel Matz. The rights of ecclesiastical institutions could be extensive within the city walls, particularly in matters of jurisdiction and exemption. But several factors generally assisted the municipal executive in its efforts to cohabit with ecclesiastical privilege or, when necessary, to combat it. Clerical absenteeism at the higher levels meant that scope for conflict was often reduced. The increasing sophistication and resources of the municipal executive permitted dogged resistance and even victory against ecclesiastics. Municipalities might also appeal over the head of the clergy to the king or his officers, although this could cut both ways. The growing advantages of the municipal executive did not abolish the moral authority of ecclesiastics within the town, and indeed that authority might still prove useful to urban governments. But it is fair to say that in most parts of the realm, the rights of the clergy did not impinge drastically or even at all on the exercise of municipal authority. Towns like Lisieux, where Jean Lesquier finds that ecclesiastical influence in urban government was still marked well into the fifteenth century, were exceptional.

The place of the nobility in French towns is often seen as minimal compared to their role in Flanders or parts of Italy. In fact, the presence of nobles in French towns was ancient and remained significant into our period. Although the proportion of nobles within the population was commonly very small – at Périgueux or Nîmes, around 1 per cent of the inhabitants in the view of Arlette Higounet-Nadal – what mattered was their weight in relation to the wealthy notables of the town. In Dijon, Thierry Dutour calculates that nobles constituted as much as 10 per cent of that leading sector between 1350 and 1410. At Tarascon, Michel Hébert finds that membership of the municipal *conseil* was shared between a group of 49 nobles and 68 *bourgeois* between 1370 and 1400. Although the nobility claimed to be distinct from other sectors of the population, their role in government indicates they were natural allies of the ruling elite and indeed often part of it. The presence of nobles in French towns clearly did not diminish the urban oligarchy: in key respects, it strengthened their dominance.

The third group which might counterbalance the power of the oligarchy were the masters of trades organised into professional associations. The organisation of tradesmen into guilds, that is to say autonomous corporations with statutes sanctioned by the crown, was a late medieval development. Royal grants of statutes are rare before the middle of the fourteenth century, but over 300 are recorded by 1530. In the long term, guilds would acquire considerable autonomy and influence within municipalities, and already in the fifteenth century they were coming to be seen by monarchs as a mechanism for assuring social peace in towns. With this kind of support, guilds would become a threat to the oligarchy's powers. But incorporation was a slow and uneven process within our period, strongest in Paris and in the north, much less marked in the south, centre or west. The late medieval emergence of guilds that were relatively free of municipal control was not, therefore, a serious problem for oligarchies in our period.

The organisation of manual workers into interest groups by trade under the municipality, rather than formal guild structures approved by the crown, was a fact of urban life long before the first autonomous corporations emerged. Masters came together in the twelfth and thirteenth centuries to take mutually beneficial decisions about their trade, to regulate matters pertaining to it, and to attend to devotional or charitable concerns. Paris is perhaps the earliest city in which trade organisations could be listed: 101 figure in the *Livre des métiers* compiled on the order of the king's *prévôt*, Étienne Boileau, in 1268. Paris is exceptional among French cities in that the trades generally fell under the jurisdiction of the king's *prévôt*. Elsewhere, trades were dependent upon municipal, not royal, authority.

Although their powers were generally limited to the regulation of their craft, in some regions the trades did attain a constitutional role in town government, particularly in Languedoc, Ponthieu, Picardy, the Amienois and Beauvaisis. At Nîmes, Alès and Lodève, the election of consuls and advisers from a population divided for electoral purposes into units known as *échelles* gave tradesmen a significant role. Often the participation of tradesmen in municipal government was greatest among the wealthiest crafts, those most likely to have connections to the notables such as the drapers, grocers and furriers. But outside the north- and south-east, little or no place was made for tradesmen in many French municipal administrations in our period. Where such a role existed, it did not necessarily win widespread acceptance. Étienne Delcambre records how a commissioner from the *Parlement* of Paris visiting Montferrand in 1440 informed one of the consuls, Étienne le Bourrelier, a saddler by trade, that he had never seen a man of his ilk holding the office of consul before, and that he should immediately resign and surrender the keys and registers in his possession. Trade participation in government had yet to become an accepted tradition, despite the fact that the trades figured strongly in the 'greater and better part' of the urban population which paid taxes across France. Of 516 citizens of Tours who were deemed to be sufficiently important to perform an oath of loyalty to Louis XI in 1471, nearly three-quarters were masters within a craft. The remaining minority consisted of merchants, lawyers and other bourgeois, from whose ranks a far greater proportion of civic governors emerged.

Urban Revolt

One suspects that statistics like the last one quoted were a source of grievance among the trades, and there is no doubt they had a part to play in urban revolt against the oligarchy in French towns in our period. Butchers played a prominent role in the revolt of Metz in 1406, the rising associated with Simon Caboche in Paris in 1413, and the *rebeyne* of Lyon in 1436. But generally speaking, urban revolts in later medieval France were not orchestrated by guildsmen seeking inclusion in government. The most prominent exception is the revolt of Tournai in 1423–8, but this was a town on the periphery of the Low Countries where guildsmen had forced themselves into government through a *révolution des métiers*, notably in Ghent and Brussels. No single trade was of sufficient economic importance in French towns to mobilise a large sector of the population, as the woolworkers (Ciompi) did in Florence in 1378. The diversified economy of the late medieval French town ensured a measure of social peace at least.

The widespread nature of revolt

But urban risings figure far more prominently in the historical record than rural revolts, a fact which has been disguised to some extent by an older historiography of the subject which tended to group rebellions in seemingly discrete chronological cycles.

There was certainly an early highpoint of unrest in the 1350s as the effects of war and taxation began to take their toll. Uprisings occurred at this time in the capital, but also in Arras, Amiens and Laon in the north, in Rouen and other parts of Normandy, in Toulouse and Lavaur in the south, and in a group of eastern towns including Villefranche-sur-Saône, Belleville and Montbrison. But we should not imagine that the years before and after this intense period of revolt were free from incident. Paris and Rouen witnessed commotions in the 1340s and early 1350s, while revolts occurred in Tournai, Paris and Valenciennes in the 1360s, sometimes in response to local tax initiatives rather than those directly from the crown.

These last events almost run into what was once considered a second great cycle of revolts associated with the taxation which funded the victories of Charles V's reign. The most famous occurred in Paris, where the rebels of March 1382 were known as the *maillotins* because of the hammers with which they armed themselves from a royal arsenal. A rising in Rouen, known by an Old French term for sedition, the *Harelle*, was one of several revolts that affected towns across the duchy of Normandy in February and March of the same year. Commotions and riotous assemblies also occurred during these months at Orléans, Bourges, Laon, Reims and Amiens. Revolts in the northern half of the kingdom were preceded or accompanied by further disruption of the social peace in southern towns, in particular at Lyon, Le Puy, Montpellier, Béziers, Alès, Nîmes and Toulouse.

The third commonly cited period of urban revolts, located between 1412–22 and linked to the struggle between Armagnac and Burgundian factions within the kingdom, was also a high watermark in a swollen tide of dissidence in the fifteenth century. Violence engulfed the capital in 1413 and again in 1418 during this 'late' phase of urban revolts, and commotions are recorded in the south (at Carcassonne and Limoux) and the north (in Soissons, Noyon and Tournai). Whereas the impact of the Navarrese party of the 1350s was limited to Paris and some northern towns connected to it by the river network, two generations later the proven importance of towns and the politicisation of urban society through assemblies and tax-paying ensured that the Burgundian–Armagnac struggle was felt in different ways in many urban centres across the realm. La Rochelle in the west, Toulouse in the south, Lyon in the east and Tournai in the north all witnessed public disorder arising from civil conflict.

But urban uprisings continued well into the fifteenth century, disrupting any clear pattern we might care to discern at the regnal level. The 1430s witnessed very many urban revolts: at Chartres, Pontoise and Paris, as well as better known rebellions in Amiens and Lyon, all during the period of renewed royal taxation discussed in an earlier chapter. Even Bernard Chevalier's view that social peace increased from around the middle of the fifteenth century is only true to an extent. As André Leguai has shown, Louis XI's reign witnessed a great number of urban revolts: at the start of his reign in Angers, Reims, Perpignan and Alençon, and towards the close, when revolts shook towns of the formerly Burgundian dominions, notably Dijon and Arras in 1477–8. Further uprisings are recorded in some central and south-western towns, notably Bourges in 1474.

At the very start of our period, when regional leagues of nobles and churchmen joined in 1314–15 to voice their discontent at royal policy, municipalities played little or no part. From the 1340s on, however, urban revolt became a sustained feature of French political culture, far more so than rebellion in the countryside.

Revolt and taxation

Insofar as a general cause of revolt might be discerned, the growing burden of taxation stands out. Highpoints of dissidence clearly match periods of heavy tax demands from the crown, notably the revolts of the 1350s, the later 1370s to early 1380s, and the 1430s. Outside these periods, locally variable taxation had its effect too. Peasant households could at least avoid the full blow of indirect taxes through their privileged role in food production and barter. For the urban rich, indirect taxes on consumables represented less of a demand on their pockets than it did for poorer folk who had to buy staple commodities. Moreover, the wealthy in towns could avoid direct taxes through the pursuit of exemptions, an advantage which the rural aristocracy enjoyed anyway. But none of these options was open to the bulk of the urban population, obliged to buy food on which indirect taxes were raised, or pay direct taxes on their possessions. This was the sector of French population which was most exposed to the upsurge in taxation in the late Middle Ages. Moreover, urban administrations were getting better at recording the tax obligations of town dwellers in *livres d'estimes*, registers of the *taille* and other assessments (even if these documents were far from perfect). Alongside taxpayers who found their outgoings increasing – and increasingly hard to avoid – there was a marginal element in the population of most towns which might be readily persuaded to participate in revolt.

The foregoing helps explain why popular anger was usually directed against the men most associated with taxes. At Rouen in August 1382 and Caen a year later, as Léon Mirot notes in his work on urban rebellions, it was the arrival of tax collectors which stirred up the populace. Members of the ruling oligarchy sometimes tacitly supported or even openly encouraged revolts against taxation, for ultimately they were tax payers too. At Montpellier in 1379, Jan Rogozinski finds that the consuls were accused by the crown of having led the rebellious crowd against its officials. At Lyon in 1436, studied by René Fédou, revolt was set in motion by an assembly of townsfolk summoned by the consuls to intimidate royal commissioners who had brought a tax demand to the city.

But very often, the governing elite of the town were themselves the agents of royal fiscality. In the case of Arras in 1355 studied by Jean Lestocquoy, popular anger at a local tax to pay for troops to send to John II ended in the defenestration of several governors by the crowd. In a highly symbolic act during the *Harelle* at Rouen analyzed by Charles Radding, the rebels seized a rich draper, paraded him round the market square dressed as a king and forced him to pronounce all taxes abolished. Here, at least, no one was in any doubt: royal fiscal power was vested in the local oligarchy. To say that revolts were directed against the king's taxes and its agents rather than against the civic elite is, in many cases, to draw too firm a distinction between the recruiting grounds of royal and municipal government.

But that very association with the king was what generally guaranteed the survival of the oligarchy and the suppression of rebellion. The most serious revolts of the period were put down by force, whatever early gains they might have achieved: at Lyon in 1436, for instance, where three decapitations, one mutilation and 120 banishments settled the affair. If, to some extent, violence was becoming an acknowledged feature of relations between the urban populace and their governors, there were clearly limits to how far one could go. In any case, the governing elite might find ways of preventing trouble before it happened. Recognised measures for nipping matters in the bud included the banning of assemblies, the control of the flow of information by demanding that visitors report directly to a magistrate on arrival in the town, and restrictions on the bearing of arms. Some towns witnessed isolated expressions of discontent but no open revolts at all in our period, such as Poitiers. Perhaps in such cases social peace was maintained, not simply though fear, but through the ability of urban institutions and inhabitants to resolve conflict and strike a balance in difficult times, as Jan Rogozinski finds in his study of fourteenth-century Montpellier.

If, when peace broke down, the hold on power of a small group of families was loosened, on the whole they managed to restore their grip, usually with the help of the king's men: for they too were often the king's men themselves. The importance of these oligarchies more widely in the kingdom can now be considered.

Extra Muros: Towns in the Kingdom

Writing in the late thirteenth century, Philippe de Beaumanoir believed the king should treat his towns as he would an underage minor. Subjection to the monarch was, in theory, the default position of the municipality – a relationship enshrined in a community's privileges which had to be renewed at the start of a reign, and which could be suspended or revoked at any point during it. In the course of our period, however, municipal authorities acquired a far greater degree of autonomy than ever before.

The locality

The most obvious sector in which French municipalities exercised political influence in the later Middle Ages was the *banlieue*, an area of variable size within the town's jurisdiction. The *banlieue* of Lille was relatively small because the authority of the counts of Flanders had been well-established in the surrounding countryside in earlier times. At Bordeaux and Toulouse, the *banlieue* extended deep into the surrounding countryside, relatively unhindered by ducal or comital jurisdictions.

As the powers of municipal authorities developed, so the inhabitants of the *banlieue* could find themselves contributing on an equal footing with townsfolk to municipal taxes, or assisting them in some other way. Between 1422 and 1429, the minutes of the council of Reims published by Sylvette Guilbert record a series of instructions to surrounding villagers issued by the magistrates: to send men to help clear the moats and archers to guard the city's ramparts; to keep a lookout for troop movements and inform the magistrates of approaching danger; to contribute to the cost of demolishing a local fortress used by brigands. Refusal would have been unwise, given that the defensive capacity of urban walls could be extended (or refused) to the persons, family, livestock, grain and property of rural dwellers in times of crisis. French towns of the late Middle Ages displayed symptoms of the 'contado syndrome' more commonly associated with their Flemish or Tuscan counterparts, with the difference that they exercised their growing authority, not in their own name, but in that of the king.

The military organisation of towns contributed along with the economic, administrative and spiritual factors discussed above to the importance of the municipality within the surrounding country-side. Control of a city afforded greater opportunity to dominate a region than simply holding local fortresses, not only for logistical and strategic reasons, but because the resistance or surrender of a major town tended to determine the actions of smaller communi-ties. It may be no exaggeration to claim (with Robert Favreau) that the resistance of Orléans in 1428 was more important in the Val-ois struggle against English arms than all the set battles of its time. Improvements in artillery weakened urban resistance to sieges from the early fifteenth century on, as evinced in Charles VII's victorious campaigns in the same duchy and in Guyenne (1449–53). But urban defences were improved to take account of developing technology. At Lille, Gilles Blieck has shown that provision was made in 1452–3 for hand-held firearms and long-range artillery to weaken an attacking force. Towns might be taken by surprise, treason or negotiation, but well-defended walls and well-stocked storerooms ensured that sieges remained lengthy, costly and therefore uncertain undertakings.

It follows that the most important measure in retaining a city, and with it the wider region, was the watch – by day over the city gates, by night along the ramparts. The watch mobilised the population like no other civic organisation. At Tours in the middle of the fifteenth century, Bernard Chevalier finds that arrangements for the watch required the services of 1,876 heads of household. Exemptions from the watch were rigorously contested by the civic authorities, while the practice of permitting replacements enabled clerics and female heads of household to be asked to contribute on an equal footing. Rather like urban processions but in an altogether more demanding and regular manner, the watch reinforced civic hierarchies. Still at Tours, the bourgeoisie and wealthier trades were entrusted with the day watch of the city gates, fully armed. The night watch over locked gates and the walls was performed without arms, and was left to lesser tradesmen and similar groups. When, in September 1467, Parisian heads-of-household responded to the king's request to present their full military force for inspection, an estimated 30,000 armed men lined up over a distance of 4 km outside the Saint-Antoine gate. Philippe Contamine notes that the exercise was repeated later that year, and again in 1469, 1472 and 1474 – a fact which emphasises the continuing insecurity of the realm (and with it the need for strong towns) long after victory in Normandy and Guyenne.

It is sometimes suggested that the military power of towns did not extend far beyond their immediate region, and that they made little contribution in terms of manpower in the field to the military effort of the king or his opponents. But retaining a town, and with it the countryside and lesser communities which looked to it, was sufficiently important and demanding work. By attending to such concerns in a convincing manner, municipal authorities usually succeeded in sparing their co-habitants from one of the most reviled of external impositions, the admission within the city gates of soldiers in the king's pay. In this respect as in others, the gap between town and country was increasing. Relative security from the soldiery may also help explain the greater willingness of urban populations to rebel by comparison with their rural counterparts.

Urban networks and the estates

The existence of urban networks is revealed in the case of Amiens by mentions in the town accounts of formal gifts of wine to official visitors from other towns. Neil Murphy (in his study of relations between northern French towns and the monarchy) has shown that in 1430–1, representatives from Abbeville, Arras and Boulogne-sur-Mer were present in Amiens for a total of 6 months of the year, while the smaller town of Doullens had at least one official in the regional capital in all but 3 months of the year.

It was natural that the civic governors should maintain contact with other communities of their region. Matters such as troop movements, the regional levying of taxation or alterations to the value of coinage affected towns together and at the same time. At Martel, recently studied by Nicholas Savy, the authorities remained in close contact with the consuls of nearby towns (Sarlat, Brive, Gourdon and Figeac), but also more distant but strategically important communities, like Aurillac. Communication, cooperation and even collaboration between urban communities were further strengthened by the absence of serious competition between them. Not, of course, that relations between towns were entirely untroubled. Raymond Cazelles cites a number of instances where towns sharing the same river entered into commercial rivalry with one another, such as the authorities of Rouen and Paris in 1315, 1380 and 1426. But in contrast to Flanders, the distance of major French communities one from the other generally precluded damaging long-term hostilities over economic matters.

Urban networks could further the interests of municipal authorities. At Saint-Flour, Albert Rigaudière finds that the consuls employed their regional contacts to promote a common stance against royal tax demands, particularly with their counterparts in Aurillac. Networks of mutual support could address more fundamental issues. From 1430 to 1433, we read in the town council minutes of Reims that the magistrates resolved three times to supply nearby Laon with food, and in June 1434 they wrote to the king's council on the matter. Pacts of mutual self-defence were negotiated and put into action. In the later 1350s, Pierre Desportes notes that the municipal authorities of Châlons-en-Champagne and Reims each promised to furnish the other with a contingent of up to 60 swordsmen, or three times that number of archers or crossbowmen, to serve within a delay of 4 days for a period of up 2 weeks over an area no greater than 40 miles from their hometown. In Guyenne, Yves Renouard has shown that military threats encouraged communities to pull together around the leadership of the municipality of Bordeaux, and in 1424 an urban coalition repulsed a French attack on the duchy.

Leadership within urban networks was necessarily local in the difficult conditions of our period. Although Paris was, as we have seen, the largest city by far, its influence in the realm probably reached its lowest point in our period. In a letter to Étienne Marcel, the leading officer of the municipality, King John proclaimed Paris 'the head of all the other towns in the kingdom'.[16] A century later, Louis XI could still state that the capital 'fed and sustained all the other towns of this kingdom, as the limbs of a body are sustained by the heart'.[17] But by Louis's time, the royal court rarely resided in Paris. Many organs of government functioned there, but Paris without the king's court was a diminished city. Jean Juvenal des Ursins was moved to write:

> Alas, city of Paris, who used to be so powerful and full of people, what has become of you? You were founded on four things: the residence of lords, . . . sovereign justice which was there for the entire kingdom, and the Châtelet which was superior; the third thing was the university, where one used to see sixteen or twenty thousand students; the fourth thing was trade . . .[18]

Admittedly this was probably in the mid-1430s, not a highpoint in the capital's history. But it was late in Charles VI's reign that the fortunes of Paris took a marked turn for the worse, particularly after the bloody return of the Burgundians in 1418. For nearly 20 years there-after, Paris was capital of the Anglo-Burgundian north. It is debatable whether consuls in the south ever paid much attention to Parisian developments, but in the second half of our period there was even less reason to do so than usual. It was the regional and not the regnal capital which set the most-heeded example within urban networks.

The primarily regional nature of urban networks was one of the factors which helped determine the development of representative assemblies, bodies which, despite their limitations, did permit munic-ipalities to extend their influence in some parts of the realm. The lists of requests drawn up by estates reflected the needs and concerns of townsmen, and meetings of representative assemblies left many traces in town accounts and council minutes. At Tours, Chevalier finds that envoys were sent to meetings of the estates of Languedoil 24 times between 1420 and 1435. As Jean-Pierre Leguay has shown, Rennes sent deputies (usually two or three in number, but sometimes as many as seven) to attend meetings of the estates of the duchy on at least 41 occasions between 1419 and 1496. The estates of Languedoc tended to fall under the sway of the representatives of Toulouse, Nîmes, Béziers and Montpellier throughout their existence. The trend was particularly marked in the period 1358–63, when assemblies of towns in the southern seneschalcies, with the blessing of John II, took a lead-ing role in tax raising, the regulation of coinage and defence. By the reign of Louis XI, the third estate's votes in Languedoc equalled those of the nobility and clergy combined, an advantage which was accen-tuated by their own regular attendance and by the more variable presence of members of the first and second estates. In Normandy under English rule, as Henri Prentout showed, the estates met on average twice a year, and in 1443 more than half of all representa-tives in attendance were from the towns. In many parts of France, above all the so-called *pays d'états* of Brittany, Provence, Burgundy and Normandy, regional estates advanced the interests of urban commu-nities and were supported by them as a result.

By contrast, summonses to attend larger representative assemblies were less frequent and less likely to elicit a positive response from towns. When Louis XI revived the estates-general in 1468, as Neithard Bulst has shown, summonses were issued to 71 towns which each sent two deputies. But by 1484, changes in electoral practice meant that urban representation was drastically reduced, with the result that over

60 per cent of the deputies of the third estate on that occasion were not representatives of the towns at all, but rather royal officers elected by region.

Municipalities and princes

Beyond the locality, then, the municipalities of France acquired a significant amount of leverage, as part of wider urban networks and through the medium of the estates in some parts of the realm. Naturally these activities brought them into contact with higher authorities, not least princes and the highest members of the nobility. Oftentimes the municipality suffered setbacks in bruising encounters with these, the most powerful elements of French political society. But there were advantages to be gained, and means of pursuing them; and in doing so, municipalities became an integral part of the political life of the realm.

The powerful local noble and his affinity was a force most town councils had to deal with at some point or another, and how that relationship developed could have a bearing upon life and politics within the town, the adjacent countryside and more broadly in the realm. A particularly well-documented case is that between successive authorities of Périgueux and the last two counts of Périgord, Archambaud V and VI, from the 1360s to around 1430. As Léon Dessalles's study of this sorry affair shows, the relationship between count and municipality was supportive at first. Archambaud V was released by the English in 1366 thanks in part to the intervention of the town. But trouble arose when the count was refused payment of a due he traditionally took from the townsfolk. A campaign of intimidation lasting several years began. The count's lands were eventually declared confiscate in 1385 by the king's seneschal in the region. But Archambaud's men made it known they thought the seneschal no better than 'the excrement of a rotten dog'. Gradually the count's excesses concentrated the attention of a distant royal administration on the needs of its *bonne ville*, particularly when Archambaud declared himself sovereign lord of the region and encouraged English forces to make use of his strongholds. Successful military action carried out by the municipal authorities with royal help in 1391 forced Archambaud to the *Parlement* to answer for his actions. But the centre's response was slow and cumbersome. The case took 4 years to pass through the *Parlement*'s procedures, by which point many more outrages had been perpetrated, and Archambaud V was near the end of his life. Even when confiscation was pronounced by the *Parlement* and Archambaud's property was sold by public auction at Périgueux, the comital affinity, now gathered around the count's eponymous son, did not give up the struggle. It took the military intervention of Jean II le Meingre, veteran of the king's wars and newly appointed as a royal marshal, assisted by a force of archers and footmen from Périgueux, to defeat and capture Archambaud VI in 1398. The following year the defeated count left for England like other restive westerners before him. As late as 1424, Périgueux still had to fight off attacks by Archambaud VI and his English allies. In the end, it was the count's death, in exile, disconnected from his local powerbase, which finally put an end to the affair.

Following its confiscation in 1399 from Archambaud VI, Périgueux was merged into the apanage lands of one of the most powerful princes in the kingdom, Louis of Orléans. Such figures had greater power to reward and punish than the likes of the counts of Périgord, and their authority was far more immediate than that of the king. Such was the perceived threat of princely power to towns, indeed, that some resisted its imposition. In Brittany, where many urban communities had backed the Valois candidate Charles of Blois, relations between the towns and Jean IV were understandably distant at first. The governors of Saint-Malo even obtained a bull from the Avignon pope Clement VII in 1394, which ceded the city to Charles VI of France – a state of affairs which lasted until the king returned the municipality to Jean V in reward for his support at Agincourt. On the edge of the Burgundian dominions, the royalist city of Tournai maintained its independence from the dukes of Burgundy at the cost of an annual tribute from 1423 to 1441, and again from 1472 to 1477.

But setting aside well-documented tensions and periods of conflict, it is important to recognise that good relations with regional princes could bring considerable political and economic advantages to municipalities, a fact which added to their growing status and rights as public authorities. In Brittany under Jean V, as Jean-Pierre Leguay has shown, existing urban rights were extended and new privileges were granted to Tréguier, Saint-Malo and Guérande. As René Lacour's work demonstrates, Poitiers became an administrative centre under Jean, Duke of Berry from the late fourteenth century on. Municipal and princely administration combined in the careers of men like Denis Gillier, mayor of the city from 1392 to 1395, and a ducal counsellor in Jean's *chambre des comptes* from 1379.

There is little doubt that the ability of princes to harness the energies and ambitions of urban elites could enhance their power

considerably. But these same urban elites generally adopted a pragmatic attitude to the demise of princely dynasties and the return of
untrammelled royal authority when it came. At Dijon, where the inter-
penetration of ducal and municipal interests was pronounced and
long-lived, there were riots at first when Louis XI seized the duchy
after Charles the Bold's demise in 1477. Quickly, however, the oligarchy of the regional capital was assimilated into royal service. One
such was Philippe Martin, mayor of the town. Martin became a *valet
de chambre* of the king and was an *élu* in the duchy, despite the fact
that he had served as a spicer at Charles the Bold's court, his brother
had been Philip the Good's *valet de chambre*, and his grandmother that
same duke's wetnurse. Successful oligarchs in later medieval France
knew to bend with the prevailing wind.

Municipalities and the king

Relations between a municipality and the king were usually the most
distant of any under discussion here. The restricted nature of royal
itineraries meant that few towns saw their monarch more than once
in a royal lifetime, and many not at all. Françoise Autrand reminds
us that between the death of Philip III and Charles VI's first journey
to the south of France in 1389, a period of just over a century, the
number of royal visits to Languedoc can be counted on the fingers
of one hand. In 1437, Saint-Flour in Auvergne received its one and
only visit from Charles VII. Given such facts the entry of a king was
clearly an important moment in the life of any urban community,
and was remembered as such by its inhabitants. As Bernard Guenée
and Françoise Lehoux have shown, the frequency and complexity of
royal entry ceremonies increased in the course of our period, creating
opportunities for symbolic communication between monarch and
urban subjects which emphasised the latter's loyalty and the former's
responsibilities. Urban corporations (usually acting under municipal
instruction) organised street theatre and dumb shows deploying the
imagery of sacred, classical, royal and local history to convey an ideal
image of relations between the king and his subjects. But these were
nonetheless rare events in the life of a single town. Tournai had the
privilege of staging three entries under successive monarchs (1355,
1368 and 1382), but it would be 82 years before the sight of another
king gladdened Tournaisien hearts.

It follows that the relationship between a monarch and his *bonnes
villes* was largely conducted through royal officers of varying types.

The monarchy continued to rely on the commissioner with a particular but temporary remit, such as the *commissaires* dispatched by Louis XI to oversee the return of the Somme towns to royal rule in 1463. The envoy from centre to locality was a perennial figure of government, but by definition he was an occasional presence. By contrast, the king's *baillis–sénéchaux* and their ancillaries were usually based in major towns. At La Rochelle, where a royal administration was located from 1372 on, Robert Favreau finds that the king's men included the seneschal's lieutenant, the king's advocate, *enquêteur*, clerk, receiver, and sergeants; the occupant of the older post of *prévôt* to whom kings had previously entrusted governance of the town, and who now exercised authority over visitors and royal port revenues; and the *châtelain* nominated directly by the king. Attached to these figures we must imagine – but are unable to quantify – a number of personnel who assisted them in their duties.

The presence of the king's men was sometimes a necessity for the defence and administration of a town, especially in the earlier part of our period. At Troyes in the 1350s and 1360s, as Françoise Bibelot demonstrated, municipal institutions of government were only slowly evolving under fiscal and military pressure. It was therefore the king's captain, Henri de Poitiers, who took charge of correspondence, the summoning of assemblies, tax-raising and the auditing of accounts. But as civic administrations emerged and developed, the presence of the king's men often became a source of irritation to municipal governors. Conflicts between municipality and royal officers frequently occur in the record. At La Rochelle once again, this time studied by Roger Little, the king's men and a number of inhabitants complained in 1422 to the *Parlement* of Poitiers that the magistrates of the town were overstepping their rights in fundamental matters such as tax-raising and justice. The *Parlement* responded with strong action: commissioners were sent to inspect the claims and, finding them to have substance, recommended suspending the magistrates' powers. Small wonder that Claude Gauvard finds the verb *résister* frequently used in letters of remission for crimes committed against royal officers, especially ones who came looking for taxes.

But it was far from certain that the king's men would win every such contest with municipal officers. Albert Rigaudière notes the case of a frustrated royal commissioner who threatened the total destruction of Saint-Flour when confronted by the civic authorities' obduracy in 1468, and perhaps there were some among the city's governors who believed such a thing were possible. A Lyon oligarch warned his colleagues in 1436 that if they did not comply with the king's wishes, he was capable of turning the city into a garden. But no royal official could be sure he would be able to focus the monarch's attention for long on a disobedient town. So long as that was the case, the royal official was better off reaching a practical compromise.

Very great leeway was generally accorded to civic administrations whose loyalty was of paramount importance to the monarchy. At Troyes, three-quarters of the assemblies of the town's council between 1429 and 1433 took place in the *salle royale* or the lodge of the *prévôt* under the eye of the *bailli* or his lieutenant, but this was at a time when the city had newly returned to the king's obedience after several years of Anglo-Burgundian rule. At Moulins, by contrast, a town that did not pass into English hands, the king's men had a more relaxed approach: Paul Baer shows that royal officers attended meetings of the council, but simply as residents of the town, not in any official capacity. At Le Puy (studied by Delcambre), no royal officer attended a deliberation of the plenary assembly of the town, nor was one present at consular elections, the auditing of accounts or the division of the *taille*. There was apparently no royal officer officially resident in the great city of Lyon before the early fifteenth century, save for one minor post commonly held by a member of the bourgeoisie. The number of royal officers increased through the fifteenth century, but Jean Déniau finds that the incumbents' powers did not interfere with the consulate.

In a sense, of course, all municipal officers were royal officers, serving the king, so in principle there was no need to interfere anyway. Once the municipality of Bordeaux was assimilated into the realm in the second half of the fifteenth century, the *jurats* of the town 'simply carried out administrative and judicial tasks, like small cogs on the local level of a monarchical system which overtook and engulfed them'.[19] But in key respects the 'royal state' was itself nothing more (and nothing less) than the sum of many such municipal 'cogs'. By governing their own town, urban oligarchs were doing the king's work; they were accountable to him, as Gisela Naegle rightly reminds us in her work on the towns and the monarchy, but they were generally free from his interference. Hence the vow taken by new advisers at Reims 'to counsel the town well and loyally, to the well-being of the king and of the town'.[20] At Troyes, new gatekeepers swore 'to guard the well-being and honour of our lord the King, and the keys of the city, without fault'.[21] At Saint-Flour, the consuls adopted a discourse of governance which was indistinguishable from that of the monarchy: they acted 'for the public good and utility'.[22] Bernard Chevalier has been criticised for arguing that a perfect *entente* existed between

municipal authorities and the king at the close of the fifteenth century. But this view has far more to commend it than the image of a
dominant monarch and subordinate towns propagated by Henri Sée
and others in his wake.

*   *   *

This closing chapter has shown that municipal authorities figured
prominently among the 'plurality of powers' which gave tangible substance to the sublime concept of royal power in late medieval France.
A small but important proportion of the French population lived in
towns, where economic circumstances were better than those affecting some other parts of Europe. Urban populations shouldered a
disproportionately large amount of the tax burden, although not
without protest as we have seen. The oligarchies which dominated
office-holding generally had a firm grip on the population within
the city walls, with the result that royal officers from the outside
found they had to work through and with the ruling group to achieve
their ends. More than ever before, the decisions taken by municipal
authorities affected the surrounding region: not just villagers nearby,
but the hierarchy of urban communities which looked to the regional
capital for support and guidance.

Once again, we are reminded of Richard Southern's aphorism that
the secret of successful government lay in 'familiar collaboration with
the right people'. As far as the crown was concerned, the 'right people' included churchmen whose support brought numerous benefits,
from processions and tax assessment at the parish level to the development of a governing ideology backed by Scripture, as we saw in
Chapter 1. They also included noble networks in the countryside,
whose power to disrupt and to serve was considerable, as we saw in
Chapters 2–4. And finally, as we have seen in Chapter 5, there were
the urban oligarchs – the most recent arrivals among the key powers which made up French political society, but perhaps not the least
of them.

Epilogue

The accession of Louis XI in 1461 offered the prospect of a return to power in the Kingdom of France for the men of the east under Philip the Good. Despite accompanying Louis to Paris in great ceremony and placing the crown upon the new king's head, the duke of Burgundy was to be disappointed. Those of his men who did attain royal office were few in number, and were soon suspected of putting the king's interests above the duke's, particularly when Louis XI succeeded in repurchasing the strategically important Somme towns from a declining Philip the Good (1463). It turned out that just like the future king John during his time in Normandy, Louis had not closely integrated with the regional elite which he lived among before coming to the throne. Just as few Normans followed John into power in 1350, so few Burgundians formed part of Louis's ruling group in the early years of his reign.

Growing Burgundian disaffection began to coalesce around Charles, Count of Charolais, Philip the Good's only legitimate heir, whose influence over his father's government grew stronger from 1464 on. The consequences might have been less serious had Louis not had to face other familiar problems, some of which he inherited, some he created. Key figures from his father's regime, the majority of them westerners as we have seen, were regarded with suspicion by the new king. The ruling group was purged, with up to three-quarters of the *baillis–sénéchaux*, captains of the *ordonnance* and office-holders in the financial administration being replaced. Although westerners did constitute the single largest group of counsellors in the reign as a whole, especially men from the Loire region, Louis's policy on his accession stands in stark contrast to the more conciliatory attitude towards westerners shown by Philip VI at the same stage. Breton elements of Charles VII's entourage were among the most heavily affected by the purge, certainly at the level of the royal council. Many left to form a potentially dangerous group around Duke François II. In Normandy, meanwhile, the noble networks which had begun to form around new royal office-holders after 1450 were profoundly disrupted when Louis targeted leading figures of Charles VII's regime there, such as the *Grand sénéchal* and captain of Rouen, Pierre de

211

Brézé. Although a reconciliation of sorts was reached with the latter, other former servants of Charles VII left royal service for good, often to Brittany. Growing unrest was therefore affecting noble networks in both eastern and western France during the first years of Louis's reign, and the king's pre-occupation with Cerdagne and Roussillon in the south did little to alleviate matters. In previous reigns, only John had found himself with little support from eastern and western noble groupings. The consequences then were severe. For all the advantages at his disposal, Louis was heading the same way.

There was a further, familiar element of danger for the ruler in these early years: the king's only brother and, until 1470, the heir to the throne, Charles of France. Charles does not appear to have orchestrated opposi-tion to the king, but his attitude – classically that of a royal brother – was sufficiently hostile for him to emerge as the figurehead for the plurality of noble powers which came together from east and west to form the League of the Public Weal (1465). The leading princes (including Brittany, Bourbon, Alençon and Charolais) and nobles who eventually took the field did so in Charles of France's name, and in support of an ideological programme of well-established reforming goals, namely the removal of the king's favourites and an end to 'the disorder of the kingdom' in matters of justice, taxation, and the church.[1] They also called for the estates-general to be summoned. The league attracted urban support (which no doubt some of these propos-als were intended to achieve), primarily in Paris and much of Normandy, although many municipalities remained loyal to a monarchy whose interests were increasingly consonant with their own. Militarily, however, the contest was a close-run affair. Louis quickly forced Bourbon's submission, but he was unable to defeat a Burgundian army led by the count of Charolais when they met at Montlhéry south of Paris in August 1465. The Treaty of Conflans which marked the end of the war saw a considerable number of concessions to the leading princes and other nobles in the realm, including the grant in apanage of Normandy to Charles of France.

For all Charles VII's successes, and despite the redistribution of the crown's considerable resources among noble networks and leading members of the royal familial community, the war of the Public Weal demonstrated that the monarchy could not simply override the interests of these powerful groups. For the next decade, Louis had to face several similar challenges, the most intense of which usually involved the participation of Charolais (who became duke of Burgundy upon his father's death in June 1467).

In these early years of his rule, despite his growing power in the Low Coun-tries and the German-speaking lands of the Empire, Charles 'the Bold' (as posterity most commonly knows him) remained a prince with interests and ambitions in France. In 1467–8, he and François II of Brittany made common cause in an attempt, assisted by Jean II, Duke of Alençon, to force Louis to make over the apanage of Normandy to Charles of France which had been promised at Conflans. This was a dangerous prospect given the propensity of Norman and Breton noble networks to ally with opponents of the king, but Louis managed to force the Bretons to submit at Ancenis and so averted the danger. Again in 1471–2, François offered support to Charles the Bold in his attempts to recover the Somme towns, which had also been restored to Burgundy at Conflans, but had reverted to the crown early in 1471. The two princes formed part of a wider coalition against the king which included Jean V, Count of Armagnac.

The death of Charles of France in 1472 brought some relief for Louis XI, but shifting noble coalitions in both eastern and western France still found allies they could call upon. It was fortunate that throughout much of Louis's early reign, conflict between the houses of York and Lancaster prevented significant English intervention in France. But the threat was never far away. In July 1468, Charles the Bold took Edward IV's sister Margaret of York as his third wife, and although the prospect of Yorkist aid reaching the dukes of Burgundy and Brittany was diminished by the temporary Lancastrian recovery of 1470–71, throughout these years, as one contemporary observed, Edward, Charles and François 'were like three heads under a single hat'.[2]

In 1474–5, the greatest threat to Valois tenure of the throne in over half a century emerged from this coalition, reportedly supported by lesser figures such as Louis of Luxembourg, Count of Saint Pol (1433–75), Charles V, Count of Maine (1472–81), Jean II, Duke of Bourbon and Jacques of Armagnac, Duke of Nemours (1464–77). Edward IV landed in France with a large army and the avowed intention of having himself crowned at Reims. In the end, his Breton and Burgundian allies were unwilling or unable to join him in the field, and Edward made a lucrative peace with Louis at Picquigny in August 1475. The treaty effectively marked the end of that phase of Anglo-French conflict known as the Hundred Years' War.

Edward's withdrawal from France was not well received at the Burgundian court, but by that stage Charles the Bold had turned his back on the kingdom anyway. The year 1474 has a better claim than 1420 as the point at which the duke of Burgundy finally gave up on the desire to dominate the Kingdom of France. That was the year Charles signed the Treaty of London with Edward IV. The duke effectively agreed to abandon the kingdom to Edward should he conquer it, in return for holding his existing lands and a few others (including Champagne) free of homage. These were the terms on which the English invaded in 1475. Charles the Bold's withdrawal from France had been gradual, but his intentions were already apparent in 1468, when he sought to curb the jurisdiction of the *Parlement* of Paris over his lands. The policy was not unanimously popular among the men of the east around Charles, some of whom considered the rejection of his rights and responsibilities as a Valois prince unnatural. Many of them were tied themselves by property and pedigree to the kingdom, and a small number of leading figures returned to their natural lord, the King of France, at this stage or later on. The memoirist Philippe de Commynes was one such, and although his was seen as a peculiarly self-serving abandonment of the duke (1472), the fact that his grandfather had also taken the road to royal service during his career is a reminder that Commynes resembled other Burgundian servants whose families had sought preferment in the kingdom.

For a few short years, the notion of a 'princely state' acquired demonstrable substance under Charles the Bold. Reforms of the ducal household and army were drawn up, and a separate *Parlement* at Mechelen, an imperial territory, was established in 1473. Negotiations with the Emperor for a crown – possibly that of the ancient kingdom of Burgundy – took place in the same year, although they were ultimately fruitless.

Charles the Bold's regime collapsed, in January 1477, when the duke met his death at Nancy fighting a coalition of the many enemies Burgundian expansion had made in the Empire. His lands passed to his daughter, Mary, who was hurriedly married to Maximilian, son of Emperor Frederick III. The wars of the Burgundian succession now began. By 1493, in a series of gains and reverses which need not be detailed here, the French crown had reabsorbed many of the formerly ducal dominions, including Picardy, Artois and Boulogne in the north, and the duchy of Burgundy in the south.

The end of Valois Burgundian power was one of several dynastic collapses which benefited the monarchy in the last quarter of the fifteenth century. As Michel Nassiet has pointed out in his study of kinship and dynastic states, these deaths in the royal familial community probably did more than any other single event to change the fortunes of the monarchy (a similar 'clear-out' at Agincourt also had a marked effect, albeit for the worse as we have seen). In Anjou, Duke René lost his son (Jean, Duke of Calabria, d. 1470) and grandson (Nicholas, Duke of Calabria, d. 1473) in quick succession, and Louis XI was ultimately able to exploit an insecure succession to annex Anjou, Maine, Bar and Provence, the last of these lands being acquired in 1481. In Brittany, François II left two female heirs on his death in 1488, the eldest of whom eventually married Charles VIII in 1491, thereby initiating the gradual absorption of the duchy which was completed in 1532. Added to the lands of the counts of Armagnac, confiscated on the death of Jean V in 1473 and only partially and temporarily restored to his son Charles (1473–97) in 1484, these gains greatly increased the monarchy's resources at the close of the fifteenth century.

In addition to the expansion of the *domaine* which resulted from these developments, Louis XI's reign witnessed a tremendous increase in the fiscal resources of the monarchy. Jean-François Lassalmonie has estimated that from 1461 to 1483, extraordinary revenues from direct taxation alone more than tripled. The principle justification for the fiscal drive of Louis's reign was the king's struggles against the leading princes, Burgundy in the van, but also the continued threat of English intervention. On his death in 1483, the king was still maintaining a standing force of nearly 4,000 mounted units (or lances) and 16,000 foot soldiers. His ability to raise the necessary revenues was achieved without any significant involvement of representative assemblies. The only time the estates-general were summoned in his reign was in

1468, when the king sought the estates' support for his decision to withhold the duchy of Normandy from his brother.

But the triumphs of the 'royal state' at the close of our period are easily overestimated. None of Louis's immediate successors was able to sustain his fiscal success, as Bernard Chevalier has shown. In the decade following Louis's death, annual revenues from direct taxation dropped by more than half from the highpoints of his reign. The pattern of French politics which had prevailed for so long, of eastern and western nobilities influenced by a strong Burgundian dynasty on one side and a potential English ally for restive lords on the other, was no longer apparent: to that extent at least, the second half of the fifteenth century witnessed fundamental change.

But a 'plurality of powers' nonetheless remained and shaped political life across the realm. Princes to whom the revenues of taxation were ceded in previous reigns were gradually replaced by royal governors of provinces. But most of the governors of the late fifteenth century were princes themselves, and all of the crown's major representatives in the provinces – governors, captains of the *ordonnance*, *baillis–sénéchaux* and so forth – were just as likely as the princes of previous generations to recruit local networks of support among the nobility and townsfolk. The cost of retaining the service and loyalty of the great men whose powers extended between centre and localities still placed enormous demands on the finances of the monarchy. In 1470, Peter Lewis has calculated, the pensions awarded to a governing elite of princes, members of the king's chivalric order of Saint Michael (founded the previous year), courtiers and others amounted to fully 35 per cent of the king's income. A 'plurality of powers' still ran the kingdom beneath its ruler: nobles, leading churchmen and townsmen foremost among them.

Notes

Introduction

1. H. Le Bras and E. Todd, *L'invention de la France. Atlas anthropologique et politique* (Paris, 1981), p. 76.
2. G. Langmuir, 'Community and legal change in Capetian France', *French Historical Studies* 6 (1970), pp. 275–86, at p. 286.
3. E. Hallam, *Capetian France 987-1328* (second edition revised by Judith Everard, Harlow, 2001); J. Dunbabin, *France in the making 843-1180* (second edition, Oxford 2000); M. Bull (ed.), *France in the central Middle Ages* (Oxford, 2002).
4. B. Smalley, 'Capetian France', in J.M. Wallace-Hardill and J. McManners (eds.), *France: government and society* (London, 1957), pp. 61–82, at p. 80.
5. Notably A. Curry, *The Hundred Years' War* (new edition, Basingstoke, 2003); C. Allmand, *The Hundred Years' War: England and France at war, c. 1300–1450* (Cambridge, 1988). Jonathan Sumption is working on a detailed history of the conflict, of which two volumes have appeared at the time of writing: *The Hundred Years' War, I: Trial by Battle* (London, 1990) and *The Hundred Years' War, II: Trial by Fire* (London, 1999).
6. E. Perroy, 'Feudalism or principalities in fifteenth-century France', *Bulletin of the Institute of historical research* 20 (1947), pp. 181–5; J. Le Patourel, 'The king and princes in fourteenth-century France', in J.R. Hale, J.R.L. Highfield and B. Smalley (eds.), *Europe in the late Middle Ages* (London, 1965), pp. 155–83; A. Leguai, 'Royauté et principautés en France aux XIVe et XVe siècles: l'évolution de leurs rapports au cours de la Guerre de Cent Ans', *Le Moyen Âge* 101 (1995), pp. 121–36.
7. D.L. Potter, *A history of France, 1460–1560. The Emergence of the Nation State* (Basingstoke, 1995), p. ix.
8. G. de Lagarde, *La naissance de l'esprit laïque au déclin du Moyen Âge*, 6 vols, first published 1934–46.
9. J-L. Gazzaniga, *L'église de France à la fin du Moyen Âge: pouvoirs et institutions* (Goldbach, 1995); V. Tabbagh, *Gens d'église, gens de pouvoir (France,*

216

216

XIIIe–XVe siècle) (Dijon, 2006). Cf. J.-P. Genet and B. Vincent (eds.), *État et église dans la genèse de l'état moderne* (Madrid, 1986).

10. P. Contamine, *La noblesse au royaume de France de Philippe le Bel à Louis XII* (Paris, 1996); M.-T. Caron, *Noblesse et pouvoir royal en France, XIIIe–XVIe siècle* (Paris, 1994). For a pertinent recent overview with bibliography see G. Prosser, 'The later medieval French *noblesse*' in D.L. Potter (ed.), *France in the Later Middle Ages* (Oxford, 2003), pp. 182–209, 229–31.

11. B. Chevalier, *Les bonnes villes de France du XIVe au XVIe siècle* (Paris, 1982) and G. Naegle, *Stadt, Recht und Krone: französische Städte, Königtum und Parlement im späten Mittelalter*, 2 vols (Husum, 2002). An important collection of essays is A. Rigaudière, *Gouverner la ville au Moyen Âge* (Paris, 1993).

12. P.S. Lewis, 'Reflections on the role of royal clientèles in the construction of the French monarchy (mid-XIVth/end-XVth centuries)', in N. Bulst, R. Descimon and A.Guerreau (eds.), *L'état ou le roi. Les fondations de la modernité monarchique en France (XIVe–XVIIe siècles)* (Paris, 1996), pp. 51–67.

13. *Idéal du prince et du pouvoir royal en France, 1380–1440* (Paris, 1981); *L'empire du roi: idées et croyances politiques en France, XIIIe–XVe siècle* (Paris, 1993).

14. 'Guerre civile et changement du personnel administratif dans le royaume de France de 1400 à 1418: l'exemple des baillis et sénéchaux', *Francia* 6 (1978), pp. 151–298.

15. *Les entrées royales françaises de 1328 à 1515* (Paris, 1968).

16. R. Cazelles, *La société politique et la crise de la royauté sous Philippe de Valois* (Paris, 1958); *Société politique, noblesse et couronne sous Jean le Bon et Charles V* (Paris, 1982).

17. B. Guenée and J.-F. Sirinelli, 'L'histoire politique', in F. Bédarida (ed.), *L'histoire et le métier d'historien en France 1945–1995* (Paris, 1995), pp. 301–12, p. 305.

18. *Charles VI: la folie du roi* (Paris, 1986); *Charles V: Le sage* (Paris, 1994).

19. L. Stone, 'The revival of narrative: reflections on a new old history', *Past and Present* 85 (1979), pp. 3–24.

20. The period 1328–1461 is a conventional one, and sits well with coverage provided by the works of Elizabeth Hallam and David Potter mentioned elsewhere in this preface. But some of the themes which inform our narrative do not sit comfortably with the closing date of 1461, and for this reason an epilogue takes our account a little further into the second half of the fifteenth century. Broadly speaking, thematic chapters concentrate on fourteenth- and fifteenth-century developments.

Chapter 1: Ruling the French in the Late Middle Ages

1. L. Pannier (ed.), *Le débat des hérauts d'armes de France et d'Angleterre* (Paris, 1877), p. 10.

2. S. Menache, ' "Un peuple qui a sa demeure à part". Boniface VIII et le sentiment national français', *Francia* 12 (1984), pp. 193–208.
3. *Maistre Nicolas Oresme. Le Livre de Politiques d'Aristote*, ed. A.D. Menut (Transactions of the American Philosophical Society, New Series, Vol. 69, part 6: Philadelphia, 1970), p. 161.
4. J. Krynen, *L'Empire du roi. Idées et croyances politiques en France, XIIIe–XVe siècle* (Paris, 1993), p. 360, my translation.
5. *Oeuvres de Georges Chastellain*, ed. J.C.B.M. Kervyn de Lettenhove, 8 vols (Brussels, 1863–8), vol. 4, 358.
6. Cited in F. Autrand, *Charles V* (Paris, 1994), pp. 539–40.
7. L. Scordia, *'Le roi doit vivre du sien'. La théorie de l'impôt en France (XIIIe–XVe siècles)* (Paris, 2005), p. 442.
8. C. Gauvard, *Violence et ordre public au Moyen Âge* (Paris, 2005), p. 90.
9. Louis IX, d. 1270.
10. Louis of Anjou, bishop of Toulouse, d. 1297, great nephew of King Louis IX.
11. Charles of Blois, claimant to the ducal throne of Brittany, d. 1364. Charles was not in fact canonized, though great efforts were made to investigate his case.
12. *Le Songe du Vergier*, ed. M. Schnerb-Lièvre 2 vols (Paris, 1982), i, pp. 153–4.
13. *La chronique d'Enguerran de Monstrelet*, ed. L. Douët-d'Arcq, 6 vols (Paris, 1857–62), vol. 3, p. 42.
14. *Oeuvres de Georges Chastellain*, vol. 5, p. 391.
15. *Oeuvres de Robert Blondel*, ed. A. Héron, 2 vols (Rouen, 1891–3), vol. 1, p. 472.
16. *Le livre des faits et bonnes moeurs du roi Charles V le Sage*, ed. E. Hicks & T. Moreau (Paris, 1997), p. 127.
17. In his preface to M. Ornato, *Répertoire prosopographique de personnages apparentés à la couronne de France aux 14e et 15e siècles* (Paris, 2001), p. 7.
18. J. Kerhervé, 'Les présidents de la chambre des comptes de Bretagne au 15e siècle', in P. Contamine & O. Mattéoni (eds.), *La France des principautés. Les Chambres des comptes* (Paris, 1996), pp. 165–204, at p. 168.
19. M. Jones, *'Bons bretons et bons Françoys*. The language and meaning of treason in later medieval France', *Transactions of the Royal Historical Society* 5th ser. 32 (1982), pp. 91–112, repr. in his *The Creation of Brittany. A Late Medieval State* (London, 1988).
20. J.-P. Genet, 'Conclusion', in *La ville, la bourgeoisie et la genèse de l'état moderne (XIIe–XVIIIe siècle)* (Paris, 1988), p. 349.
21. J. Strayer, 'The laicization of French and English society in the thirteenth century', *Speculum* 15 (1944), pp. 76–86.
22. J.-L. Gazzaniga, 'Les clercs au service de l'état dans la France du XVe siècle. À la lecture de travaux récents', in J. Krynen & A. Rigaudière (eds.), *Droits savants et pratiques françaises du pouvoir (XIe–XVe siècles)* (Paris, 1992), pp. 253–78, at p. 254.
23. *Lettres de Louis XI, roi de France*, ed. J. Vaesen & A. Charavay, 12 vols (Paris, 1883–1909), vol. 6, p. 9.

24. Translated in L. Taylor, *Soldiers of Christ. Preaching in late medieval and reformation France* (New York–Oxford, 1992), p. 104.

25. From the treatise 'How one should hold Mass', cited in J. Chiffoleau, 'La religion flamboyante (v. 1320–v. 1520)', in J. Chiffoleau et al., *Du Christianisme flamboyant à l'aube des Lumières (XIVe–XVIIIe siècle) (Histoire de la France religieuse, 2)* (Paris, 1988), p. 60.

26. Cited in H. Martin, 'Les prédications déviantes, du début du XVe siècle au début du XVIe siècle, dans les provinces septentrionales de la France', in B. Chevalier & R. Sauzet (eds.), *Les réformes. Enracinement socio-culturel* (Paris, 1985), pp. 251–66, at p. 264.

27. Cited in V. Tabbagh, 'Les évêques du royaume de France en 1438', in his *Gens d'église, gens de pouvoir (France, XIIIe–XVe siècle)* (Dijon, 2006), pp. 87–186, at p. 135.

28. Cited in N. Offenstadt, *Faire la paix au Moyen Âge. Discours et gestes de paix pendant la Guerre de Cent Ans* (Paris, 2007), p. 173.

29. J. Chiffoleau, 'Les processions parisiennes de 1412. Analyse d'un rituel flamboyant', *Revue historique* 284 (1991), pp. 38–76, at p. 71.

30. P. Rézeau, *Les prières aux saints en langue française à la fin du Moyen Âge*, 2 vols (Geneva, 1982–3), vol. 2, p. 192.

31. Cited in F. Autrand *Charles VI* (Paris, 1986), p. 204.

32. J. Le Patourel, 'The king and the princes in fourteenth-century France', in J. Hale, J. Highfield & B. Smalley (eds.), *Europe in the late Middle Ages* (London, 1965), pp. 155–83, at p. 158.

33. B. Guenée & J-F. Sirinelli, 'L'histoire politique', in F. Bédarida (ed.), *L'histoire et le métier d'historien en France, 1945–1995* (Paris, 1995), pp. 301–12, at p. 303.

34. D. Potter, 'Introduction', in *France in the Later Middle Ages* (Oxford, 2003), pp. 1–22, at pp. 10–11.

35. M. Harsgor, 'Maîtres d'un royaume. Le groupe dirigeant français à la fin du Moyen Âge', in B. Chevalier & P. Contamine (eds.), *La France de la fin du XVe siècle. Renouveau et apogée* (Paris, 1985), pp. 135–46.

36. *Journal de Nicholas de Baye*, ed. A. Tuetey, 2 vols (Paris, 1885–8), vol. 1, pp. 25–7.

37. *Extraits analytiques des anciens registres des Consaux de la ville de Tournai (1385–1422)*, ed. H. Vandenbrouck, *Mémoires de la Société historique et littéraire de Tournai*, 7 (1861), pp. 88–9.

38. E. Hamy (ed.), *Le livre de la description des pays de Gilles le Bouvier, dit Berry* (Paris, 1908), p. 30.

39. G. Sivéry, 'La description du royaume de France par les conseillers de Philippe Auguste et par leurs successeurs', *Le Moyen Âge* 90 (1984), pp. 65–85.

40. Philippe de Beaumanoir, *Les Coutumes de Beauvaisis*, ed. A. Salmon, 3 vols (Paris, 1899–1974), vol. 1, p. 5.

41. Trans. in E. Cohen, *The Crossroads of Justice. Law and Culture in Late Medieval France* (Leiden, 1993), p. 28.

42. Ibid., p. 19.

43. *Ordonnances des Rois de France* (Paris, 1723), vol. 4, p. 252.
44. F. Braudel, *The Identity of France, I: History and Environment*, trans. S. Reynolds (New York, 1986), pp. 250–1 (writing of the Mediterranean, but the point is more valid in our period for the Atlantic).
45. P. Arabeyre, 'La France et son gouvernement au milieu du XVe siècle d'après Bernard de Rosier', *Bibliothèque de l'École des chartes* 150 (1992), pp. 245–85.
46. P.S. Lewis, 'The centre, the periphery and the problem of power distribution in later medieval France', in J. Highfield & R. Jeffs (eds.), *The Crown and Local Communities in England and France in the Fifteenth Century* (Gloucester, 1981), pp. 33–50.
47. R.W. Southern, 'The place of England in the twelfth-century Renaissance', in his *Medieval Humanism and Other Studies* (Oxford, 1970), pp. 158–80, at p. 179.
48. *Alain Chartier. Le Quadrilogue invectif.* Translated and annotated F. Bouchet (Paris, 2002), p. 20.

Chapter 2: Rural France, c. 1300–c. 1500

1. H. Denifle, *La désolation des églises, monastères et hôpitaux en France pendant la Guerre de cent ans*, 2 vols (Paris, 1897–9; repr. Brussels, 1965), vol. 2, p. 829.
2. R. Muchembled, *Culture populaire et culture des élites dans la France moderne (XVe–XVIIIe siècle)* (Paris, 1978), p. 54.
3. R. Boutruche, *La crise d'une société. Seigneurs et paysans du Bordelais pendant la Guerre de cent ans* (Paris, 1947), p. 331.
4. N. Wright, *Knights and Peasants. The Hundred Years War in the French Countryside* (Woodbridge, 1998), p. 87.
5. G. Fourquin, *Les Campagnes de la région parisienne (du milieu du XIIIe au début du XVIe siècle)* (Paris, 1964), pp. 138–40, p. 152.
6. *Le terrier de Jean Jossard, coseigneur de Châtillon d'Azergues 1430–63*, ed. R. Fédou (Paris, 1966), p. 53.
7. See 'Further Reading' at the end of this book.
8. *Le terrier de la famille d'Orbec à Cideville (Haute-Normandie)*, ed. D. Angers (Montréal-Rouen, 1993).
9. M. Le Mené, *Les campagnes angevines à la fin du Moyen Âge (vers 1350–vers 1530). Étude économique* (Nantes, 1982), p. 164; L. Tricard, *Les campagnes limousines du XIVe au XVI siècle. Originalité et limites d'une reconstruction rurale*.
10. C. Dyer, *Standards of Living in the Later Middle Ages. Social Change in England, c. 1200–1520* (Cambridge, 1989), p. 47.
11. G. Prosser, 'The later medieval French *noblesse*', in D. Potter (ed.), *France in the Later Middle Ages* (Oxford, 2003), pp. 182–209, 229–32, at p. 231.
12. Y. Bezard, *La vie rurale dans le sud de la région parisienne de 1450 à 1650* (Paris, 1929), p. 48.

13. *The Chronicle of Jean de Venette*, ed. R. Newhall & trans J. Birdsall (New York, 1953), p. 51.
14. M.-C. Marandet, *Le souci de l'au-delà: la pratique testamentaire dans la région toulousaine (1300–1450)*, 2 vols (Perpignan, 1998), vol. 1, pp. 321–2.
15. L. Carolus-Barré, 'Jeanne, êtes-vous en état de grâce?', *Bulletin de la Société nationale des antiquaires de France* (1958), pp. 203–8, at p. 205.
16. P.S. Lewis, 'Introduction', in idem (ed.), *The Recovery of France in the Fifteenth Century* (London, 1971), pp. 11–22, at p. 11.

Chapter 3: Royal France, c. 1328–c. 1380

1. *Chronique de Jean Le Bel*, ed. J. Viard & E. Déprez (Paris, 1904), p. 179.
2. R. Cazelles, *La société politique et la crise de la royauté sous Philippe de Valois* (Paris, 1958), p. 150.
3. *Chronique normande de Pierre Cochon*, ed. C. Beaurepaire (Rouen, 1870), pp. 57–8.
4. M. Vale, *The Angevin legacy and the Hundred Years' War* (Oxford, 1990), p. 54.
5. W. Ormrod, 'The west European monarchies in the later Middle Ages', in R. Bonney (ed.), *Economic systems and state finance* (Oxford, 1995), pp. 123–60, at p. 144.
6. J.B. Henneman, *Royal taxation in fourteenth-century France. The development of war financing, 1322–56* (Princeton, 1971), pp. 303–7.
7. E. Perroy, *La Guerre de cent ans* (Paris, 1945), pp. 100–1.
8. *La Chronique des quatre premiers Valois*, ed. S. Luce (Paris, 1862), p. 19.
9. P. Lewis, 'Decayed and non-feudalism in later medieval France', *Bulletin of the Institute of historical research* 37 (1964), pp. 157–84, at p. 175 (repr. in his *Essays in later medieval French history* [London, 1985], No. 5, at p. 59).
10. D'A.J.D. Boulton, *The knights of the crown. The monarchical orders of knighthood in later medieval Europe 1325–1520* (second edition, Woodbridge 2000), p. 185.
11. P. Contamine, *Guerre, état et société en France à la fin du Moyen Âge* (Paris, 1972), pp. 152–3.
12. R. Cazelles, *Société politique, noblesse et couronne sous Jean le Bon et Charles V* (Paris, 1982), pp. 493–5.

Chapter 4: Royal France, c. 1380–c. 1461

1. *Journal d'un bourgeois de Paris (1405–49)*, ed. A. Tuetey (Paris, 1881), p. 133.
2. M. Rey, *Les finances royales sous Charles VI. Les causes du déficit* (Paris, 1965), p. 612.
3. Ibid., p. 573.
4. J.R. Major, *Representative Government in Early Modern France* (New Haven & London, 1980), pp. 26–7.

5. *Chronique d'Enguerran de Monstrelet*, ed. L. Douët d'Arcq, 6 vols (Paris, 1857–62), vol. 2, p. 66.

6. B. Guenée, *La folie de Charles VI. Roi bien-aimé* (Paris, 2004), p. 262.

7. *Oeuvres de Georges Chastellain*, ed. J. Kervyn de Lettenhove, 8 vols (Brussels, 1863–6), vol. 8, p. 324 n. 1.

8. *Extraits analytiques des anciens registres des Consaux de la ville de Tournai, 1431–76*, ed. A. de La Grange, in *Mémoires de la Société historique et littéraire de Tournai* 23 (1893), p. 181.

9. *Proceedings and Ordinances of the Privy Council of England IV*, ed. Harris Nicholas (London, 1835), p. 223 (my rendering).

10. *Christine de Pizan. Ditié de Jeanne d'Arc*, ed. A. Kennedy & K. Varty (Oxford, 1977), v. 159–60.

11. *Perceval de Cagny. Chroniques*, ed. H. Moranvillé (Paris, 1902), pp. 205–6; 'Testimony of Raoul le Bouvier as to events at Arras, given 6 November 1451', in J. Dickinson, *The Congress of Arras 1435. A study in medieval diplomacy* (Oxford, 1955), p. 231.

12. *Actes des états généraux des Pays-Bas, I: actes de 1427 à 1488*, ed. S. Cuvelier (Brussels, 1948), p. 188.

13. B. Ditcham, ' "Mutton guzzlers and wine bags": foreign soldiers and native reactions in fifteenth-century France', in C. Allmand, ed., *Power, culture and religion in France, c. 1350–c. 1550* (Woodbridge, 1989), pp. 1–13, at p. 4 (citing the *Book of Pluscarden*, ed. F. Skene [Edinburgh, 1890], p. 354).

14. N. Sussman, 'Debasement, royal revenues and inflation in France during the Hundred Years' War, 1415–22', *Journal of Economic History* 53 (1993), pp. 44–70, at p. 69.

15. J.R. Major, *Representative institutions in Renaissance France 1421–1559* (Madison, 1960), p. 25.

16. R. Little, *The Parlement of Poitiers: war, government and politics in France, 1418–36* (London, 1984), p. 194; cf. M.G.A. Vale, *Charles VII* (Berkeley, 1974), pp. 49–51.

17. P. Contamine, 'Lever l'impôt en terre de guerre: rançons, appatis, souffrances de guerre dans la France des XIVe et XVe siècles', in idem, J. Kerhervé & A. Rigaudière (eds.), *L'impôt au Moyen Âge*, 3 vols (Paris, 2002), vol. 1, pp. 12–39, at p. 35.

18. R. Favreau, 'La Praguerie en Poitou', *Bibliothèque de l'École des chartes* 129 (1971), pp. 277–301, at p. 300.

19. P. Contamine, 'The French nobility and the war', in K. Fowler (ed.), *The Hundred Years' War* (London, 1971), pp. 135–60, at p. 151.

Chapter 5: Municipal France, c. 1300–c. 1500

1. *Le Paris de Charles V et de Charles VI: vu par des écrivains contemporains*, ed. Le Roux de Lincy & L. Tisserand (Caen, 1992; partial re-edition of Paris, 1867), pp. 82–166.

2. *Oeuvres de Georges Chastellain*, ed. J. Kervyn de Lettenhove, 8 vols (Brussels, 1863–6), vol. 4, p. 182.

3. A. Higounet-Nadal, *Périgueux aux XIVe et XVe siècles. Étude de démographie historique* (Bordeaux, 1978), p. 340; P. Desportes, *Reims et les rémois aux XIIIe et XIVe siècles* (Paris, 1979), p. 579.

4. *Le livre de la description des pays de Gilles le Bouvier, dit Berry*, ed. E.-T Hamy (Paris, 1908), p. 46.

5. B. Chevalier, 'Les villes de la Loire', in his *Les bonnes villes, l'État et la société dans la France de la fin du XVe siècle* (Orléans, 1995), pp. 43–67, at p. 60.

6. R. Fédou, *Les hommes de loi lyonnais à la fin du Moyen Âge* (Paris, 1964), p. 102.

7. A. Bossuat, *Le bailliage royal de Montferrand (1425–1556)* (Paris, 1957), p. 152.

8. B. Chevalier, 'La religion civique dans les bonnes villes: sa portée et ses limites. Le cas de Tours', in A. Vauchez (ed.), *La religion civique à l'époque médiévale et moderne (Chrétienté et Islam)* (Rome, 1995), pp. 337–49, at p. 349.

9. R. Favreau & J. Glenisson, 'Fiscalité d'État et budget à Poitiers au XVe siècle', in *L'impôt dans le cadre de la ville et de l'état* (Brussels, 1962), pp. 114–49, at p. 122.

10. J. Turlan, *La commune et le corps de ville de Sens (1146–1789)* (Paris, 1942), pp. 38–9.

11. A. Rigaudière, *Saint-Flour, ville d'Auvergne au bas Moyen Âge. Étude d'histoire administrative et financière*, 2 vols (Rouen, 1982), vol. 1, p. 433.

12. B. Guenée, *L'opinion publique à la fin du Moyen Âge d'après la 'Chronique de Charles VI' du Religieux de Saint-Denis* (Paris, 2002), pp. 102–3.

13. A. Voisin, 'Autour d'une élection de maire à Dijon sous Philippe le Bon (1450)', *Annales de Bourgogne* 13 (1941), pp. 97–108.

14. *Histoire de la France urbaine*, ed. G. Duby et al., vol. 2 (Paris, 1980), p. 513.

15. *Extraits analytiques des anciens registres des Consaux de la ville de Tournai, 1385–1422*, ed. H. Vandenbrouck, in *Mémoires de la Société historique et littéraire de Tournai* 7 (1861), p. 120.

16. Cited in B. Guenée, *Un meurtre, une société: l'assassinat du duc d'Orléans, 23 novembre 1407* (Paris, 1992), pp. 121–2.

17. Cited in B. Chevalier, *Les bonnes villes de France du XIVe au XVIe siècle* (Paris, 1982), p. 60.

18. *Écrits politiques de Jean Juvenal des Ursins*, ed. P.S. Lewis, 3 vols (Paris, 1978–93), vol. 1, p. 257.

19. M. Bochaca, *La banlieue de Bordeaux. Formation d'une juridiction municipale suburbaine (vers 1250–vers 1550)* (Paris-Montréal, 1997), p. 165.

20. *Registre de délibérations du Conseil de la ville de Reims (1422–36)*, ed. S. Guilbert (Reims, 1990–1), p. 232.

21. 'Le plus ancien registre des délibérations du Conseil de la ville de Troyes (1429–33)', ed. A. Roserot, in *Collection de documents inédits relatifs à la*

ville de Troyes et à la Champagne méridionale publiés par la Société académique de l'Aube, vol. 3 (Troyes, 1886), pp. 165–474, at p. 208.

22. A. Rigaudière, *Saint-Flour, ville d'Auvergne au bas Moyen Âge. Étude d'histoire administrative et financière*, 2 vols (Rouen, 1982), vol. 1, p. 524.

Epilogue

1. J. Krynen, 'La rébellion du Bien public', in M.T. Fögen (ed.), *Ordnung und Aufruhr im Mittelalter. Historische und juristische Studien zur Rebellion* (Frankfurt, 1995), pp. 81–97, at p. 87.

2. B.-A. Pocquet du Haut-Jussé, *François II duc de Bretagne et l'Angleterre, 1458–88* (Paris, 1929), p. 149.

Guide to Further Reading

Peter Lewis's *Later Medieval France: the polity* (London, 1968) provides a section of 'Bibliographical indications' referring to the more important studies that had appeared to that point, especially but not exclusively relating to political history, and a good number of these titles remain central to the study of our period. More recently, a section of 'Further Reading' accompanies the collection of essays edited by David Potter, *France in the later Middle Ages 1200–1500* (Oxford, 2003), with a particular emphasis on material available in English. Repetition of titles cited in either volume or in the notes accompanying this book is kept to a minimum in the following guide (which, needless to say, cannot be a bibliography of the works consulted for the present volume).

Bibliography, Sources and Orientation

The main guide for new research remains the *Bibliographie annuelle de l'Histoire de France* (*BAHF*), published annually since 1955 by the Centre national de la recherche scientifique (CNRS), currently still produced in hard copy but ultimately to be made available as an electronic resource. In the meantime, a valuable tool in the last category is the *Bibliographie de la Société des historiens médiévistes de l'enseignement supérieur public* (http://shmesp.ish-lyon.cnrs.fr/). A leading site for French medievalists with links to on-line resources is Ménestrel (http://www.menestrel.fr/). For an introduction to the sources, the most comprehensive and widely available work is still Auguste Molinier's *Les sources de l'histoire de France des origines aux guerres d'Italie*, especially volumes 3 (*Les Capétiens, 1180–1328* [Paris, 1903]), 4 (*Les Valois, 1328–1461* [Paris, 1904]) and 5 (*Introduction générale. Les Valois (suite), Louis XI et Charles VIII (1461–94)* [Paris, 1924]). A revision of this work was carried out under the direction of Robert Fawtier from 1964 on, published as *Les sources de l'histoire de France des origines à la fin du XVe siècle. Refonte de l'ouvrage d'Auguste Molinier*. For a site devoted to the study of French sources of the period, consult the *Bibliographie des éditions et études de sources documentaires françaises médiévales* (*BÈDE*) (http://elec.enc.sorbonne.fr/bede/), maintained by the École des Chartes. Succinct and informative guides to authors of the period can be found in M. Zink (ed.), *Dictionnaire des lettres françaises. Le Moyen Âge* (Paris, 1992).

For twentieth-century developments in research, one can explore many topics by reading the surveys collected in *L'histoire médiévale en France. Bilan et perspectives*, ed. M. Balard (Paris, 1991), supplemented by thematic volumes published by Seuil containing essays (also with valuable bibliographies) by leading scholars. These volumes include J. Dupâquier et al. (eds), *Histoire de la population française*, vol 1 (Paris, 1988); G. Duby et al. (eds.), *Histoire de la France rurale*, vols 1 & 2 (Paris, 1975); G. Duby et al. (eds.), *Histoire de la France urbaine*, vol. 2 (Paris, 1980); and J. Le Goff et al. (eds.), *Histoire de la France religieuse*, vols 1 & 2 (Paris, 1988). Relevant historiographical matters are treated in the essays in F. Bédarida (ed.), *L'histoire et le métier d'historien en France 1945–95* (Paris, 1995) and S. Berstein and P. Milza (eds.), *Axes et méthodes de l'histoire politique* (Paris, 1998).

Ruling the French

Political thought and ideologies in our period are illuminated in Jacques Krynen's work (1993) cited in the notes above, and that of Colette Beaune (trans. 1990). On law and justice, both shading into wider political matters, an important collection of Albert Rigaudière's work is *Penser et construire l'état dans la France du Moyen Âge* (Paris, 2002), while a great deal can be found in Claude Gauvard, '*De Grace especial'. Crime, état et société en France à la fin du Moyen Âge*, 2 vols (Paris, 1991). On institutions, especially seen now from a prosopographical perspective, studies include Françoise Autrand *Naissance d'un grand corps de l'état: les gens du Parlement de Paris* (Paris, 1981); J. Kerhervé, *L'état breton aux XIVe et XVe siècles. Les ducs, l'argent et les hommes*, 2 vols (Paris, 1987); P. Contamine and O. Mattéoni (eds.), *La France des principautés. Les chambres des comptes, XIVe–XVe siècle* (Paris, 1996); O. Mattéoni, *Servir le prince. Les officiers des ducs de Bourbon à la fin du Moyen Âge* (Paris, 1998); and *Les serviteurs de l'état au Moyen Âge, XXIXe congrès de la Société des historiens médiévistes de l'enseignement supérieur public* (Paris, 1999). On writers and intellectuals a recent general work with bibliography is J. Blanchard and J-C. Mühlethaler, *Écriture et pouvoir à l'aube des temps modernes* (Paris, 2002). Work on the church and its relationship to the state includes essays by Vincent Tabbagh and Jacques Verger mentioned in the notes above (with valuable bibliographies), but also H. Millet, *Les chanoines du chapitre cathédral de Laon (1271–1412)* (Rome, 1982); V. Tabbagh, *Gens d'église, gens de pouvoir (France, XIIIe–XVe siècle)* (Paris, 2006); X. de La Selle, *Le service des âmes à la cour: confesseurs et aumôniers des rois de France du XIIIe au XVe siècle* (Paris, 1995); and the essays in J.-P. Genet, *État et église dans la genèse de l'état moderne* (Madrid, 1986). This last volume is part of a substantial project, *Origines de l'état moderne*, which resulted in several other important collections of essays under the auspices of the CNRS: see J.-P. Genet, 'La genèse de l'état moderne: les enjeux d'un programme de recherche', *Actes de la recherche en sciences sociales*

118 (1997), pp. 3–18. On language, see most recently Serge Lusignan, *La langue des rois. Le français en France et en Angleterre* (Paris, 2004). The Capetian context discussed in the closing section can be taken further in J. Bradbury, *The Capetians* (London, 2007).

Rural France

If it is really true that 'l'histoire rurale n'est plus à la mode', as Jean Jacquart wrote in his *Les fermiers de l'Île-de-France: l'ascension d'un patronat agricole, XVe–XVIIIe siècle* (Paris, 1994) (p. 13), then nonetheless the contribution of French scholars to the subject since Marc Bloch's *French rural history: an essay on its characteristics* (1931; trans. London, 1966) has been immense. The only regional study to be translated into English is not necessarily the most representative, namely Guy Bois's *The crisis of feudalism: economy and society in eastern Normandy, c. 1300–c. 1550* (1976; trans. Jean Birrell, Cambridge, 1984), but some of the recent work is surveyed in the early parts of E. Le Roy Ladurie, *The French peasantry 1450–1660* (orig. 1977; trans. Oxford, 1987). Further important regional studies are mentioned in the notes above, particularly those by Robert Boutruche (1948), Guy Fourquin (1965), Pierre Charbonnier (1980), Michel le Mené (1982) and Jean Tricard (1996), and a wide range of topics is addressed, roughly speaking from north to south, in A. Girardot, *Le droit et la terre. Le Verdunois à la fin du Moyen Âge* (Nancy, 1992); M. Belotte, *La région de Bar-sur-Seine à la fin du Moyen Âge* (Dijon, 1973); J.-P. Leguay and H. Martin, *Fastes et malheurs de la Bretagne ducale, 1213–1532* (Rennes, 1982); R. Germain, *Les campagnes bourbonnaises à la fin du Moyen Âge (1370–1530)* (Clermont-Ferrand, 1987); M.-T. Lorcin, *Les campagnes de la région lyonnaise aux XIVe et XVe siècle* (Lyon, 1974); J. Lartigaut, *Les campagnes du Quercy après la guerre de cent ans (vers 1440–vers 1500)* (Toulouse, 1978); M. Berthe, *Le comté de Bigorre. Un milieu rural au bas Moyen Âge* (Paris, 1976).

   In addition to Charbonnier's work of Guillaume de Murol (see notes above), aspects of noble lordship (broadly defined) in the countryside are examined in J.L. Goldsmith, *Les Salers et les d'Escorailles, seigneurs de Haute Auvergne* (Clermont-Ferrand, 1984); M.-T. Caron, *La noblesse dans le duché de Bourgogne 1315–1477* (Lille, 1987); and M. Walsby, *The counts of Laval. Culture, patronage and religion in fifteenth- and sixteenth-century France* (Aldershot, 2007). A valuable collection of essays is *Seigneurs et seigneuries au Moyen Âge. Actes du 117e congrès national des sociétés savantes* (Paris, 1995).

Royal France

'History by reign' lost its footing in France until Raymond Cazelles (writing on political society under the first three Valois kings) and Françoise Autrand (in her biographies of the third and fourth Valois kings), both cited in the notes above, demonstrated how it might be done. The reign of Charles VI has long been one of Bernard Guenée's preoccupations, especially (in addition to works cited in notes above) in his *Un meurtre, une société. L'assassinat du duc d'Orléans, 23 novembre 1407* (Paris, 1992) and *La folie de Charles VI, roi bien-aimé* (Paris, 2004). With the notable exceptions of Malcolm Vale's book on Charles VII (see notes) and Jean Favier's *Louis XI* (Paris, 2001), the fifteenth century is less well served, although an overview of events can be found in R.J. Knecht, *The Valois Kings of France 1328–1589* (London, 2004). Studies of members of the royal familial community are sometimes pressed into the mould of the 'princely state', such as Richard Vaughan's four biographies of the Valois dukes of Burgundy, now re-edited with updated bibliographies (2002), but also include F. Autrand, *Jean de Berry* (Paris, 2000) and R. Famiglietti, *The French monarchy in crisis, 1392–1415, and the political role of the Dauphin Louis of France, Duke of Guyenne*, 2 vols (New York, 1982). The central question of taxes and public finances can be explored in greater detail now in J.B. Henneman, 'France in the Middle Ages', in R. Bonney (ed.), *The rise of the fiscal state in Europe, c. 1200–c. 1815* (Oxford, 1999), pp. 101–22; *L'impôt au Moyen Âge: L'impôt public et le prélèvement seigneurial, fin XIIe-début XVIe siècle*, ed. P. Contamine, J. Kerhervé and A. Rigaudière, 3 vols (Paris, 2002); and J.-F. Lassalmonie, *La boîte à l'enchanteur. Politique financière de Louis XI* (Paris, 2002). The most recent survey of the nobility is P. Contamine, *La noblesse au royaume de France de Philippe le Bel à Louis XII. Essai de synthèse* (Paris, 1997), but two volumes in particular explore this group's role within the political life of the realm: M.-T. Caron, *Noblesse et pouvoir royal en France XIIIe–XVIe siècle* (Paris, 1994) and J.B Henneman, *Olivier de Clisson and political society in France under Charles V and Charles VI* (Philadelphia, 1996). Nobility and war are very much the subject of Philippe Contamine's *Guerre, état et société à la fin du Moyen Âge* (Paris-The Hague, 1972). Finally, representative assemblies constitute an area where non-French scholars have led the way in more recent times. In addition to the work of Peter Lewis and John Russell Major cited in the notes above, Neithard Bulst has looked at later assemblies in *Die Französischen Generalstände von 1468 une 1484. Prosopographische Untersuchungen zu den Delegierten* (Sigmaringen, 1992).

Municipal France

For a long time Henri Sée's influence was profound over this subject (*Louis XI et les villes* [Paris, 1890]), but the work cited in the notes above by Bernard Chevalier on Tours (to which we must add his *Tours ville royale 1356–1520: origine et développement d'une capitale à la fin du Moyen Âge* [Leuven-Paris, 1976]), Robert Favreau on Poitiers (to which we must add *La ville de Poitiers à la fin du Moyen Âge. Une capitale régionale*, 2 vols [Poitiers, 1978]), Albert Rigaudière on Saint-Flour, and Pierre Desportes on Reims (among others), has renewed the subject in the last two generations. For printed guides one can use the full bibliographies which accompany Chevalier's *Les bonnes villes de France* (cited in notes) and Gisela Naegle's *Stad, Recht und Krone. Französische Städte, Königtum und Parlement im Spätenmittelalter*, 2 vols (Husum, 2002). The fullest on-line resource is Dr Naegle's *Bibliographie thématique sur les villes françaises, le droit et la royauté à la fin du Moyen Âge* (http://www.menestrel.fr/spip.php?.rubrique443), which includes bibliographies of the older literature, where much of interest can still be found.

The Church and Religion

The *Histoire de la France religieuse* (vols 1 & 2) cited in the first section of this guide above contains selective but representative bibliographies up to 1988, so what follows deals mainly with work that has appeared since then.

Regional surveys include the *Histoire des diocèses de France* (1967–) and, especially for our period, N. Lemaître, *Le Rouergue flamboyant. Le clergé et les fidèles du diocèse de Rodez 1417–1563* (Paris, 1988); P. Paravy, *De la Chrétienté romaine à la réforme en Dauphiné. Évêques, fidèles et déviants, vers 1340-vers 1530* (Paris-Rome, 1993); and D. Viaux, *La vie paroissiale à Dijon à la fin du Moyen Âge* (Dijon, 1988). On confraternities, C. Vincent's study of Normandy (1988) led to her wider *Les confréries médiévales dans le royaume de France* (Paris, 1994). On preaching, Hervé Martin's work on Brittany (1975) led to his *Le métier de prédicateur en France septentrionale à la fin du moyen âge 1350–1520* (Paris, 1988). Institutional matters of varying descriptions are treated in M. Aubrun et al. (eds.), *Entre idéal et réalité. Actes du colloque international 'Finances et religion du Moyen Âge à l'époque moderne'* (Clermont-Ferrand, 1994); P. Guichard et al., *Papauté monachisme et théories politiques. Études d'histoire médiévale offertes à Marcel Pacaut*, 2 vols (Lyon, 1994); J.-L. Gazzaniga's collected essays, *L'église de France à la fin du Moyen Âge. Pouvoirs et institutions* (Goldbach, 1995); and *Crises et réformes dans l'église de la réforme grégorienne à la préréforme. Actes du 115e congrès national des sociétés savantes* (Paris, 1991). Important studies of the clergy include the following collections of essays: *Le clerc séculier au Moyen Âge. XXIIe congrès de la Société des historiens médiévistes de l'enseignement supérieur public (Amiens, 1991)* (Paris, 1993); F. Bériac and A.-M. Dom (eds.), *Les prélats, l'église et la société XIe–XVe siècles. Hommage à Bernard Guillemain* (Bordeaux, 1994); and M.-M. de Cevins and J.-M. Matz (eds.), *Formation intellectuelle et culture du clergé dans les territoires angevines (milieu XIIIe-fin du XVe siècle)* (Rome, 2005). On the rural world, essays on French subjects figure in P. Bonnnassie (ed.), *Le clergé rural dans l'Europe médiévale et moderne. Actes des XIIIe journées internationales d'Histoire de l'Abbaye de Flaran 1991* (Toulouse, 1995) and *L'église au village. Lieux, formes et enjeux des pratiques religieuses (Cahiers de Fanjeaux no. 40: Toulouse, 2006).* On the urban world, see P. Boucheron and J. Chiffoleau (eds.), *Religion et société urbaine au Moyen Âge. Études offertes à Jean-Louis Biget* (Paris, 2000) and S. Cassagnes-Brouquet et al. (eds.), *Religion et mentalités au Moyen Âge. Mélanges en l'honneur d'Hervé Martin* (Rennes, 2003).

Index